RISK MANAGEMENT SYSTEMS

Risk Management Systems

PROCESS, TECHNOLOGY AND TRENDS

Martin Gorrod

palgrave
macmillan

First published 2004 by
PALGRAVE MACMILLAN
Houndmills, Basingstoke, Hampshire RG21 6XS and
175 Fifth Avenue, New York, N.Y. 10010
Companies and representatives throughout the world

PALGRAVE MACMILLAN is the global academic imprint of the Palgrave Macmillan division of St. Martin's Press, LLC and of Palgrave Macmillan Ltd. Macmillan® is a registered trademark in the United States, United Kingdom and other countries. Palgrave is a registered trademark in the European Union and other countries.

ISBN 1–4039–1617–9

This book is printed on paper suitable for recycling and made from fully managed and sustained forest sources.

A catalogue record for this book is available from the British Library.

A catalog record for this book is available from the Library of Congress.

Editing and origination by Aardvark Editorial, Mendham, Suffolk

10 9 8 7 6 5 4 3 2 1
13 12 11 10 09 08 07 06 05 04

Printed and bound in Great Britain by
Antony Rowe Ltd, Chippenham and Eastbourne

Contents

List of figures

List of tables

Preface

The aim of this book is to provide a 'whirlwind' tour of risk management, and the processes and technical issues facing the risk manager and risk technologist within a typical investment bank. The recent climate, both regulatory and economic, has meant that monitoring and managing risk, both in terms of financial risk and the risk of projects and process failures, is more important now than ever before. The impending Basel 2 Accord is extending the regulatory monitoring of risk to be more complex and complete in its analysis. Constant ongoing innovation within the financial marketplace is resulting in ever more complex financial transactions and processes. But pressure on margins and costs means that these must be achieved with reduced budgets and in shorter timescales, if first mover advantage is to be achieved.

It is difficult for any individual to be an expert in all the technical and business issues within a financial institution, but the nature of risk management, with its extreme breadth and coverage, means that this is increasingly becoming a requirement for those involved in the risk management process. Risk management is becoming more integrated not only across the different types of risk but also into the control and management of the business processes within the financial organization. This book will help those in this unenviable position, by offering a complete overview and understanding of these issues. Part I provides an introduction to exactly what risk management is and the current regulatory and external market drivers that are impacting the development of risk management systems. This should help any technologist to understand the scope of the area he is working in and provide the risk manager with another perspective on his field.

Part II goes on to highlight the issues in developing risk management systems, covering the entire software lifecycle. The development of any system is not only about technology but also about understanding the business environment and the uses that system will be put to. It also requires processes and approaches to ensure that any risk management project succeeds. Risk is inherent in the software development process and needs to be managed just as the proposed system will need to manage (other) risks within the organization. This section of the book should help the risk manager to understand the complexity of the software development process so that it can be more efficiently managed and controlled. It should also help risk technologists to appreciate other stages of the software development process, so that they have a fuller understanding of their importance within this process. The software development process is broken down in a fairly formal manner which provides a more rigorous and structured perspective on the different steps in this process. The aim is to improve understanding and the quality of any approach and, in so doing, help to reduce development risk.

Finally, Part III highlights some of the business and technical drivers that will impact the development of the next generation of risk management systems. This is a personal view, selecting some of the key drivers that I have witnessed as a consultant in the investment banking arena.

I would like to thank a number of individuals for their comments and assistance in writing this book. The genesis of it came from a number of ideas that evolved out of courses and presentations produced by myself, Jeremy Tugwell and Peter Devlin. I would also like to thank many of my colleagues from Bankers Trust, Merrill Lynch, Credit Suisse First Boston and Iris Financial, with whom I worked and who helped to provide an environment that allowed these ideas to develop.

I would especially like to thank my wife Sarah for her patience and assistance with the writing of this book, Peter Devlin for his help in proofreading many of the chapters and providing valuable feedback, Bryan Davidson for many useful conversations and observations, Andrew Gill for countless technology discussions and comment, as well as Rebecca Bond for providing numerous stylistic pointers both in this book and many other articles. Any remaining omissions or inaccuracies within this book, however, remain mine. Finally I would like to thank everyone at Palgrave Macmillan and the team at Aardvark Editorial for their help and support in bringing this book to publication.

To the best of my knowledge, all appropriate acknowledgements and copyright notices have been included, but if any have inadvertently been omitted the publishers will be pleased to make the appropriate changes in future versions of this book.

List of abbreviations

.NET Microsoft's web services strategy for distributed applications and system connectivity
ACID atomicity, consistency, isolation and durability
ATS alternative trading system
BA business analyst
BIS bank of international settlements otherwise known as the Basel committee on banking supervision
CAPM capital asset pricing model
CBD component-based development
CMM capability maturity model
COM component object model
COM+ extension of the component object model
CORBA common object request broker architecture
DCOM distributed component object model
DNA distributed interNet applications architecture
DOM distributed object-orientated middleware
EAI enterprise application integration
ECN electronic communication network
ERD entity relationship diagram
FX foreign exchange
GL general ledger
GUI graphical user interface
HSM hierarchical storage management
IDL interface definition language
IR interest rate
IRB internal ratings-based (methods)
ISDA International Swaps and Derivatives Association, Inc.
IT information technology
J2EE java 2 platform, enterprise edition
KRI key risk indicator
LTCM Long Term Capital Management
MOM message-orientated middleware
MTS Microsoft transaction server
NDA non-disclosure agreement
OLAP online analytical processing
OLTP online transaction processing
ORML operational risk mark-up language
OTC over-the-counter (or customised)
P&L profit and loss
PC personal computer
PM project manager
QA quality assurance
RAG red, amber, green
RAID redundant array of independent disks

RAROC	risk-adjusted return on capital
RMI	remote method invocation
RPC	remote procedure call
RUP	Rational unified process
SMART	specific, measurable, achievable, relevant and timely
SOAP	simple object access protocol
SPR	software problem report
SQL	structured query language
STP	straight through processing
TP	transaction processing
TQM	total quality management
UAT	user acceptance testing
UML	unified modelling language
WSDL	web services description language
XML	extensible mark-up language
XP	extreme programming

PART I

An Introduction to the Risk Management Process

CHAPTER 1

What is risk management?

In the current volatile markets at the beginning of the new millennium, where newspaper headlines inform us how much money has been wiped off the stock market in a bad day or lost in the bankruptcy of a company, risk management is a key phrase. But what do we mean by risk management and why are regulators so concerned with this topic?

Risk management is the application of analysis techniques and the definition of measures to quantify the amount of financial loss (or gain) an organization is exposed to, when certain unexpected and random changes and events occur. These events range from changes in observable or derivable market data (such as prices, or price volatility), process related failures, or credit (payment default type) events. Risk is therefore all about uncertain rather than definite outcomes. This uncertainty is not an undesirable thing. It is, however, important that the organization is aware of the impact of any outcomes that may occur and their implication for its profitability. For these risk measures or metrics to be of use, the calculated risks and actual losses arising should correlate. If this is not the case, the information on which the risk analysis is based, or the analysis itself, is either incorrect or inaccurate and must be rectified for the information to be of use. Even where it is thought that the risks are well understood, the risk manager needs to be constantly looking for previously unidentified risks, or inherent assumptions and failings in the calculation and management of those risks. This is especially true when these risks may only become evident in extreme market conditions. If these risks are not identified and controlled, the organization is likely to suffer the same fate as that of Long Term Capital Management (LTCM), the US hedge fund that came close to financial collapse due to unexpected market events and behaviour in 1998.[1]

Financial markets enable participants to raise capital and exchange risks, so that one participant's risk becomes another's potential reward or offsets a risk they already have. Market participants then structure and trade these risks so as to either remove (that is, *hedge*) or take on additional risk in return for a given benefit or expected return; this latter activity is known as *speculating*. Risk may also be retained or additional risk taken on if there is a belief that the market is mispricing the cost of taking on this risk. This activity is known as *relative value* or *richness/cheapness analysis* and can have varying levels of sophistication. The aim of this trading strategy is to try to benefit from any mispricing by buying or selling the instruments involved on the assumption that the market will correctly price them in the future (resulting in a greater than expected return). If these mispricings result in a transaction which leaves no residual risk but rather a guaranteed return or profit, then this is called *arbitraging*. Arbitraging can also cause (through variations in supply and demand resulting in changes in prices) the mispricings to disappear and so plays a vital role in the financial markets in ensuring different financial instruments are fairly priced.

The brokers or intermediaries in this process earn commission by linking the two sides of a transaction together, exposing themselves to the minimum level of indirect risk while participating in the process. Market makers, where they exist in certain financial markets, add *liquidity* to the market by always being willing to either buy or sell a given financial instrument. These market participants are all taking different risks and making profits based on their unique business model. For example, market makers will try to maintain a relatively flat trading book with limited downside risk, but will make their profit from the bid/ask spread (the difference between the price financial instruments are bought and sold at). As a result, the participants in financial markets all have unique definitions and appetites for risk and require different tools to manage it. This explains why asset managers, hedge funds, corporate treasury departments and investment banks all require different tools and information to manage and control their risk profile while supporting their business model. It is therefore difficult to provide a 'one size fits all' approach to risk management. In particular, even within investment banks, each trading style results in its own unique risks that may differ greatly from those of its competitors.

Directly or indirectly, people will only take on additional risk if they believe they can profit from it. However, no one will knowingly take on risks that could (in the event of probable market events) result in the destruction of the organization. It is this systematic risk that regulatory authorities focus on, ensuring that the failure of any one financial institution does not result in a domino effect that causes the entire financial system to collapse. The importance of risk measurement in this process cannot be underestimated. It is only once risks can be measured that they can be managed and controlled.

The role of technology in risk management cannot be overstated. More complex organizational processes and financial instruments, together with rapidly changing external market conditions, have led to the requirement for more advanced models and faster computers to ensure all the risks are captured, modelled and understood in a timely manner. Even when trading simple financial instruments, the number of positions (or net transactions) and their different characteristics require complex visualization and reporting tools in order to ensure that there are no excessive concentrations or unexpected correlated exposures.

In the past, the unique requirements of an organization, its IT environment and source of competitive advantage have led to the assumption that unique solutions and sets of tools are required to manage risk. Such ground-up approaches have had a high likelihood of failure, with everything from process to underlying systems up for redevelopment. Consolidation in the financial industry, together with convergence in opinions and approaches, has however shown that this may no longer be the case. Although the context of this problem (whether technological, business model, organizational structure or political) is still often unique, the general core concepts and development approaches are becoming more standardized. As a result, the time is fast approaching for financial institutions to concentrate on what is unique to them and leverage what is now commonly accepted as generic or best practice in the industry. Much of the functionality required to create a risk management solution may already exist within the organization or can be purchased from external software vendors.

SOURCES AND DRIVERS OF RISK

The occurrence of unexpected losses within the organization is driven by the evolution of various internal or external risk events (Figure 1.1). These risk events range from changes in the market prices of traded instruments, an increase in traded volumes, or the bankruptcy of a company. In themselves, these events need not result in a financial loss. Whether this occurs, and the magnitude of any loss will depend on the specific sources of risk within the organization. For example, the bankruptcy of a company like Enron[2] will only result in losses for those organizations that hold positions in Enron equity, bonds or outstanding loans to the company. A financial institution that has no exposure will have no unexpected loss.

Although all financial institutions are exposed to the same external risk events and may have many internal risk events in common, the possibility and size of a financial loss (that is, risk) will depend on the unique set of sources of risk within the organization itself, and will differ greatly from organization to organization. It will depend on the instruments traded and any risks retained, as well as on the people, processes and technology.

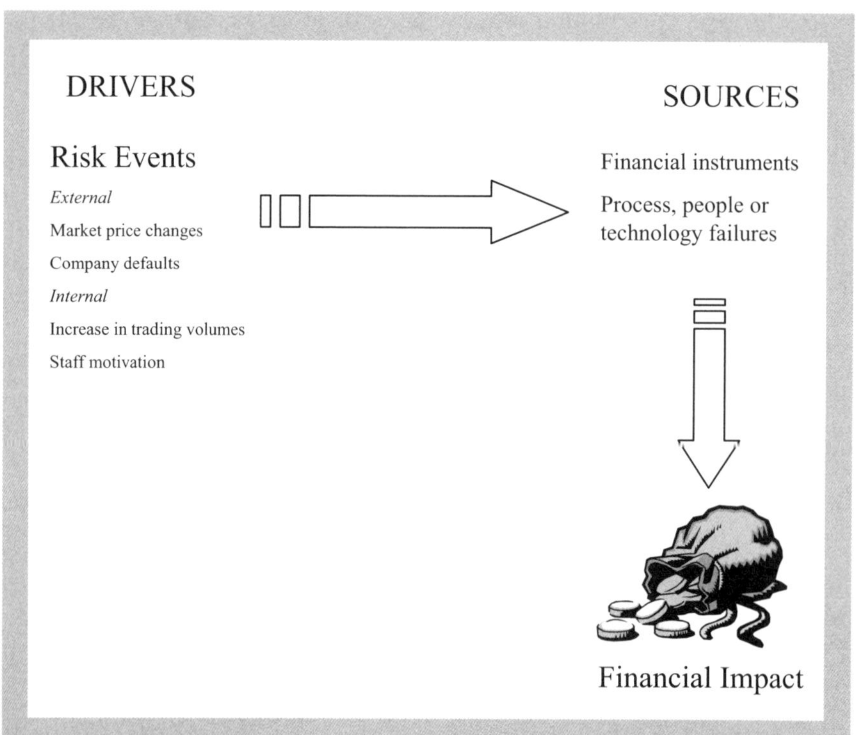

Figure 1.1 Sources and drivers of risk in an organization

Risk reduction and mitigation typically focus on the sources of risk, since these are internal to an organization and therefore under its control. Internal risk drivers, which are often associated with operational risk, may also be influenced. For example, if a system cannot handle significant trading volumes without a high-level of risk of failure, it is possible for the organization to reduce this trading volume until the problem has been addressed.

Risk management, however, focuses on both the sources as well as the drivers of risk events. It brings these dimensions together in order to determine what losses could occur, the events that cause them to occur and the likelihood of those events occurring. As a result, risk can be viewed and broken down in to either of these dimensions. At the most generic level, risk within an organization is typically thought of in terms of the following categories of risk events:

Credit risk
This is the risk arising from changes in the (perceived) credit quality or likelihood of a company or counterparty involved in a financial transaction to default on its liabilities.

Market risk
This is the risk arising from changes in underlying market variables (not credit related) such as commodity, bond or equity prices, interest rates, option volatility and so on.

Operational risk
This is the risk arising from events that cause losses or reduced future income that result from people, process and technical or systems failure, buildings and infrastructure failings and other external events such as natural disasters. The term is often used to describe any type of risk that is not classified as market or credit risk.

Market risk and credit risk differ dramatically from operational risk in that they are typically related to pricing issues and risks directly arising from a financial transaction. There can, however, be problems in categorizing risk as either market or credit risk. The price of a credit derivative or an equity share can be viewed as either credit or market risk, as although the price is quoted in the market this will be impacted by various credit events affecting the underlying company. As a result, these risks are often referred to under the generic title of *pricing risk.*

Risks may also be viewed in terms of the sources of risk, which will be directly attributable to an actual loss should a given risk event occur:

- Product/instrument type
- System or staff responsible for source of risk
- Business line
- Geographical region.

Risk hierarchies are often used to break down risks and actual losses according to either various decompositions of the sources or the type of event that gives rise to that risk or loss. The structure of any hierarchy will depend on the organization's requirements; for example, it may be broken down by business line and then into credit, market or operational risk type events, or market risk broken down by geographical region. For losses arising from sources of operational risk, there may however be problems in quantifying intangible losses such as reputational damage or the extent of liabilities arising from future legal action.

The management of these three primary risk event groups (market, credit and operational risk) supports the organization in its quest for profit (Figure 1.2). In its aim to be profitable, each pillar must be well constructed and support the organization in managing the risk of unexpected losses.

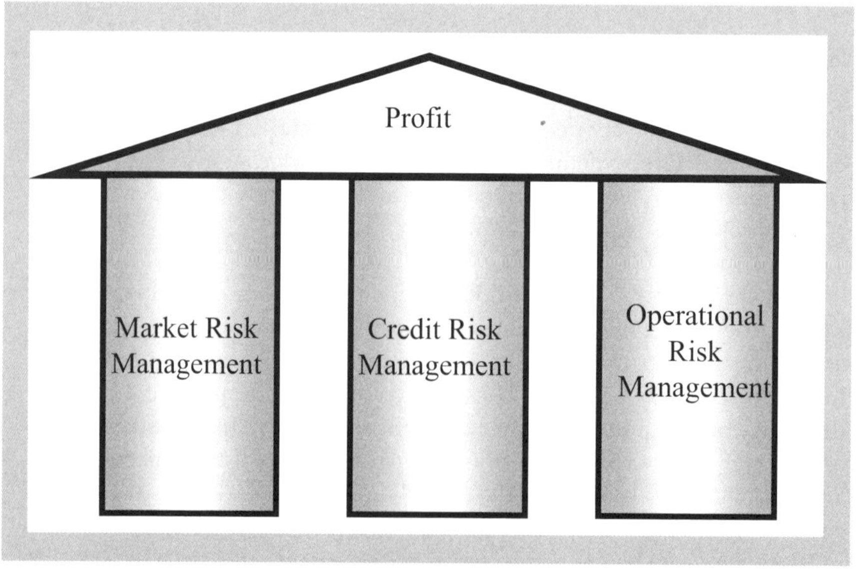

Figure 1.2 The risk management temple supporting profit

Deconstructing each pillar, it is possible to break this requirement down into its constituent parts. In order to effectively manage risk it must be:

- *Defined:* How risk is defined and what events cause this risk to occur
- *Monitored:* Organizational structure and processes for monitoring and controlling risk within the organization
- *Measured:* Access to data and measurement of the risk arising
- *Mitigated* and *communicated:* A process for removing risk where necessary or where the risk is unacceptable as well as communicating the risks that are being taken.

Failure in any of these levels will result in a weak pillar that will crumble and collapse, with a sudden and unexpected loss that will have disastrous impact on the organization (Figure 1.3).

The role of technology in the risk management process is to assist the organization throughout each risk pillar; to support in the obtaining of risk data, to measure risks, communicate the results and to help miti-

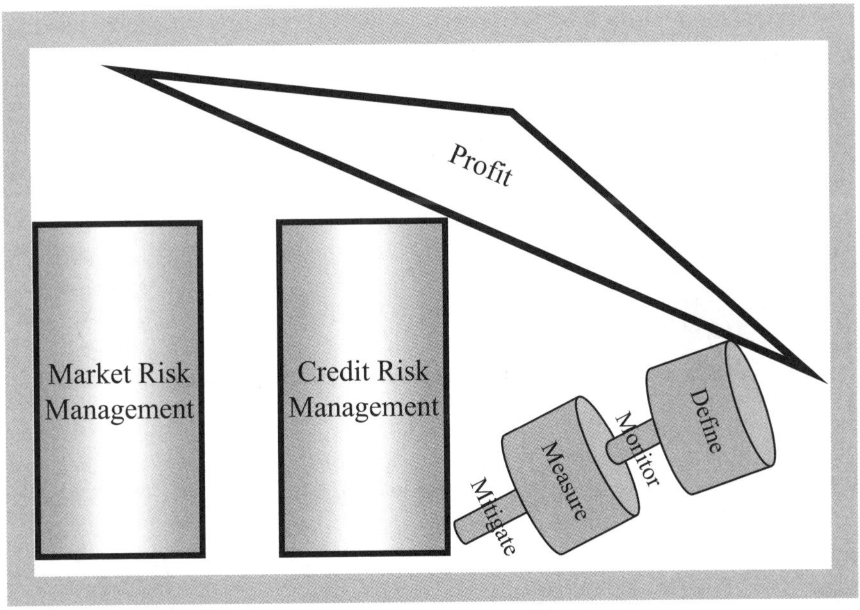

Figure 1.3 Inadequate risk management support can result in organizational collapse

gate operational risk. Measurement of risk will require the gathering of information concerning the current state of the company (comprising financial positions, loss data, current process flow) as well as external and internal information concerning the likelihood and occurrence of various risk events.

RISK AND RETURN

Organizations focus on leveraging any strengths or competitive advantage they have in order to obtain the maximum amount of profit or return for a given level of risk; the higher the level of risk taken, the greater the expected profit or return (Figure 1.4). The given level of risk that the organization is willing to accept should be defined as part of the risk management process and indicates the organization's appetite for risk. The aim of each business unit is then to maximize the level of return for the defined level of risk that can be taken.

Economic and financial models tell us that markets provide different levels of return for different types and levels of risk.[3] For example, based on the capital asset pricing model (CAPM),[4] the market does not reward participants for taking on equity-specific risk and not adequately diversifying their portfolios. Economic capital calculations are often used to explicitly convert the level of risk to the amount of capital that is required

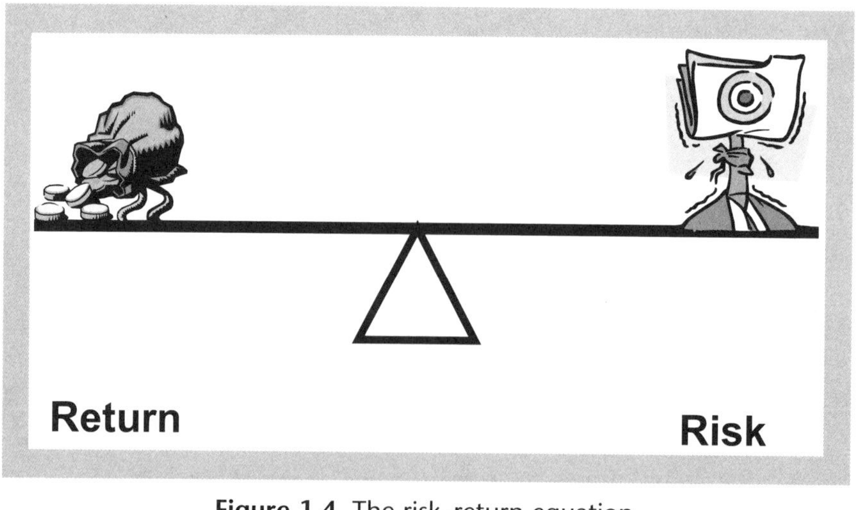

Figure 1.4 The risk–return equation

to support that risk taken by the organization, in line with the institution's target financial strength. Economic capital provides management with a standardized unit for comparing and discussing opportunities and threats. Economic capital numbers can also be multiplied by an institution's equity hurdle rate (the minimum acceptable rate of return required), to offer a 'cost of risk' number that is comparable to other kinds of bank expenses. This and associated approaches such as risk-adjusted return on capital (RAROC)[5] are often used to 'charge' for capital used by a given business line. Economic capital calculations are then used by senior management to ensure both that capital is correctly allocated, and, using profit and loss (P&L) figures, that an adequate return is being obtained for its use.

Given that risk management is important and excessive risk above the organization's risk appetite should be reduced wherever possible (especially operational risk which tends to have a negative impact on current or future profitability), one could be forgiven for believing resources should always be aimed at risk reduction wherever possible. Indeed, for organizations where the measurement and reduction of risk is viewed as paramount, this is indeed what happens. This behaviour, however, highlights a number of key points from Kaplan and Norton's research on balanced score card approaches to measuring performance within the organization.[6] Their research highlighted that:

What you measure is what you get
People modify their behaviour so as to achieve the targets they are measured against. They also tend to ignore those targets they are not measured against.

No single measure can be completely appropriate
It is difficult for a single number or measure to truly define any desired behaviour or encapsulate risk.

Any measures used must provide a balanced view
The solution to the above is to use a number of different measures and monitor and combine them in a balanced manner.

The first two points have interesting implications for risk management; financial institutions and traders tend to trade in a manner that maximizes their expected return given their risk limits or any regulatory constraints. If some forms of risk are monitored and others are not, then it is not unusual to see excessive transactions that exploit this. Traders will seek to obtain additional return by taking on this unmeasured, and uncharged for, risk. This is clearly not an ideal situation for the organization. The second implication is that any single view of risk is unlikely to completely capture all the risks within an organization. Multiple views and approaches are therefore critical, in order to ensure that all risk exposures are understood and monitored.

As a result, if all that is ever measured is risk and risk reduction is the key performance indicator, then the organization will focus all its resources on risk reduction at the expense of everything else. This includes spending more on removing risks than could ever be lost should that risk be realized. There are many views of the organization. For example:

- *Risk reduction:* How do we reduce all types of unwanted risk?
- *Financial:* How does the organization survive?
- *Internal:* How does the organization obtain competitive advantage in the market?
- *Stakeholder:* How do our customers and shareholders view us?

Any financial institution will have many different perspectives and these may change over time depending on market and internal conditions. This is often the source of many of the political and structural issues that the IT manager will face in implementing a risk management solution. In particular, most organizations will ensure that any approach to risk management not only considers the risk/reward calculation but also:

- Avoids risk reduction at the expense of survival
- Focuses on strategy and vision rather than on possibly inappropriate controls.

As has often been noted, the only manner in which risk can be completely removed is to withdraw the financial institution from the market. Although this is an extreme step, it can be a valid strategy if the total expected return (after considering all costs and risks) from being in a particular market is inadequate to cover capital costs. This is the strategy that Bank of America took in March 2003 with its European equity market making and research businesses.[7]

The balanced scorecard does however highlight that any risk management and also any IT project management process must always try to:

- Articulate goals
- Define measures for each goal
- Monitor
- Define a metric for combining the different measures
- Aim to align key aspects of any measures in a coherent manner
- Take remedial action if the measures deviate from those desired or expected.

The alignment and concurrent use of the terms *operational efficiency* and *operational risk* are examples of how operational risk and other efficiency-based measures are being combined; by reducing operational risk, organizations are also aiming to improve operational efficiency at the same time. Given that there are many options for reducing operational risk within an organization, prioritizing those that also improve efficiency (that is, improve return) is clearly the best approach. The only outstanding issue is how to quantify the efficiency improvement and how to measure the risk reduction.

When considering any IT projects within the organization the aim should be to:

Make the risk/reward equation more explicit
This will require project managers to clearly specify any benefits and risks.

Encourage the efficient use of budgets
Budgets should be allocated to those projects that provide the greatest benefit for an acceptable level of risk.

Change IT spending in risk management from being a cost centre to being a profit centre
Using technology to control and reduce risk has a clearly defined benefit. As a result, technology spending should not always be seen as a cost to the organization.

Unfortunately, there are difficulties in that:

- There are no standard approaches for achieving the previously listed aims.
- Quantifying and comparing different types of operational risk mean that it is difficult to formalize the risk/return calculation.

- Approaches for comparing risk tend to focus on well-behaved distributions rather than the impact of extreme risk events that can destroy the organization. Losses arising from fraudulent traders and stock market crashes may be very unlikely but their impact can be catastrophic.
- Defining return when it is not specifically identifiable in any profits. For example, efficiency gains and preventing losses from occurring can be difficult to quantify.
- There is a danger of overfocusing on current costs and risks at the expense of strategic survival.

RISK MANAGEMENT AND RISK MITIGATION

The risk management process breaks down into a cycle of continual improvement in identifying, monitoring, managing (including risk mitigation) and testing, as outlined in Figure 1.5. Many of the activities highlighted in Figure 1.5 should become clearer through the rest of this book. Any risk management process and systems must support this cycle, continually evolving as new risks are identified and as risk policy evolves. There are three approaches to managing risk within the organization:

1. To do nothing because the risk is inherent in the business, or the cost of reducing the risk will outweigh the benefits of any risk reduction. This is all part of the process of allocating the risk appetite of the organization. It assumes that the level of risk is acceptable and that the current capital base can absorb any losses.
2. Contingency-based approaches where the impact of events is reduced by offsetting sources of risk through hedging or insurance.
3. Risk reduction arising from limiting the impact of risk events through the removal of those sources of risk. This may be by exiting the business, outsourcing and transferring liabilities, reversing or securitizing financial positions,[8] improving processes or other operational risk reduction techniques that remove sources of risk within the organization.

Whatever the approach taken, it is important that the cycle continues as a constant ongoing process.

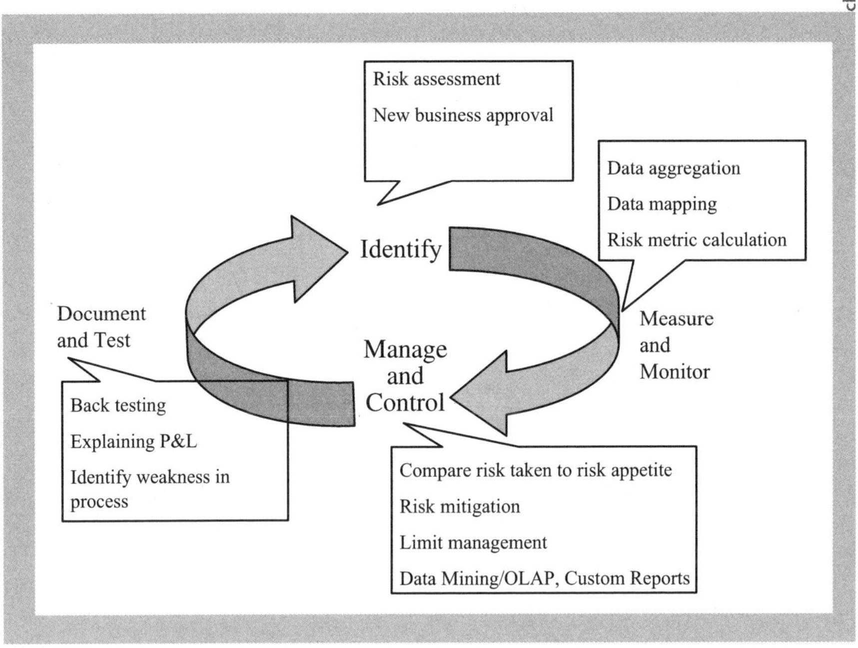

Figure 1.5 Risk management improvement cycle

It is neither possible nor desirable to mitigate all risks within the organization. Instead they should be understood and categorized as to whether they are avoidable or unavoidable based on the source of the risk and the risk policy. Avoidable risks should be prioritized and addressed, whereas unavoidable risks can only be either transferred through outsourcing, or removed through termination of the business. Where risk is retained, adequate planning should be undertaken to deal with any event that might occur.

APPROACHES TO IDENTIFYING AND MEASURING RISK

There is a continuum of possible approaches to identifying and measuring risk, ranging from the qualitative to the quantitative (Figure 1.6), which will be discussed further in Chapter 3. Quantitative approaches are typified by those where the data used in the risk analysis can be precisely modelled and measured. Where it is not possible to accurately calculate or categorize risks, more qualitative approaches can be

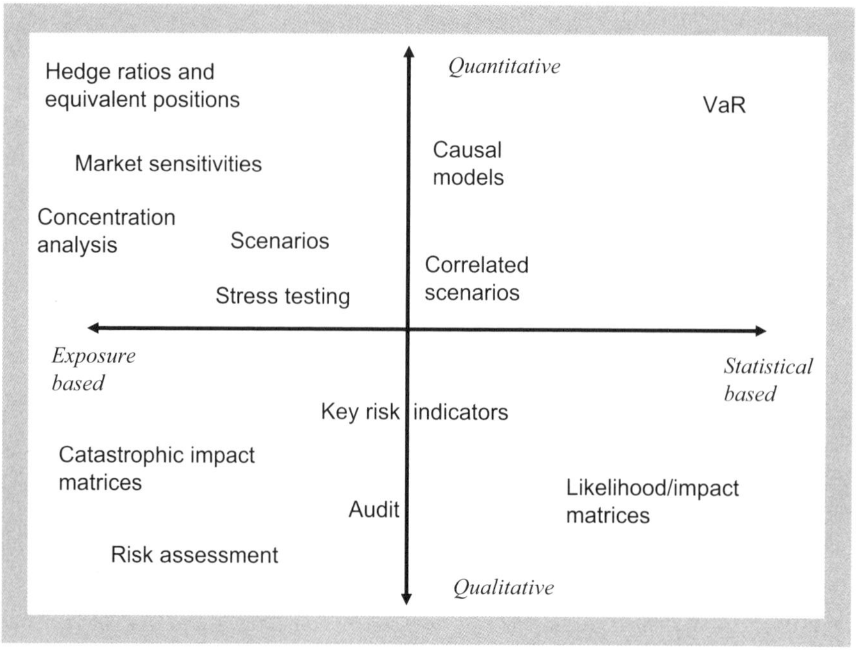

Figure 1.6 Continuum of approaches to risk management

used with broad categorizations of the likelihood, level and source of any risk. These approaches can however lead to highly subjective assessments. The precise position of each methodology in Figure 1.6 will depend on the precise implementation; the positions should be taken as being only indicative.

Quantitative approaches are generally preferable to qualitative approaches, simply because they are more tractable for mathematical models and can enable risks to be analysed in a more objective manner. Whichever approach is taken, it is important to obtain the data as objectively as possible. Human judgement is notoriously fallible,[9] leading to a number of common potential biases in the data used to measure risk:

Availability bias

- Events are believed to be more frequent if they come to mind easily
- The likelihood and impact of dramatic events tend to be overestimated (and those that are less dramatic are underestimated).

Overconfident bias

- People tend to be overconfident in their own opinions
- People tend to believe that they are correct more often than is justified.

Confirmation bias

- People tend to stick to their initial judgements
- Notice confirming evidence
- Dismiss contradictory evidence.

Hindsight bias

- People feel they were more certain about their decisions and judgements than they actually were at the time.

Despite this, even if risks are viewed as subjective and unquantifiable (such as reputational risk), it is important that they are not ignored, but are captured and monitored in some manner. The greater maturity of risk modelling within credit and market risk will tend to result in more quantitative approaches to risk management, whereas the less well-defined area of operational risk will often still rely on qualitative-type approaches and can be more susceptible to subjective judgements.

Statistical approaches to risk focus on the likelihood (or probability) of various risk events occurring, and the magnitude of any loss when they do occur. They are characterized by predicted probability distributions of expected returns or statistical measures such as confidence intervals, order statistics, variance and expected values,[10] which associate the magnitude of a possible loss with different probability levels. Statistical approaches are typically of more use at the portfolio rather than the individual position level, considering the correlation and offsetting movements of hedge positions to give an aggregated loss profile. They also highlight the link between risk and volatility (or variance): the wider the distribution of returns about the mean (or expected value), the higher the level of uncertainty and risk. There is, however, a danger in using single statistical measures to summarize complex risks within an organization. As a result, although a single figure can act as a warning indicator (when compared over time), it is important to understand how the risks within the organization combine to generate this figure.

Exposure-based approaches concentrate on sources of risk and the possible magnitude of any loss given that a defined event occurs. They are characterized by market sensitivities that indicate changes in the value of financial instruments due to market price changes or as hedge instrument positions that have an equivalent risk.[11] The exposure-type analyses tend to dominate in flow-based (high volume, high liquidity) trading where traders and credit departments are concerned with hedging and removing unwanted exposure. This is achieved by trading instruments with offsetting risks or by managing credit lines and collateral so that counterparty exposure is constrained or minimized.

Exposure-based approaches are also used at the senior management level to ensure that risk is adequately diversified across different markets, and guard against low probability, catastrophic or extreme market behaviour (such as market crashes). This will ensure that such events do not result in too significant a loss that could destroy the organization. Statistical and expected loss measures, however, tend to dominate at the senior management level, as well as being used by regulatory authorities to ensure that financial institutions maintain enough capital to cover unexpected or extreme market events. These measures are also used to quantify risk when charging economic capital to individual desks and business lines.

APPROACHES TO MANAGING RISK

How an organization is risk managed very much depends on its business model, the instruments it trades in and the regulatory environment, as well as what risks are being taken and how they are modelled. For example, a brokerage that doesn't take its own *proprietary* positions but does have significant settlement risk has a very different risk profile from a hedge fund or proprietary trading desk that retains significant trading positions over a long period of time. In this book we will focus on the complex problems faced by the security houses and investment banks that typically have to handle high trading volumes and complex structured instruments across many types of financial instruments. Many of the ideas transfer to other types of organizations but, as mentioned previously, they will have their own unique risk characteristics, which must be captured and monitored.

Investment banking is all about taking risks – whether market, credit or operational – and then monitoring, controlling and modifying those risks in order to obtain the desired risk profile with the maximum return. As a result, systems that support the monitoring of this risk and ensure that it is kept within predefined limits are an essential business control. These limits may be based on various decompositions of the risk within the organization; by counterparty, type of financial instrument or asset class, country, maturity of transaction, and so on, resulting in complex limit monitoring hierarchies. This control aspect of risk management leads to it being performed independently of the business areas responsible for generating those risks. This may also be a regulatory requirement.

Risk management occurs at various levels within a bank, with each level providing the risk information relevant to the management at that level, and also acting as an information filter (Figure 1.7). This effectively reduces information overload for more senior management but ensures that those at each level have the correct detail of information to manage the risks they are responsible for. Although the precise hierarchy and number of levels vary from organization to organization, the general approach is to have:

- *At the organizational level,* the senior management will be monitoring the overall risk profile of the organization. They will be viewing high-

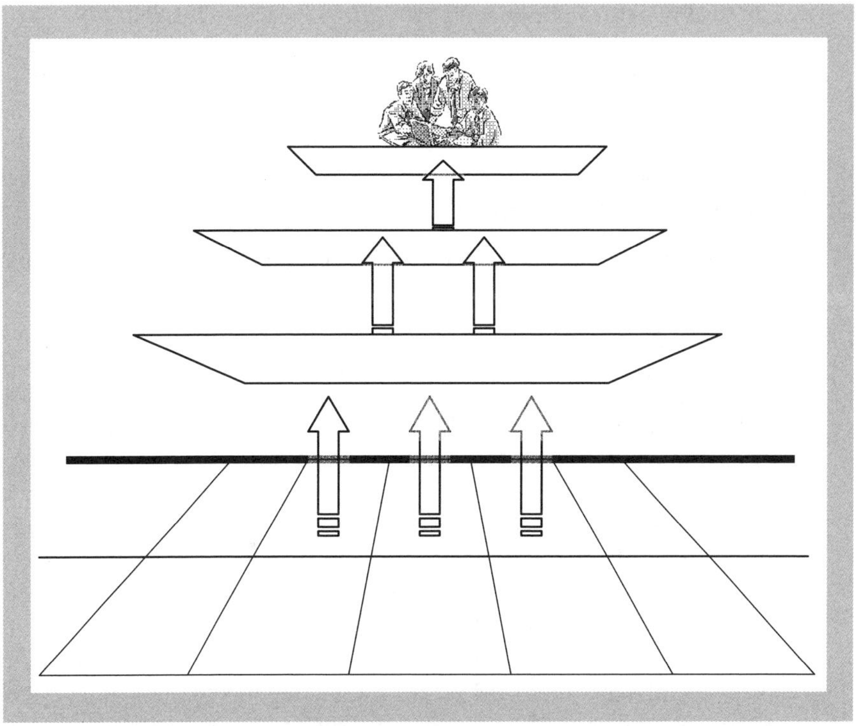

Figure 1.7 Risk management hierarchy and information filtering

level risk and concentration measures, ensuring that trading in different locations and business lines does not result in an unacceptable aggregate risk profile where the occurrence of certain events can result in a significant loss. Because of the volume of distinct individual risks that make up the aggregate risk profile for the organization, these will have been mapped into a smaller number of equivalent risks. Typically, there will be a focus on potential loss calculations, through the use of statistical methods, as well as on the running of scenarios that *stress* the sources of risk within the organization to ensure unlikely events do not result in unacceptable losses. This information enables them to instruct business heads to modify these exposures or to place macro-level hedges, and generally to decide how risk capital should be deployed, based on observed risk and return. This is also the level at which regulatory risk reporting and capital calculations are performed. Although the requirement is generally for high-level, aggregated information, there is often a need to be able to 'drill down' into finer detail if required.

- At the *desk and/or business level* senior heads of trading will be looking at the breakdown of the higher level risk measures for their individual business unit(s). They will monitor how risk capital is being utilized as well as how any risks have changed over time or will vary as other risk events occur, and how individual sources of risk combine into an aggregated risk profile. At this level and below, risk ownership usually occurs. The business is responsible for and owns the risk – and has responsibility for ensuring that those risks are managed correctly.
- Finally, at the *trader/desk level* the focus is on monitoring positions and analysing relative value, risk exposures and hedge equivalent positions so that a trader can either take on, remove or hedge excessive risk.

Throughout this hierarchy, risks are controlled by comparing risk levels against defined limits. The limit structure should cover all the risk types mentioned previously but tends to focus on credit (including counterparty credit limits) and market risk. As part of a balanced approach to risk management, some of these limits may be defined as hard (cannot be broken) or soft (may be temporarily exceeded with management approval). This ensures that controls to limit risk do not inadvertently prevent certain highly profitable transactions being performed. As it is difficult for a formalized limit structure to completely control the risks taken within an organization, a risk management department will support this process. This department will analyse the risk information and ensures all risks are understood and acceptable to the organization.

The risk management process is also validated by ensuring that the reported exposures or risks are consistent with actual events and any resulting P&L. For example, if the risk management process predicts that $100 million may be lost once in every 10 days then any such losses should not exceed this frequency. Similarly, when viewing exposures, if the risk management process predicts that a 1 per cent move in interest rates will result in a $1 million loss then, if this move does occur, the predicted loss should also occur. At the organizational level, *back testing* validates actual P&L against calculated (expected loss) risk levels, to ensure that the reported risk is statistically valid. Regulators use this information to ensure the correctness of the risk management process and impose additional constraints and reserves on organizations that repeatedly underestimate their risks.

It is important to note that different event data and risk measures may be utilized at each level. Traders may wish to risk manage their books based on modified (and hopefully more conservative) data or utilize market data that reflects the trading style adopted. For example, if a fixed income trader is trading government bonds and hedging the risk exposure using bond futures, then risk is likely to be shown in terms of future equivalent positions and hedge ratios. While this is a valid (and required) strategy within a business line, it is difficult to aggregate or compare the risks taken by different desks when different risk calculations are being used. As a result, the higher up the organizational risk hierarchy we move, the more important it is to:

1. Utilize holistic models that enable the comparison of the risks arising from different styles of trading in different asset classes
2. Use comparable models and data so that risk exposures that should offset each other, do indeed do so.

Even where the same type of instrument is traded in two different business areas (for example interest rate swaps are used for hedging in both the foreign exchange (FX) derivatives and interest rate derivatives areas), unless the swaps are priced and risk parameters calculated using the same underlying market data and models, then two identical and opposite positions may not show the same levels of risk. This can become a major issue where it is possible to net/offset risk exposures between business lines, since the two calculated levels of risk will differ.

DRIVERS FOR CHANGE

Systems and processes evolve because they have to. This may either be driven by unique internal drivers such as organizational change and new business models, or be enforced by external drivers such as regulatory requirements, market conditions, competition or client needs. Financial institutions have had to deal with market consolidation and falling trading margins for some time. However, recent research as part of the Finexpo 2003 conference in London[12] highlighted a number of additional key issues that are currently impacting the investment banking community. They include:

Cost reduction
Financial institutions are cautious given the current market conditions and are trying to improve profitability by reducing costs. This is likely to lead to an emphasis on leveraging existing technology within the organization and focusing on projects that improve the efficiency of current processes. These projects will need to also have a rapid impact on profitability or cost saving.

Constrained budgets and reducing IT staff numbers
Budgets are expected to be slightly down on previous years, together with staffing levels. This is placing even further strain on IT resources.

Increased outsourcing
Although tactical outsourcing is expected to increase, organizations appear uncertain about the benefits of outsourcing entire processes or departments.

Regulatory compliance
External regulatory changes, such as Basel 2, are driving risk management changes (especially in credit and operational risk). There are also internal demands for better business intelligence and tighter controls.

Straight through processing (STP)
Improved and more efficient internal processes that require minimal manual intervention. This is being driven by regulatory pressure and the desire for potential cost savings.

In addition, market volatility has increased in many markets with liquidity reducing in others. This has tended to make financial institutions much more risk averse. Despite some of the cautious opinions in the survey, there was a general optimism that IT can assist organizations to mitigate the worst effects of the current market conditions. This research is painting a picture where the risk IT manager is faced with:

- Changes in the regulatory environment, driving new risk management requirements
- A need for improved and timely information to more effectively manage risks
- A drive for increased operational efficiency
- Having to support rapidly evolving business models in an increasingly competitive and volatile marketplace
- Wanting to reuse existing internal resources but having to provide scalable risk management solutions that address current as well as future needs.

The regulatory environment and Basel 2

Whereas financial institutions focus on maximizing returns for the level of risk taken, and mitigating those risks that are viewed as unacceptable, the regulatory environment is concerned with:

- Ensuring the integrity of the markets and that customers are protected from inappropriate practices
- Mitigating systemic risk.

Systemic risk is the risk that some market event will result in a series of correlated shocks throughout the financial system that will negatively impact the wider economy. Typically this is thought of in terms of a significant loss in one institution impacting its ability to meet liabilities to other market participants, and so on, until the entire financial system is under threat.

There have been recent examples of both these types of risks and events in the markets recently. The current US litigation concerning the role of analysts and the financial institution's relationships with the companies covered in the analysts' reports has resulted in widespread changes to the role of research within investment banks, in order to ensure that research is unbiased by other activities (and that as a result clients are not misled).[13] The Sarbanes-Oxley Act (www.sarbanes-oxley.com) has been passed in the US to increase the requirement for board-level members to understand and ensure the accuracy of the figures reported in company accounts. This should reduce the likelihood, and impact on financial institutions, of the uncovering of financial irregularities such as those at Enron and WorldCom.

All these regulatory changes impact the environment that financial institutions operate in, both highlighting as well as trying to reduce risks within the financial system. They may also increase the operational risk for financial organizations, by resulting in fines for regulatory failings, or reputational damage.

Outside the US, the Bank of International Settlements (Basel Committee on Banking Supervision or BIS) has been producing a number of directives to improve the collaboration between banking regulators in different countries, and to assist them in the setting of similar regulations with respect to banks' international operations. Although the Basel Committee directives were originally produced for the G-7 countries, they have since been adopted in over 100 countries. The BIS does not have statutory or regulatory responsibilities, so the precise details and the timing of the implementation of any accord are left to local regulatory authorities in each country. As a result, the precise regulatory risk requirements are likely to vary depending on the regulatory authority.

The initial Basel Capital Accord (1988), for credit risk, achieved international convergence in the measurement of bank capital adequacy and established a minimum regulatory capital requirement for credit risk. Regulatory capital is available as a cushion against large, low probability loss events and, as a result, has a different role to that of economic capital (which is aimed at measuring risk in terms of economic realities, rather than regulatory accounting rules). Eligible capital comprises:

1. Issued shareholder equity and retained earnings (defined as Tier 1 Capital)
2. General provisions and issued subordinated debt as defined in the Accord (Tier 2 Capital)
3. Some short-term issued subordinate debt (Tier 3 Capital).

The aim is to ensure that assets that have higher levels of risk associated with them require higher levels of capital to be maintained. The minimum regulatory capital requirement is then given as a percentage of the risk-weighted assets, which can be compared against the actual regulatory capital of the organization.

The initial Basel Accord is, however, less relevant than it was due to changes in the markets and the business models of banks (partially arising from implementation of the Accord). This has seen banks take on more market risks that are not adequately provisioned for in the initial Accord, although this deficiency was addressed in an amendment to the Accord in 1996. This amendment did not, however, address the differentiation between different types of credit risk and the benefits of credit diversification, so that banks that reduced their credit exposure through this approach were not adequately compensated by a reduced capital requirement.

The new Basel Accord (known as Basel 2) is aimed at addressing a number of deficiencies of the initial accord, requiring a more complex treatment of credit risk (through the introduction of new methodologies and internal models) and the inclusion of operational risk. The capital requirement for operational risk is likely to be a powerful driver for organizations to focus on reducing it.

The implementation of the impending Basel 2 Accord is currently a top priority within all global financial institutions and is again aimed at mitigating systemic risk within the global financial markets. As well as providing a more complete measurement of risk, Basel 2 focuses on a three-pillar approach to ensure safer banking practices:

- Pillar 1: minimum capital requirements based on the existing approach for market risk and new approaches for credit and operational risk
- Pillar 2: supervisory review of institutions' capital adequacy and frameworks for internal assessment and audit processes
- Pillar 3: market discipline through a transparent disclosure process of capital adequacy and risk control processes.

The approaches to measuring risk in the three different risk categories are shown in Table 1.1. The Accord will encourage the use of increasingly complex approaches through the likelihood of a reduced capital requirement.

The Accord has prompted many financial institutions to re-evaluate their existing systems to ensure that regulatory compliance and risk are effectively managed. Risk management technologies built to comply with the first Basel Accord for credit risk were typically based on the use of

Table 1.1 Approaches to risk measurement in the new Basel Accord

Risk Class	Increasing complexity in approach →		
Market	**Minor changes to existing methodology**		
	Standardized	**Internal ratings-based methods (IRB)**	
Credit	Additions to Basel 88 approach	**Foundation approach** Breakdown by exposure category with parameters determined by both institution and input from regulator	**Advanced approach** As for **Foundation** but all parameters calculated by institution
Operational	**Basic indicator approach** Use of a single risk indicator or aggregate activity measure multiplied by a fixed multiple or alpha	**Standardized approach** Different business units are assigned different risk indicators or aggregate activity measures which are multiplied by a fixed multiple or beta determined by the regulator	**Advanced measurement** approach Internally calculated, based on a more complex analysis of the current risk taken within organization

a data warehouse and monolithic applications. As the regulatory environment evolves to be much more complex and demanding, these systems are unlikely to be able to address the needs of financial institutions.

THE MOVE TO REAL TIME AND ON-DEMAND RISK INFORMATION

When the risk profile of the organization is constantly changing, knowing the current market and credit risk a trader is responsible for, in real time, has always been essential. Trading financial instruments without knowing the risks being taken leaves the trader exposed to risk events in an unknown and therefore unpredictable manner. The focus at the trading desks has therefore always been to provide an integrated, high performance environment where traders are aware of the risks they are exposed to at all times. If the risks taken are excessive, this information enables the trader to reduce or remove those risks or modify the risk profile to one that is more acceptable. Risk control monitoring at the desk level has been essential for managing this process.

The flow of information further up the organization, across trading areas and business lines, has however been a more delayed process. This has tended to make the organization-wide risk management process more a reactive than a proactive one. Regulatory risk calculations are only performed at the end of each trading day and senior managers often do not need to monitor intra-day risk unless other lower level control processes have failed or risks have significantly changed (in either magnitude or likelihood). It is this need to review total risks within an organization when certain major risk events occur, or the sources of risk within an organization significantly change, that alters this requirement. As a result, there is a growing need to be able to view on demand the current risk taken within an organization. This move to on-demand intra-day risk information gathering raises a number of data issues which will be addressed throughout this book. Currently, many organizations spend a large amount of their time 'cleaning' and correcting information received from various systems, in order to obtain a true and correct snapshot of the organization as of some moment in time. Often, the effort required in this process demands that this moment in time is some point further in the past than many risk managers would like.

By improving the risk management processes and technology it is possible to move closer to near real time risk monitoring throughout the risk hierarchy. This can have many benefits for business processes throughout the organization. If intra-day risks are constantly monitored throughout the trading day, there will be fewer surprises in the end-of-day risk analysis and calculations. Unexpected changes in the risk profile can also be investigated to ensure that they are not due to failures or incorrect data in the source systems. It is also possible to rectify these problems while financial markets are still active and able to be used to reduce any market risk. Otherwise, this will have to wait until the end of the trading day when reports will have been produced and some of those financial markets are closed. This process can also provide additional competitive advantage, ensuring that regulatory risk and economic capital are used as efficiently as possible. This enables the organization to trade up to its global regulatory risk limits or reapportion capital between different business units intra-day, rather than having to maintain a margin for error based on the use of out of date information. This changing use of risk management information throughout the organization will drive organizational risk management from being seen as a costly reactive process to one which can add value. But for all this to occur the need to efficiently obtain high quality data from across the organization in a timely manner must be addressed.

The changing business models within financial institutions with more cross asset class risk being traded within each business unit is also resulting in problems for localized limit monitoring; similar risks are taken in different business units which produce an aggregate exposure that cannot be determined by looking at any area in isolation. With the increasing overlap of specific types of risk across different business lines, there is also a need to ensure that the aggregate exposure within the organization is controlled. Currently many limit monitoring processes (counterparty exposure is a common exception) are only performed at the business line level or at the end of trading as part of an end-of-day risk management process. This has meant that the available risk limits within the organization cannot easily be dynamically shared across business lines if one area wishes to use the unused risk limits of another business area. With global real time risk management, all this becomes possible.

Notes

1 R. Lowenstein, *When Genius Failed* (Fourth Estate, 2001)
2 'The amazing disintegrating firm', *The Economist* (6 December 2001)
3 F. Cowell, *Practical Quantitative Investment Management with Derivatives* (Palgrave, 2002)
4 S. Beckers, 'A survey of risk measurement theory and practice', in *The Handbook of Risk Management and Analysis,* C. Alexander (ed.) (John Wiley and Sons, 1996) p. 173
5 T. C. Wilson, 'Calculating risk capital', in *The Handbook of Risk Management and Analysis,* C. Alexander (ed.) (John Wiley and Sons, 1996) p. 195
6 R. S. Kaplan and D. P. Norton 'The balanced scorecard – measures that drive performance', *Harvard Business Review* (Jan–Feb 1992) 71–9
7 J. Merriman and A. Tudor, 'Bank of America to cut up to 100 jobs in London', *Yahoo! Finance UK* (Wednesday March 19 2003, 03:10 pm)
8 A. K. Bhattacharya and F. J. Fabozzi (eds), *Asset-backed Securities* (FJF, 1996)
9 D. J. Isenberg 'How senior managers think', *Harvard Business Review* (Nov–Dec 1984) 81–90
10 R. Hogg and A. Craig, *Introduction to Mathematical Statistics* (Prentice Hall, 1995)
11 J. C. Hull *Options, Futures, and other Derivatives* (Prentice Hall, 1997)
12 Finextra.com, *Financial Technology Strategies 2003* (Finextra Research, January 2003)
13 J. Geralds, 'Wall Street analysts probe widens', *IT Week* (11 April 2002)

CHAPTER 2

The risk management challenge

The risk management challenge addresses the requirement to model and measure the risk inherent in the business model of the organization in a manner that accurately reflects the risks taken. Once measured, these risks can be effectively managed, controlled and mitigated. Risk management at the individual process or product level can be reasonably easy to manage for simple financial products. The complexity arises when we need to obtain and combine risk information for different types of risks in a wide range of instruments or operational processes in order to discover the overall risk profile for the organization or business unit. This is complicated by a legacy of risk management systems within which information resides. Risks are also not always additive and the consistency, quality and availability of data may pose significant problems to the risk developer, who will be subjected to numerous internal and external constraints (see Part II).

MODELLING RISK

Modelling the real world

Risk models provide a simplified representation of the 'real world' in which events can be analysed. These models act as a proxy for real world processes and possible events. The outputs are interpreted to provide an indication of actual risk arising from various sources within the organization (Figure 2.1). The bases of these models are typically statistical or probabilistic approaches. They will include assumptions concerning how events impact possible losses, as well as the probability distributions and correlations between those distributions. Many statistical assumptions are based on the independence of some events, and the processes having *'standard'* distributions (for example, being normally or lognormally distributed).[1] Risk modelling within the financial organization is performed in one of two ways:

- *Top down*
  These models combine risk information at the business or enterprise level, without analysing the individual sources of risk, in order to obtain an implied estimate of risk within the organization. Top-down approaches are inherently simpler to implement than bottom-up processes, but cannot readily capture the benefits or the effects of risk mitigation within the organization. They have the advantage of taking a more holistic approach to operational risk, highlighting

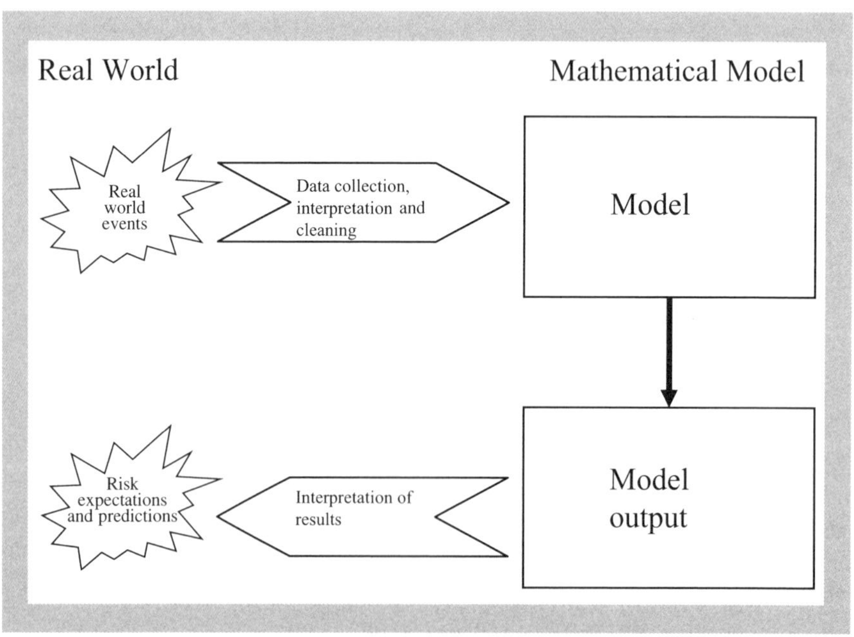

Figure 2.1 Modelling risk and relating it to the real world

issues across business units, and have less onerous data requirements. They are however usually more qualitative in their approach.

- *Bottom up*
  These approaches model the actual sources of risk, together with the events that result in losses within the organization. They are more complex but enable the impact of risk mitigation and other changes in the sources of risk, or probability of various risk events, to be modelled. They have the advantage of providing detailed low-level analysis of the actual sources and events that result in losses. The complexity of these approaches does however mean that they need to be performed by staff who understand the detail of the sources of risk being modelled. This low-level granular approach can however result in information overload and can be time consuming to perform. Focusing only on low-level detail can also miss some of the more important business unit interrelationships and correlations that can result in significant losses.

For pricing risk, a bottom-up approach is typically utilized with the approaches to modelling individual risk positions combined into an aggregate risk exposure (Figure 2.2).

In a bottom-up approach the risk models can be broken down into two types:

- Those used to determine the risk in individual sources of risk, such as those arising from individual positions or from a specific internal process
- Those used to combine individual risk exposures into the total exposure for the individual trader, business unit, region, organization and so on.

The complexity usually arises when trying to combine the various risks into an aggregate risk profile. From a quantitative perspective, this essentially involves determining how individual exposures or probability distributions of returns combine into an overall aggregate risk profile or multivariate distribution. Determining this distribution will require an understanding of the correlation or possible interaction of events. If any but the simplest distributions are involved, complex dependency structures will be required in order to understand how these marginal distributions combine into a total risk profile.

In order to combine the risks in each individual position into an aggregate profile, the risk metrics must be comparable or easily transformable to a common measure. Ideally a common framework should be used

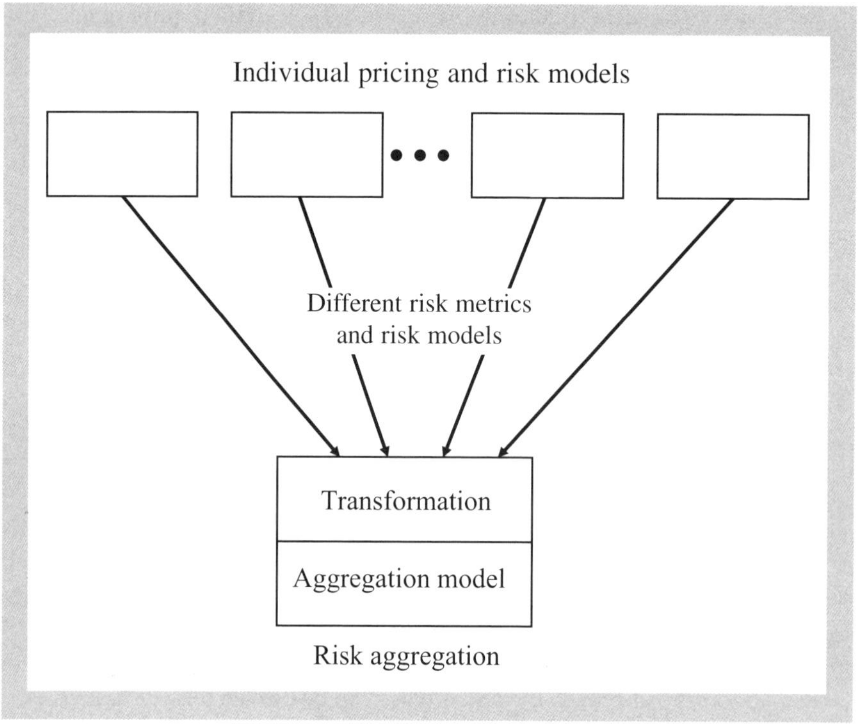

Figure 2.2 Risk model aggregation

throughout all the risk models, so that assumptions within one model are compatible with those in other models. Significantly inconsistent assumptions may lead to misleading results. One reason why exposure and scenario based approaches are viewed as complementary to more statistical methods is that they permit the analysis of certain extreme types of events that may be more likely than predicted from simple (assumed) statistical distributions.

Uncertainty in modelling risk

Any risk model from which we can calculate the risk associated with a financial instrument or operational process should be complete enough to ensure that all key risks to the organization are accurately reflected. Operational risk and uncertainty enters the risk management process due to deficiencies and failings in the processes and the models used. Models take various inputs (which may either be based on observable data or be subjectively determined), process these and produce a measure of risk (Figure 2.3). The models used within financial institutions can be categorized as:

Direct models
Prices and risks are directly derivable from observable data. For example, the price of an equity share and the impact of changes in that price are directly observable and can be obtained from equity exchanges.

Industry standard models
These are models which are generally accepted and commonly used within the industry. There is less implementation risk associated with using these models as they can be tested against commonly available and comparable models.

Proprietary models
These are models which are unique to the organization. As a result they are difficult to test and validate against other third party implementations and tend to be compared against (Monte Carlo) simulation methods (see Chapter 3) or independent reimplementations, possibly using mathematical analysis tools.

There are a number of points in this process where inaccuracies or errors may result in incorrect or inaccurate risk information:

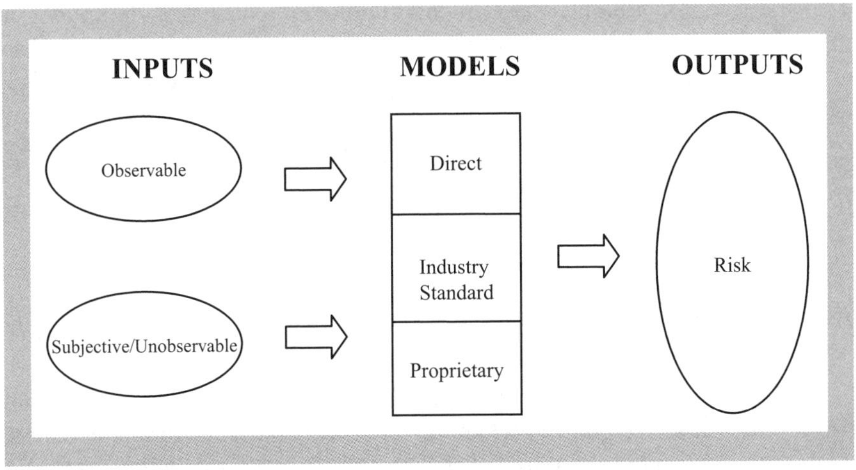

Figure 2.3 Input and model uncertainty

1. Uncertain input data, especially subjective parameters
2. Poor quality, inaccurate or incorrect input data
3. Mis-specification, incorrect assumptions or imprecise model
4. Incorrect model implementation
5. A combination of all of the above.

These deficiencies will introduce additional risk into the process, which should be quantified. This will often result in additional capital reserves being calculated to augment any other capital calculations performed as part of the risk process. The effort expended in developing models or improving data quality to enhance the quality of risk information should take into account the points listed above; there is little point in developing the 'perfect' model if it is not possible to obtain accurate input data to utilize it, just as there is no point in expending time on determining the input parameters to a high level of accuracy if the model is too simplistic to utilize this information, or the output of the model is not sensitive to that parameter.

It is this uncertainty in the input parameters that may result in traders needing to set their own model parameters in addition to using standard organizational values. Uncertainties or inaccuracies in the models used may also mean that traders may wish to use a different or more complex model in order to manage their risks. Uncertainty in the input parameters can be analysed by looking at the change in the model output as the input parameters vary, providing some indication of the possible error in the model outputs. Similarly, the impact of different modelling assumptions or numerical implementations of a model can be investigated by comparing the values generated by different models or model implementations. Even when the price of a financial instrument is directly observable in the marketplace, there are often varying levels of price transparency. A transparent market is one where it is possible to simply obtain a true and fair representation of the 'best price' available for that instrument in the market. This will depend on a number of factors such as:

- *Liquidity:* Instruments which trade infrequently will not have an up to date, current tradable price.
- *Fragmentation of market:* Instruments that trade in a single location will have a single point at which the best available price can be obtained; the exchange an equity is listed on will always provide the best price

in the market, whereas fixed income securities do not trade in any single location but are bought and sold in one-on-one sales or on electronic markets.

- *Size of position:* The prices obtained in the market for some financial instruments may not be achievable if the size of the position is exceptionally large.

Historical and predictive model inputs

Input parameters to models, when based on observable data, are either derived from historically observed behaviour or from observing current events or processes. For example, the probability of a credit default occurring can be based on observed frequencies of default for similar companies or derived from current observed credit default swap spreads.[2]

When historical data is used, the inherent assumption is that past behaviour is likely to repeat itself in the future. As a result, historical information can act as a source of information for backtesting and validating models, but it can be an ineffectual signpost for what will occur in the future. This is especially true if internal business process change when modelling operational risk or if financial markets undergo a step change in behaviour when modelling credit or market risk.

Even if there is not a major step change in the external markets, utilizing historical data as inputs into a risk model can introduce a time-lag effect. As external events occur, these are retrospectively included in any risk calculation. This means that when market conditions result in potentially higher levels of risk, these will only increase any calculated level of risk after the event, when that data is included in any risk calculation. If historical data is only periodically updated for use in risk analysis, this can result in sudden jumps in the level of calculated risk based on this reassessment of external events.

Model calibration

Many models need to be calibrated to the market. This is especially true (and also very problematic) with operational risk models and can be computationally complex as well as time consuming. The aim of calibration is to derive the unobservable model input parameters given the observed model outputs (possibly only for certain well-defined cases or financial instruments). This requires the unique determination of the input parameter(s) given the model output, or for assumptions to be made about the possible range of values the input parameter(s) may take. Examples of this process can be seen where implied volatilities are deduced from observed option values by matching option prices.[3] These implied volatilities are then used to price other less liquid instruments. Similarly, model multiples in operational and portfolio market risk may be deduced by comparing expected and observed risk levels and calibrating between the two.

DATA REQUIREMENTS FOR RISK MANAGEMENT

One of the major challenges in risk management is obtaining the requisite data that, as well as quantifying the sources and events which result in risk within the organization, also identifies the returns and losses arising from those risks (Figure 2.4).

The information concerning the sources of risk within the organization will be spread across the entire organization. It will consist of financial transactions as well as operational related information concerning

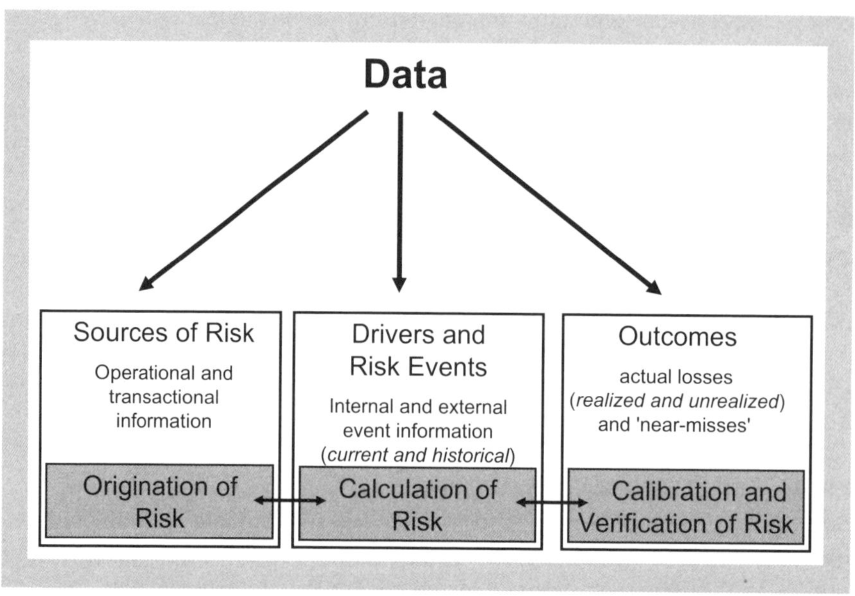

Figure 2.4 Data requirements for risk management

processes, people and technology. In order to calculate the risk arising from these sources of risk, data concerning external and internal events (both current and historical) is required as input into the risk models. Finally, data regarding the actual losses or returns attributable to different sources of risk must be obtained in order to validate, calibrate and test the implemented risk measures.

THE RISK MANAGEMENT HIERARCHY

Risk management on the trading desk and business unit

Silo and monolithic trading systems

At the bottom of the risk management hierarchy, on the individual trading desks, there have historically been two extremes of approach to developing trading and market/credit risk management systems (Figure 2.5):

1. The first was to implement a *monolithic* all-encompassing global trading system that provided a single approach and storage location for *all* transactions across the bank, its locations and desks.
2. The other was the more commonly seen 'stove pipe' or *silo* approach, where each business area (and possibly location) developed a tailored solution to address that area's individual needs.

The approach taken will have been driven by:

The manner in which budgets and costs were allocated
Where budgets and management structure were more devolved, a legacy of silo applications will have been created, so that systems development is aligned with the profit centre (business unit) responsible for funding it. Centralized budgets or management control tends to encourage resource sharing and the development of centralized systems.

The ability of a single system to address all the requirements for trading the desired range of financial instruments
If traders are responsible for a wide range of different financial instruments then all-encompassing cross asset class systems tend to be developed.

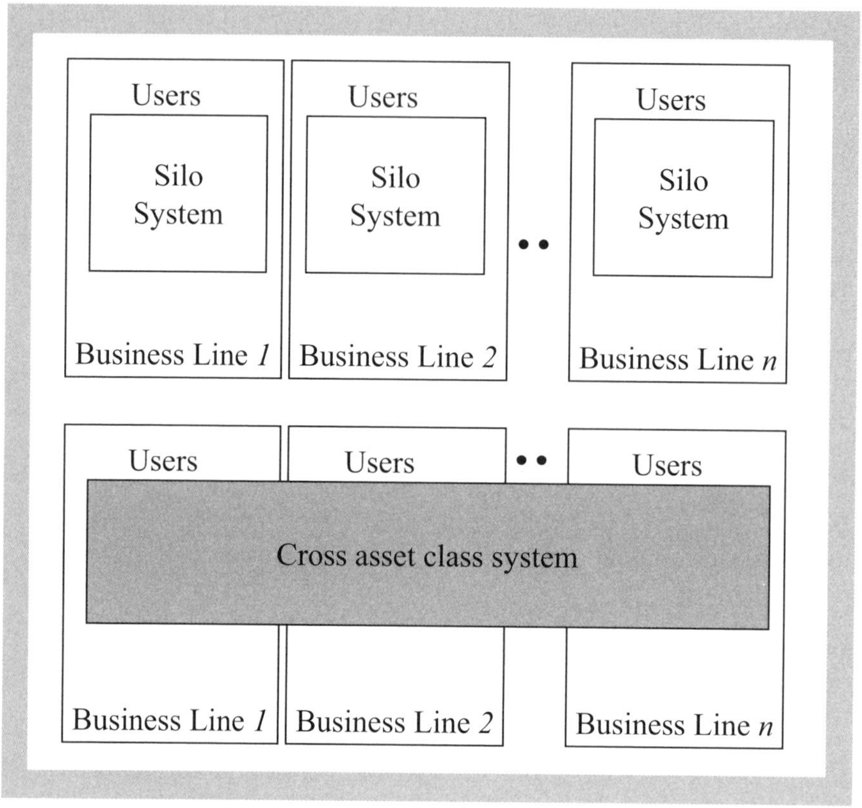

Figure 2.5 Two extreme approaches to system development

The dominant technology paradigm and costs associated with supporting such approaches at the time the solution was developed
Where a centralized mainframe processing paradigm has dominated, there is a tendency to develop centralized applications that can easily be shared across business lines. More distributed development and processing paradigms tend to have resulted in the development of silo applications.

Each approach has its own unique advantages and disadvantages as detailed in Table 2.1.

The performance implications of trying to use a single code base to support the global requirements of all traders in a monolithic solution can result in extremely complex and poor performance solutions. While they may address many of the generic requirements in the markets traded, they are complicated by the addition of location and

Table 2.1 Advantages and disadvantages of silo and centralized system solutions

Centralized systems	
Advantages	*Disadvantages*
■ Single location/system for all transactional information	■ Unresponsive to individual trader needs
■ Standard functionality used by all traders	■ Broad range of requirements which are difficult to project manage
■ High levels of code and functionality reuse	■ Significant global co-ordination (both technically and managerially)
■ Reduced costs and easier to maintain	■ Difficult to address individual trader or local regional requirements
	■ Difficult to efficiently support a diverse set of requirements and business models
	■ Often a lack of a single business sponsor
Silo systems	
Advantages	*Disadvantages*
■ 'Best of breed' approach	■ Expensive due to the rebuilding of common functionality
■ Efficiently implement unique trader or location specific requirements	■ Costly to maintain multiple solutions
■ Few contradictory requirements	■ Little functionality or code reuse
■ Single business sponsor	■ Non-standard approaches
■ Funded by business unit which will benefit from the system	■ Multiple technologies and development platforms
■ More limited requirements which are easier to project manage	■ Greater integration requirements within the organization

user-specific functionality which, although available to all, may only be used by a small subset of the user base. For example, a trading system developed for US traders may have to handle higher trading volumes, but only needs to consider instruments that trade in the US and settle in a single location in US dollars. By contrast, a solution developed for Europe or Asia will need to handle the multiple currencies, settlement locations and other non-standard demands of a multitude of international markets and clients. Developing a solution that can handle the complexities of the European or Asian markets will, however, add additional functionality, which may have negative performance implications if the solution is also to be deployed in the US.

The many, often contradictory, requirements and frequent lack of a clear business sponsor for a centralized approach and system often doom such approaches to failure before they even begin. It is therefore not surprising that most financial institutions have taken an approach that is somewhere between the extremes mentioned. The precise manner in which boundaries between systems and trading areas have been defined has often been driven by internal organizational and structural issues. As a result, market and credit risk information has been distributed across a number of different front office systems.

The distribution of risk information across many systems does not in itself result in an intractable data management problem. However, taking the silo approach to its illogical conclusion of ultimate trader flexibility at the expense of all other controls and management issues resulted in the 'spreadsheet madness' witnessed in many investment banks during the 1990s. This situation resulted from traders developing and using individually tailored spreadsheets to rapidly structure, trade and risk manage deals (see Chapter 10).

Although flexible, these unscalable 'stove pipe' solutions resulted in little reuse of software or methodology in other areas of the bank, non-standard valuation and risk management approaches, and can prove impossible to control and maintain. The difficulty in integrating these spreadsheets into other internal systems also resulted in processes that were manually intensive, non-scalable and prone to frequent process failure.

Approaches to silo trading system development

One of the key problems for a single monolithic system supporting all instrument types and trading models is that there are typically two types of financial instruments traded:

- High-volume, commodity type 'flow' instruments (for example equities, bonds, FX and so on)
- Lower volume, highly customized and structured instruments (often known as over-the-counter or OTC derivative transactions).

Innovative new financial instruments typically fall into the second category. They have higher margins and costs associated with them (due to the overhead in trading and managing such unique transactions). However, over time successful structures and customized instruments do become more standardized and clearly parameterized using standard financial language and documentation. As part of this standardization process, volumes will increase and move into the first category. This has often required a rewrite of the associated systems in order to handle the change in business model. An example of this can be seen in the credit derivative markets. Initially each transaction was uniquely defined and required complex legal documentation. As volumes increased, along with a desire to reduce costs, the definition of the contract and the terms within the contract became standardized. This led to the ISDA credit definitions,[4] which are now commonly used in most credit derivatives transactions.

The different volume and customization characteristics of these two groups of financial instruments result in two different extremes of systems being developed to support trading in them. For higher volume products, trades must be rapidly captured or entered into this system and managed by the trader. This leads to a requirement for highly automated trade capture and management systems (and the ability to enter partially completed trades with the main risk management characteristics completed) with visualization, filtering, sorting and reporting tools that enable the trader to manage high volumes of data.

At the other extreme, customized low-volume transactions require an environment where everything in the transaction can be modified to the precise requirements of the client. Often the risk in these transactions is significantly more complex and so a trader will require tailored visualization and reporting of a range of risk measures. A system that displays this level of flexibility, can be extremely difficult (and expensive) to develop and so tends to lend itself to ad hoc tools that permit the trader to develop and implement this functionality as and when required. For the risk system developer, these two types of system have significantly different challenges associated with them. Trying to reconcile both these contradictory requirements in a single system is exceptionally difficult; the data model would need to efficiently handle the high-volume standardized transactions while also being extensible and flexible enough for current and future structured transactions. The user interface would also need to be able to permit the rapid entry of data for standardized instruments while being able to support the customization of many of the features of the instruments.

Cross asset class trading and structuring

The development of silo applications has also led to further problems as the evolution of the financial markets has resulted in increasingly complex business models and financial structures. Different business units now often hedge using instruments normally associated with other business units and handled in other silo trading systems. Recent examples have seen a move towards combining government bond trading, corporate bond trading and 'flow' credit derivative trading together with the use of interest rate swaps as liquid hedging instruments into a single trading platform. This enables each desk using such a system to easily utilize the functionality and instruments usually associated with other trading areas. For example, the interest rate risk that is inherent in government bonds is also present in corporate bonds and can be hedged using interest rate swaps and bond futures. The credit risk inherent in corporate bonds is also the underlying risk in the credit derivative market and can be hedged using asset swaps or equity type transactions, due to the interrelationship between credit quality and the underlying value of the company. The traders within each business area, however, often have differing requirements and approaches to viewing these instruments. What is required are systems that possess all the advantages of both silo and monolithic system approaches, without any of the disadvantages.

This increasing interaction of what historically have been seen as separate financial markets, as well as the desire to differentiate the organization by being able to customize transactions using the most appropriate combination of different types of instrument, has begun to break the silo-based approach to trading system development. There is now an increasing realization, even at the trading desk level, that it must be possible to aggregate risk and reuse functionality that has been typically associated with different systems. This has led to the extraction of information from individual silo systems and the combining of the aggregated risk into a single real time risk management view on the trading desk (Figure 2.6). Frequently this process has been performed in an ad hoc manner within and across different business units, resulting in a bottom-up approach to building trading and risk systems.

In addition, there has also been a need to be able to link together transactions in different systems, in order to associate them with a single financial structure. Such approaches have resulted in new user

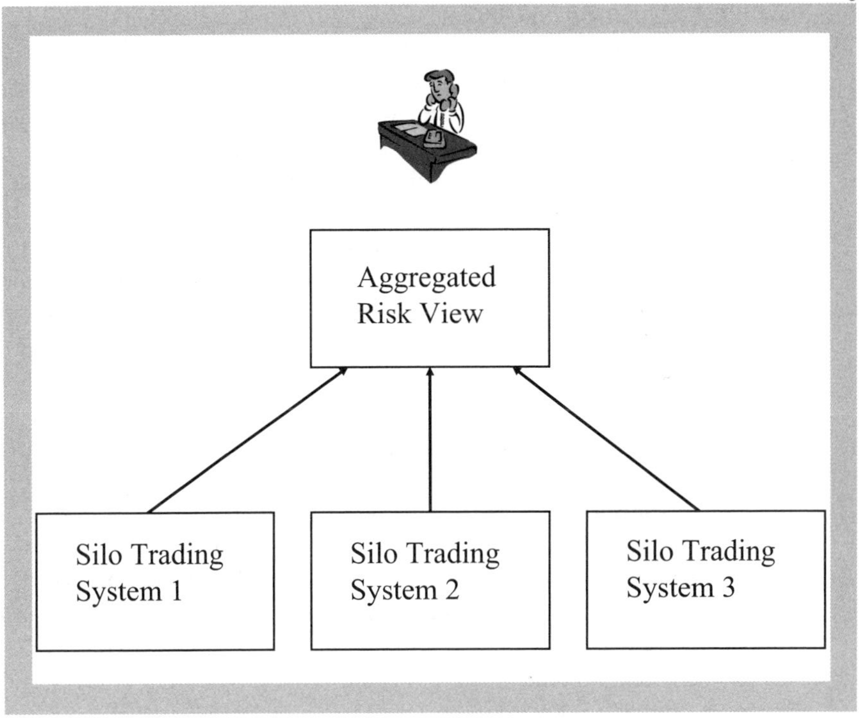

Figure 2.6 Risk aggregation at the desk level

interfaces that provide a common method of accessing a number of silo trading systems behind this interface. Traders may perform macro-level hedges at the aggregate portfolio level or associate the hedge trade directly with a structure of an individual position (that is, a micro-level hedge). The requirement to view the risk broken down in such a manner is placing increasing demands and dependencies on the individual trading systems within organizations. For risk aggregation within the business unit level, a single system is typically responsible for each instrument type. The issue of aggregating information is then one of forwarding financial transactions onto the appropriate system, calculating risk in each of these systems and combining the risk into a consolidated view of the business unit. However, when different (possibly inconsistent) approaches to calculating risk are used by different systems, the process can exhibit some of the complexities associated with business level aggregation.

Business level aggregation

The correlated nature of many of the risks taken in different business units means that individual risk exposures are likely to combine into a significant aggregate risk profile for the organization. For example, in crises such as the bankruptcy of Enron, many financial institutions held a large amount of Enron corporate bonds but also had sold credit protection on Enron, had outstanding loans, OTC derivatives with Enron as the counterparty and even held a significant amount of Enron shares. Each of these instruments may have been traded in different business units, which can result in a significant aggregate credit exposure to a single company, even if each of the individual exposures is not significant.

As a result, any initial assessment of exposure that looks at a single system or geographical location can be very misleading. When information is aggregated across multiple systems, whether to support trading activity or for business level risk management, there is a need for consistency in certain pricing and risk management approaches. Although, at the trader level, different risk metrics, models or input parameters may be used to aid the trader in their decision making, this becomes more problematic as information from different traders and business units is aggregated (see Table 2.2).

Table 2.2 highlights the need to ensure some level of consistency in pricing and risk management between each trading system. The use of different models or risk metrics and input parameters within the organization leads to two issues:

1. Reconciling the risk information produced at different levels of the organization; the inability to reconcile risk information used to calculate economic capital or enforce risk limits with that as understood by the individual trader is likely to result in significant issues within the organization.

2. Inaccuracies and netting problems when combining information calculated using inconsistent models and data into an aggregated view of risk within the organization.

As a result, most financial institutions tend to standardize the modelling approaches used. They may permit different pricing models only where differences or inaccuracies are well understood, or do not impact the risk metrics calculated higher in the risk hierarchy. The

Table 2.2 Complexity of the reconciliation issue between different levels of the risk hierarchy

		Input parameters	
		Same	**Different**
Pricing and risk model	**Same**	No reconciliation or aggregation issues	Differences can be rationalized in terms of sensitivities to input parameters. Comparable prices and risk information can be obtained by choosing a consistent set of input parameters.
	Different	Complex if more than a simple transformation is required to convert results from one model to another. This will require an understanding of the different assumptions inherent in each model and their impact on the risk metrics. Comparable prices and risk information are most easily obtained by recalculating price and risk information using a common set of models.	Highly complex – both the differences in the two models and the sensitivities of each to input parameters need to be understood. Aggregation can be achieved by selecting one of the models in preference to the other and using a common set of input data.

use of different input parameters can be managed and is often permitted within many organizations as a key trader requirement. It is however, relatively easy for the trader to investigate and understand any discrepancies resulting from differences in these parameters. The end-of-day or end-of-month reconciliation of these figures is usually handled as part of the control function to ensure that any reported P&L or risk information is a true and fair reflection of the actual portfolio.

Integrate the enterprise

The reality of integrating risk management technologies across the enterprise, inclusive of all asset classes and geographic locations is a complex task. Not only are systems likely to be physically located in different places but they are also likely to have been developed over different time periods using different technologies, often using the current 'in vogue' technology of the time. The result of this distributed development and deployment environment is that there are major challenges in obtaining and consolidating data represented with different data model semantics and syntax, and stored using different technologies.

This 'fruit machine' challenge is one of the major problems in risk management design; whereas one system may be sending a cherry, another an apple, and a third a gold bar, the risk system architect wants to be able to see just a line of all cherries, apples or gold bars, rather than a losing mix.

From a risk modelling perspective, risk aggregation provides further problems. Due to the correlation between risks arising in different parts of the organization and the non-linear nature of some risk metrics, risk aggregation is often not a simple summation process across the organization. Additional information is required in order for these risks to be combined in a coherent manner.

However, once all an organization's risk exposures can be viewed in a single location or application, regulatory reporting becomes a far simpler task. Senior management is also able to make much more informed decisions. The greater the volume of information available on an organization's funding costs, existing risk profile and capital requirement, the easier it becomes to enter into transactions which reduce risk and accurately reflect the costs involved.

TRANSACTIONAL AND WAREHOUSING SYSTEMS

Front office systems are transactional systems designed to support an organization's day to day operational activities. They will only maintain data that is directly relevant to this task, which is likely to be incomplete for all risk management needs, even if a single centralized system is developed. If other data that is relevant to the risk management process is forced into these systems, there is likely to be a detrimental performance impact. Their transactional nature means that they are optimized for inserting and updating current information, in order to provide an up to date, current view of transactional activity and risk. They hinder efficient access to and complex processing of snapshots of data at different points in the past. Carrying out such unoptimized data retrieval in order to perform contemporaneous analyses across multiple systems is likely to have a significant impact on trading system performance and response times. Because of these limitations data warehouses are often used to record complete and consistent snapshots of historical information for general retrieval and analysis, away from the transactional environment. A comparison of the contradictory requirements between transactional and data warehouse systems can be seen in Table 2.3.

So although rapid risk calculations on current positional data are unlikely to be problematic using transactional systems, the complex calculation and analysis of risk information using significant amounts of historical information will be. This is problematic for online analytical processing (OLAP) tools that 'slice and dice' information in a number of dimensions and enable analysts to gain insight into the data through fast, consistent, interactive access of a wide variety of possible views of information. Data mining tools may also be used to answer more abstract queries and provide the non-trivial extraction of implicit, previously unknown information from data.

As a result, there is a tendency to replicate data into other systems or data warehouses, where it is held in a common data representation and format, to be efficiently accessible away from the trading environment. The duplication of information can however result in further problems:

Table 2.3 Comparison of data requirements for transactional and data warehouse systems

	Data warehouse system	Transactional system
Aim	Information retrieval and analysis	Support operational activities
Data	Data required to manage and analyse the business	Data required to run the business
Type of data	Historical and descriptive	Incomplete, current view of business operations
Data Model	Single consistent data model representing risk within the entire organization	Optimized local data model to support operational activities

- Possibility of introducing yet another set of inconsistent models, market data and risk measures, if risk calculations are replicated away from the trading environment. This approach can however ensure that all risks are recalculated in a consistent manner.
- Tendency for the design to become embroiled in the search for the 'holy grail' of a data model that can efficiently represent all financial transactions. There is also the possibility of data model 'wars', where different models used within the organization compete for supremacy.
- Reconciliation issues with other systems.

Where multiple front end systems are used to feed a risk management database or data warehouse, the combining of this information can require significant effort in post processing: cleaning, standardizing and remapping data into a common format. The common experience is often that most of the effort in data collection is spent extracting, cleaning and uploading information, which acts as a barrier to real time information reporting.

This makes the issue of aggregating risk information into a single location even more complex than just mapping between data models and performing additional risk calculations (Table 2.4). It also means that corporate level risk management is often only performed once a day, based on market closing positions. Although this is acceptable for regulatory risk reporting, it means that intra-day risk positions essen-

Table 2.4 Comparison of complexity and requirements at each level of the risk hierarchy

	Trader/Desk level	Business level	Organization level
Timeline	Real time	Near real time	Once a day
Frequency	Constantly updated	Frequent intra-day updates	On demand, but typically end of each day
Risk management	Hedging and exposure analysis	Exposure analysis and limit monitoring	Capital adequacy, concentration, expected loss, capital charging
Complexity of risk models	Simple	Medium	Complex

tially go unmonitored. This can result in traders being able to take on significant intra-day risk without it being noticed by the risk management group. In fact, if the trader is clever enough and passes positions around the globe into local books, there is a chance it may never be picked up in the risk reporting process! What is clearly required is an approach where intra-day risks can be monitored in a more timely manner, across all asset classes (as well as ensuring data is correctly entered). This information monitoring can then be used to feed a data warehouse for more complex and historical risk analysis and reporting.

SOURCES OF RISK AND LOSS INFORMATION

Although risk associated with trading activity is monitored in front office trading systems as part of the trading operation, other areas within the organization may be more appropriate sources for ensuring the completeness and accuracy of all its risk information.

Organizational structure

Financial institutions characterize their operations in terms of front office, middle and back office (Figure 2.7). Front office characterizes the trading and sales environment where direct trading interaction with clients and financial markets occurs. This is where financial transactions are initiated and the part of the organization most focused on intra-day real time risk management. It is also the area most exposed to semantic volatility or changing definitions and requirements. This is mainly because new instruments, changing business models and market requirements all drive front office requirements. The higher the level of semantic volatility, the more likely the information captured and the functionality of those systems is likely to change, with associated impacts on the maintenance of any risk management infrastructure. Behind the front office are the middle and back offices. The middle office is typically a control function that validates the front office transactions, their recording in internal systems, booking, validation of risk and P&L (the role of product control) and ensures that they are correctly processed from an accounting standards perspective (financial control). The back office is then responsible for the settlement and processing of those transactions as well as the

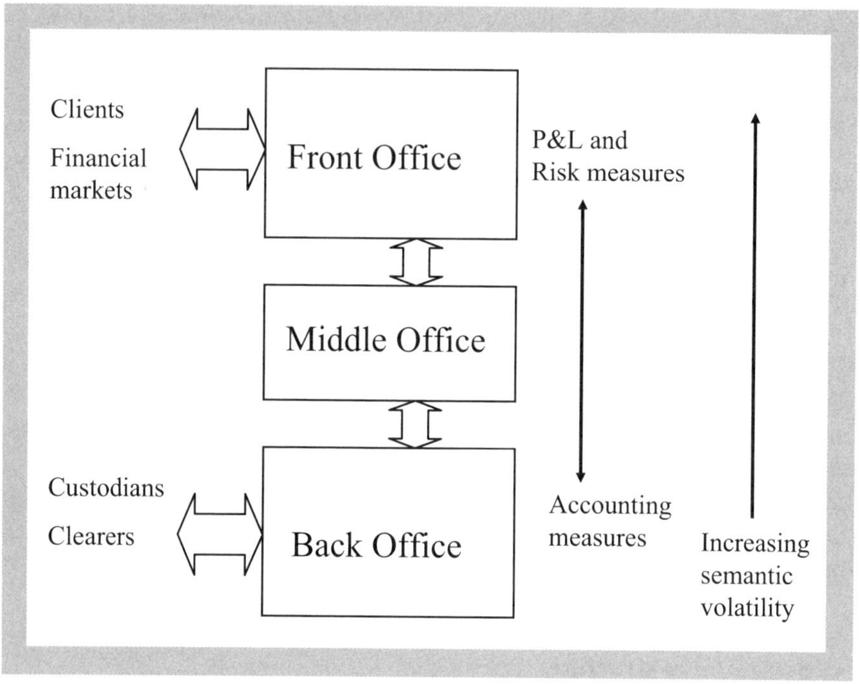

Figure 2.7 Typical organizational structure

recording of this information in the general ledger or GL (the firm's books and records system).

Information sources

Information concerning the financial transactions undertaken in an organization, and the resulting risks, can be obtained at many internal points. However, it is important to note that certain risk data and specific views of that information can be more easily obtained from some areas (typically the area viewed as owning that information) than others. For market and credit risk resulting from trading operations, this will be most easily obtained from the front office systems or where it is validated in the middle office. Data concerning client collateral that can offset certain counterparty exposures can be obtained from the credit department. Operational risk is prevalent throughout the organization, and often manifests itself when the organization interacts with the outside world (in settling financial transactions). As a result, sources of operational risk are often visible in the back office, which can then be tied back to events in other parts of the organization that were responsible for originating that risk. Indications of operational risk may also be obtained from reports and risk assessments generated by the audit department or operational risk function, data corrections rates recorded throughout the organization, data inconsistency issues from reconciliation systems within the product control area and so on.

Certain information, such as market or credit risk will not be available in back office systems because it is not of interest to them. Back office systems will, however, provide an accurate record of P&L and other accounting related information, such as actual cash (Nostro) positions, which are recorded in the GL. Also, different parts of the organization will focus on different risks. For example, front office traders may not always view translation risk (the risk due to FX moves on P&L netted into the organization's reporting currency), preferring to focus on local (trading) currency risk. However, the treasury department will be concerned with where funding occurs and the transfer of profits into the base currency, putting in place appropriate FX hedges.

The key lesson is that there is rarely a single point or system within the organization where the risk manager can go to obtain all the information required to risk manage the organization as a whole. The precise details of which systems to utilize, and at what point in the organization this should occur, will depend on the organization. The types of risks monitored and the manner in which they are measured will also often vary throughout the organization.

DATA MANIPULATION

Risk decomposition

If only a single type of instrument is traded that naturally aggregates, the process of viewing the total risk within the portfolio is trivial. For example, a spot FX trader will buy or sell various currencies. The amount bought or sold in each currency can simply be aggregated to show a net balance across all the currencies traded. However, for most trading desks, and especially when aggregating risk across the organization, there is no longer an obvious way to aggregate positions in different instruments. This necessitates the decomposition of the risks in each instrument into their constituent parts. For example, a forward

FX (or FX derivative) trader will be taking both spot FX risk as well as interest rate risk. This risk decomposition requires a mapping of instrument exposures into a set of underlying risk factors (or sources of risk). Individual risks then result in a number of equivalent risks (Figure 2.8) that can be aggregated with other equivalent risks, enabling the overall risk exposure to be more effectively managed. The breakdown of risk into these underlying risk factors, and the definition of what those factors are, requires detailed analysis of the instruments traded. Typically, the breakdown into risk factors is driven by the manner in which the instruments are monitored or financially modelled on the trading desk. As a result, this decomposition should reflect the trader's understanding of how the instrument trades as well as the fundamental drivers behind the instrument. For example, a corporate bond's price will be driven by a combination of liquidity, interest rate levels and the underlying company's perceived credit quality, together with any specific credit considerations inherent in the bond. Given that it is impossible to model or have behavioural parameters for everything, there will inherently be some loss of detail as part of this process. If the decomposition into risk factors is performed correctly, there should be minimal loss in accuracy in the calculation of subsequent risk measures using these factors. Care should however be taken when a business unit trades certain specific risks. These are risks

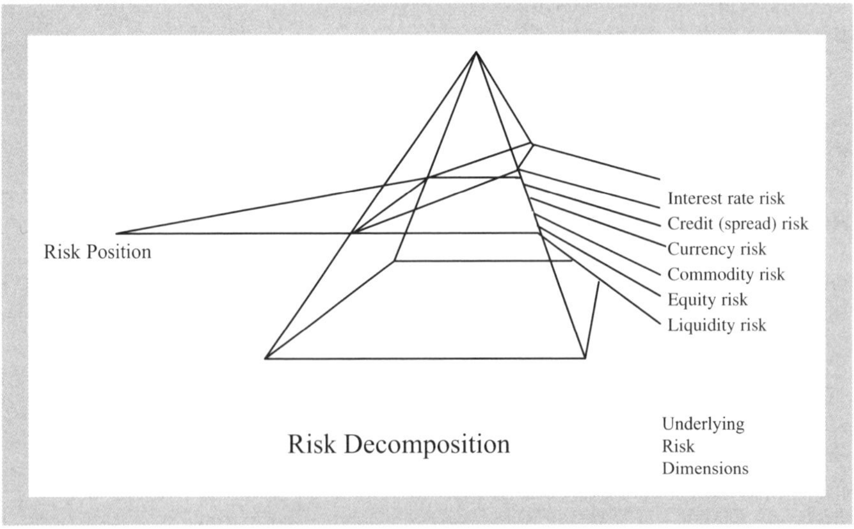

Figure 2.8 Risk decomposition process

that cannot be attributed to general market movements but are specific to the asset being managed. Too generalized a risk decomposition process can result in these risks being omitted.

Risk bucketing

Although the decomposition of instrument risk into a common set of risk factors enables risks to be aggregated and consolidated on the individual trading desk, the number of risk factors used across an entire organization can result in a data explosion. These factors may also not be used consistently across the organization leading to a complex risk mapping problem. All this can lead to an intractable data and risk modelling problem. To address this, the risk factors used by each desk are bucketed or allocated to some observable or derivable market driver (and associated risk events). This bucketing process involves risk allocation and the making of a number of assumptions. Risk factors mapped to the same bucket will be perfectly correlated and therefore expected to have similar behaviour. The impact of these assumptions and the mapping process performed will very much depend on the type and magnitude of any risks and the trading/business models within the organization. This risk bucketing process requires a reasonable amount of analysis concerning the behaviour of the different risk buckets and the types of risks traded within each portfolio. The bucketing process should not result in the loss of any key risk information but should capture the essence of the risks that drive and dominate possible losses within the organization. Possible approaches include:

- *Equity:* map to national (or sector) indexes; model individual stocks; use a principal component approach
- *Commodities:* map to an equivalent futures or cash position
- *FX:* map to currency buckets and interest rate sensitivities
- *Distressed (high yield) securities:* map to equity-type risk factors since they behave more like equities than interest rate instruments
- *Bonds:* map to an equivalent bond in the nearest maturity bucket or specified date range or break down into a number of risk equivalent interest rate positions
- *Individual future cashflows*: map to maturity buckets.

Table 2.5 Examples of the advantages and disadvantages of different approaches to risk mapping

Mapping	Advantages	Disadvantages
Individual equity stocks	Accurate representation of risk	High volume of position information and requirement for event information
Sector indices	Moderate data requirements	Does not capture equity specific risk
Market/country indices	Lowest level of data requirements	Does not capture firm specific or sector specific risks
Factor analysis (principal component analysis)	Reasonable data requirements Captures some specific risk	Fails to capture all firm specific risk More complex event data analysis requirements

The aim must be to ensure that any assumptions made do not result in risks being missed or the bucketed risks being unrepresentative of the actual risks taken. Balanced against this requirement is the need to put in place a process that is manageable (in terms of data volumes and data mapping complexity) and achievable. A more simplistic process that works is clearly preferable to a highly accurate and complex one that will not be implementable. Similarly, there is no advantage in using a complex approach that adds little in accuracy for the types of portfolios managed. For example, equity risk can be broken down in a number of ways, each resulting in different levels of data and loss of information, as seen in Table 2.5.

DATA ISSUES

Data types

Data within the organization can be broken down into the following types:

Transactional
This is data concerned with financial transactions. Transactional information must be persisted (stored permanently) and its integrity maintained.

Non-transactional
This may be:

- *Dynamic*
  Data that frequently changes during the trading day, such as market data or other pricing or event type information. Except at key points in the trading day (such as end of day, opening prices, snapshots associated with complex risk calculations), or for historical analysis, there should be no requirement to persist this information
- *Static*
  Static data is information that is persisted and remains constant over a reasonable time period (although updates and additions may occur at any time). This data is typically associated with instrument definitions, client details, process flows and so on.

Data quality

In order for the risk management information produced to be of use, the quality of data input into the process must be as high as possible. The major challenge in corporate risk management is collecting transactional data and the loss events associated with its processing. The typical problems encountered when obtaining this information can be characterized by the '4Cs of data quality', where data should be:

Complete
Ensure that all data required for input into the risk management process is captured.

Consistent
If risk data is obtained from multiple systems, any calculated values should have been modelled in a consistent manner. For example, if an instrument is traded in multiple locations using different pricing algorithms, the resultant prices and risk measures should be consistent between those locations.

Correct (or accurate)
The risk data captured should be correct. This requires system validation and efficient error detection. This is most often achieved through

exception-based monitoring, which is the automatic highlighting of potential errors at the earliest possible point. Exception monitoring is much more efficient and less likely to result in errors being overlooked compared with utilizing a more manual verification and detection process.

Current
Data must be obtained in a timely manner (where timely depends on the usage and requirements for the data). All data should also always refer to the same time epoch, otherwise offsetting risk transactions entered into multiple systems may not offset each other (for example hedge transactions), leading to misleading risk analysis.

Failure to obtain high quality data for the risk management process will result in a significant increase in operational risk.

Because of the importance of obtaining high quality data, effort should not be expended on developing complex methodologies that are highly accurate and informative, only for them to add no value due to the poor or incomplete quality of the data used. It is often better to adopt simpler risk management approaches higher up the organizational hierarchy and use the implementation of these to enforce and implement greater position and data gathering discipline. The nature of aggregating together data that has not been combined before will result in issues and discrepancies that will not have previously been observed. These data issues can take a significant amount of effort to resolve. It is better to understand these as soon as possible rather than to build the perfect risk management solution only to then find that it adds no value due to the quality of information available from the surrounding systems. Data discrepancies and errors are a reality in any complex system, and so it is important that data can be corrected or modified in order to ensure that high quality data can be achieved. Ideally these corrections should be applied to the source of any data, but if this is not possible there must be the ability to modify the data as it is used further downstream. This process should ensure that there is a full audit trail in order to reconcile any differences in source systems and aggregated data analysis.

Static data

A common problem within financial institutions is that just as trading systems have been developed as silo applications, so have the maintenance and storage of the associated static data. The creation of multiple instances of fragmented static data can result in significant reconciliation and inconsistency issues between geographical locations and different business areas. This can significantly complicate the aggregation of risk information and increase operational risk within the organization. Consistent and correct static data is essential for risk management. It is responsible for providing consistent instrument definitions used in risk calculations as well as information concerning counterparties to transactions that permit credit risk to be aggregated. Any instrument definitions should provide information on *fungibility*. Fungibility is the standardization and interchangeability of financial instruments on the same terms. This enables parties in a transaction to reverse out the risk associated with the instrument by entering into an offsetting transaction in an identical (fungible) instrument. This is especially important in markets where multiple instrument identifiers represent the same fungible instrument. Although a trader will be concerned with not only the instrument to be traded but also the marketplaces any transaction should be executed on, the risk manager is only concerned with whether risks in different instruments can offset each other. Similar issues arise when netting risk exposures to clients; the ability to net this risk across different transactions will depend on any legally defined netting arrangement with the client as well as the use of common client identifiers in transactions across different business units.

To address these issues of fragmented and distributed ownership of static data, many organizations have moved towards the centralizing of this information and the use of data guardians who are responsible for maintaining and 'cleaning' this data to ensure it is correct. Even where centralization of information has not been possible, data guardians can ensure the consistency of data in each static data store and, where different identifiers are used, maintain cross-reference tables. These cross-reference tables can then be used to map any identifiers into a common representation in order to highlight when identical risks may be netted against each other.

Because static data now tends to be more controlled, there is an inherent increase in time before new data is entered or updates are incorporated. This can be problematic if the trading operation requires this information immediately before it is able to transact business. It often perversely leads to the development of localized static data stores that are less controlled but augment the centralized and controlled static data and are periodically merged into the main store. Whatever approach is taken for static data within the organization, it will need to handle a number of data issues:

- Use of unique internal identifiers to handle changes in external references to data (such as the client name or identifier for an account).
- Merging of identifiers or multiple securities. For example, in the fixed income market, multiple tranches of bonds are often issued, which merge into a single fungible instrument on a specified date.
- Ability to set up instruments, which have not yet been assigned an external identifier, such as those trading in the 'grey market' prior to being officially issued. OTC instruments, because of their unique characteristics, tend to be represented within the trading system as part of transactional data rather than as static data. As there are no standard identifiers or characteristics for these instruments, this does not represent any major problem except that each system involved in processing the instrument must be able to represent the salient points of the transaction for it to be able to perform its processing. Static data is then only used to represent the standardized aspects of these OTC transactions. This approach can address some of the delays in setting up new highly customized one-off instruments within a controlled static data store.

THE DESIGN LEGACY

There are, unfortunately, few 'green field sites', where a blank sheet of paper is available to develop systems that standardize and reuse functionality where necessary but also provide an efficient and responsive tailored solution to the individual traders. As a result, any universal type of approach to enforce a process or technology that does not take into account the historical evolution of the organization and the context the systems and technology utilized have to operate in is likely to fail. What is required is a context-specific approach that understands what the current systems are capable of and why they have evolved in that manner, but which also addresses the challenges detailed previously.

Within each organization, there are likely to exist systems and tools for managing pieces of the risk management puzzle and for collecting the required information. What is typically missing is the ability to bring this information together in a complete and consistent manner. This key data management issue, and the delivery of systems to address it, is at the heart of many problems within risk management.

Notes

1 J. C. Hull, *Options, Futures and other Derivatives* (Prentice Hall, 1997)
2 J. James, 'Credit derivatives, how much should they cost', *Credit Risk* (October 1999)
3 See note 1
4 2003 ISDA Credit Derivatives Definitions (ISDA, 2003)

CHAPTER 3

Functional requirements for a risk management solution

In order to analyse user requirements and specify and design a system, it is important to understand the business context and models underlying the business processes to be implemented. For risk management systems this is essential as only by understanding the risk policy, business model and the risks taken can a solution be developed which captures all the appropriate information. This understanding will ensure that any solution is correctly developed first time, without significant misunderstandings, and has some degree of flexibility or future-proofing in areas where requirements are likely to be changed in the future. Current market conditions are also demanding a move away from the paradigm of 'disposable software'. Developing systems that rapidly become obsolete and too costly, or difficult, to modify to meet new requirements is no longer acceptable. Instead a more strategic approach to system specification and design is required so that these systems can be easily extended to handle any new requirements.

The communication gap between users and those involved in the development process has been cited as a common cause for project failure (Figure 3.1). Because of the different backgrounds and context of end users and developers, it is all too easy for assumptions made by one to not be appreciated by the other. These inherent assumptions typically result in functionality being incorrectly implemented or missed from the

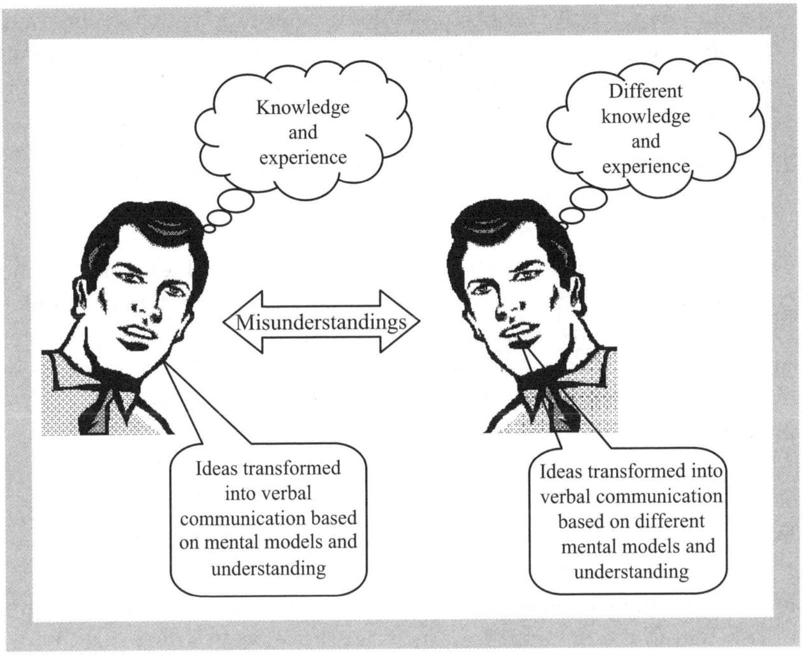

Figure 3.1 The communication gap between users and developers

implementation. The easiest way to bridge this communication gap is to ensure a common understanding and framework from which a deeper understanding can grow.

RISK IDENTIFICATION AND MEASUREMENT

Key to the risk management process is the identification and analysis of risks within the organization, together with their visualization and reporting. Within the risk management continuum, there are a number of different approaches to identifying and measuring risk. Many of these approaches build upon other approaches, providing a complex hierarchy of modelling approaches, with those used for analysing aggregate risk profiles equally being applicable to individual sources of risk. There are typically two approaches used to measure risk within the organization:

1. *Empirical approaches* that indicate the magnitude of risk but not the underlying causes or the effect of any individual event on the risk

profile. As a result it is not possible to determine which events may result in a specific loss or the precise magnitude of that loss. All that can be determined is the relative likelihood of an unexpected loss occurring.

2. *Predictive models* that link drivers and events to sources of risk in a manner that enables risk to be mitigated.

Essentially, the first approach is purely looking at the outcome of the chain of events and sources of risk without determining the causal links. Predictive models decompose these links in order to provide a greater understanding of how losses arise. We will now consider each of these approaches to identifying and measuring risk from a generic, risk independent perspective.

Event, sensitivity and equivalent risk-based approaches

From a quantitative perspective, the value or expected loss from a source of risk within the organization, such as a position in a financial instrument or operational related loss, depends on some function of observable or unobservable (but deduced) variables or events. These might be market prices, default events or process related variables such as trading volume and staffing levels:

$$\textit{expected value/loss} = f(x_1, \ldots, x_n)$$

This expected loss or return does not represent risk since it is the result of 'expected' sequences of likely events impacting sources of risk within the organization; risk arises when the actual outcome is different from that which was expected. Expected losses from operating a business unit should be priced into the cost of transactions. So, for example, if a trade processing system has a 5 per cent error rate which results in an expected daily loss of $10,000 then this cost will need to be factored in to the pricing of all trades. Similarly, if in a credit portfolio 5 per cent of the companies are expected to default, there will be an expected loss due to credit default. When the occurrence of certain unexpected events results in a significantly different level of loss, this additional loss indicates the risks in the business.

Risk sensitivity or exposure to a given event occurring can be defined as the change in value due to a given change in an input variable. For small changes in the function variables, this will be equivalent to the first order (partial) derivative of the price with respect to that variable (since loss is equal to any negative change in price). Under the assumption that the function f is well behaved and locally symmetrical about the point, we have:

$$loss_i = \frac{\partial f(x_1, \ldots, x_n)}{\partial x_i}$$

The sensitivity or possible losses arising from changes in the input variables can be derived either numerically (by changing the input variables and recalculating the function to give the change in value) or analytically, by differentiating the equation f with respect to the required variable.

One of the complexities of operational risk is that this quantitative approach relies on well-specified models for determining possible losses arising from operational risk events that can be difficult to derive.

From a hedging perspective, the trader or operational risk manager will use this calculation, and assuming the model to be a correct representation of real world behaviour, trade a hedge instrument or take out insurance that has an offsetting sensitivity or gain should this event occur. Equivalent risk positions are calculated by indicating the size of position in an equivalent (more liquid) instrument that would have the same level of risk should the event or change in pricing variable occur. This calculation may be made more complex in that the inputs to the function f may not always be observable and may be sensitive to other events or variables. Instead, unobservable input parameters may be derived from other models, resulting in a chain of models, the outputs of one being the inputs into another (see Figure 3.2).

When considering two different sources of risk where there is no causal relationship between the two beyond their both depending on (possibly) the same input parameters, these risk sensitivities can be added together due to the linearity of the differentiation operation:

$$\frac{\partial(A + B)}{\partial x} = \frac{\partial A}{\partial x} + \frac{\partial B}{\partial x}$$

While this is still true when modelling operational risk and considering how the operational risks in two independent business areas combine, it is however not true when viewing operational risk within different parts of an interrelated process, due to the causal links between them. This is part of the reason why operational risk can be so difficult to manage, and requires the causal nature and dependency of one process on internal events that may be generated by an earlier process failure to be fully modelled.

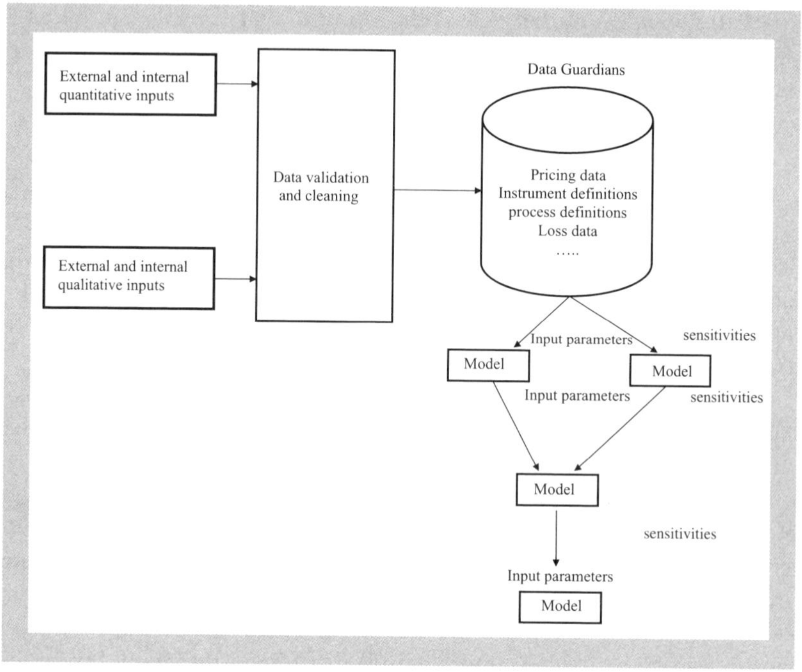

Figure 3.2 The dependency chain of pricing and risk models

Event and process simulation or modelling

Complex mathematical techniques are often used to simulate the actual or likely occurrence of certain events or changes, and to deduce the uncertainty and distribution of future returns under these assumptions. Some of the most common modelling approaches include:

- *Fuzzy logic* (ideal for modelling people processes)
- *Actuarial* or *statistical analysis*
- *Game theory* for people behaviour in modelling operational risk
- *Causal and structural models:* These approaches are used in more detailed analysis to link events to losses (building a network of causal effects). They are frequently used in operational risk modelling for investigating actual process and workflows. They use Baye's theorem and conditional probabilities to calculate the effective probability of losses occurring. They can be time consuming to set up and often only consider a narrow range of events and risks.

- *Process models and simulation:* This approach is used to model the linkage between different processes to investigate through simulation, or 'what if' analysis, the price or possible loss distribution arising from sources of risk. Statistical/probabilistic process models based on hedging strategies and/or expected event process behaviour are used to derive the price and market or credit risk of complex financial instruments.

A wide range of different models are used to price financial instruments or to calculate expected credit or operational losses. Specific details of these can be found in financial modelling and operational risk management textbooks[1,2] and are beyond the scope of this book. For all but the most simplistic direct models where the outputs are directly derivable from observable variables, the general concept is to model key financial variables or the occurrence of credit events as random processes and to derive the expected value (and other sensitivities and statistical measures) for various types of payouts based on the evolution of these random processes over time.

Where these models are used to determine the value of financial instruments, they are often used as the basis for calculating event, sensitivity or equivalent risk metrics, as discussed previously.

Value at risk

Value at risk (VaR) is an approach that uses various probabilistic modelling approaches to determine the probability distribution for the overall returns or losses (over a defined time period) for a portfolio, or the entire organization, based on the statistical evolution of a number of correlated events (Figure 3.3). By looking at the expected frequency or probability of loss (or profit), it is possible to deduce the nth per cent worst-order statistic; that is, the maximum amount that may be lost n per cent of the time. This approach is typically applied to market and credit risk, but could be applied to more frequent operational losses.

The market VaR figures typically imply the amount of proprietary risk an organization is taking and so can be used to ensure that the trading model for a business unit is indeed being followed; for example, a brokerage operation should not be taking significant proprietary risk.

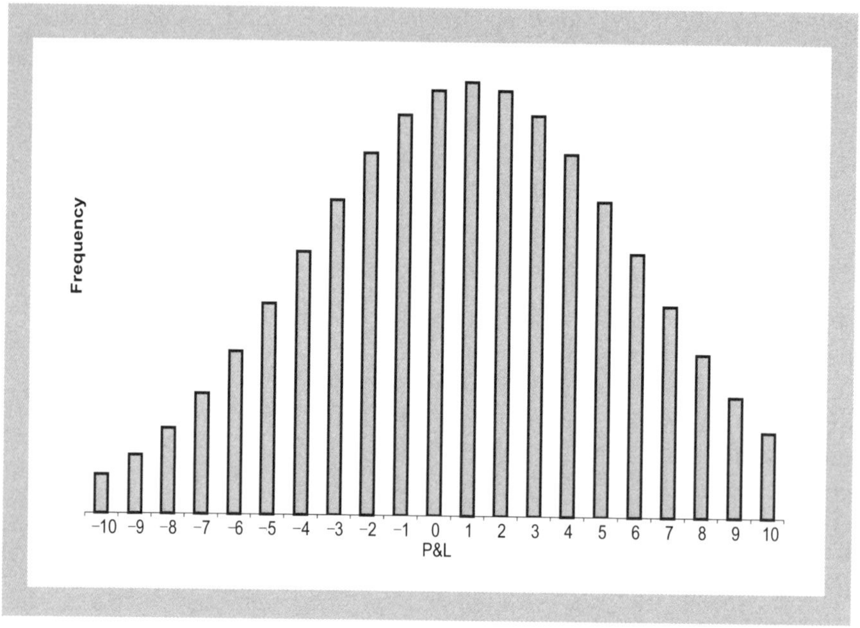

Figure 3.3 Example of an expected distribution of P&L

Stress testing

Stress testing is used to analyse the impact of low probability events that could result in excessive losses or gains. It is used to augment VaR type analyses by investigating the impact of unusual and extreme events. These types of events must be further investigated in case they are more probable than anticipated. The problem with stress testing, however, is that it is often difficult to assign any probability to such unlikely events; all it will indicate is whether such an occurrence could have disastrous implications for the organization. Stress testing will typically shift certain pricing variables, ignoring the implications or implied correlations that should result in changes in other variables.

Graphical representations of stress testing are often used to investigate the behaviour of the portfolio away from current market conditions. For example, plotting P&L or hedging information against changes in the underlying pricing variables is often used to search for unexpected and significant increases in the level of losses or possible difficulties in hedging the portfolio in the future.

Scenario analysis

Scenarios are especially important when there is little data concerning the likelihood of events and can help in fully understanding a process. Scenarios can be based on decision tree approaches (see Chapter 5), highlighting where and when decisions are made and processes can be influenced. They can also form the basis for disaster and business continuity planning. When reporting this information to traders, it is also useful to provide example situations when this has occurred in the past, together with the actual events that occur in each scenario.

Scenario analysis is similar to stress testing but is based on a more complete evolution of all the input variables, as would be expected if such events were witnessed in the real world. Changes in one part of the market will occur together with correlated changes in other pricing variables. Examples of typical scenarios are the market crash in 1987, Russian Crisis in 1997, exchange connectivity failure, company defaults and so on. As well as scenarios being based on actual observed events, anticipatory scenarios of what could happen given current external and internal drivers should also be considered to give full scenario coverage.

One of the major problems with scenario analysis (and also many other portfolio analysis approaches) is that they typically assume a static portfolio; the implications of increased dynamic hedging or selling off of positions is not included in the analysis.

Impact probability matrix/risk mapping

Impact probability matrices and risk mappings are visual techniques used to highlight and prioritize high impact, high probability losses that can create significant financial damage to the organization (Figure 3.4). They are often used to visualize qualitative risk assessments, especially for operational risk, but can also be used in the credit and market risk areas to highlight events or scenarios that would have a major impact on the organization. For quantitative approaches, they can be viewed as a specific graphical representation of the probability of loss distribution, such as that derived as part of the VaR analysis.

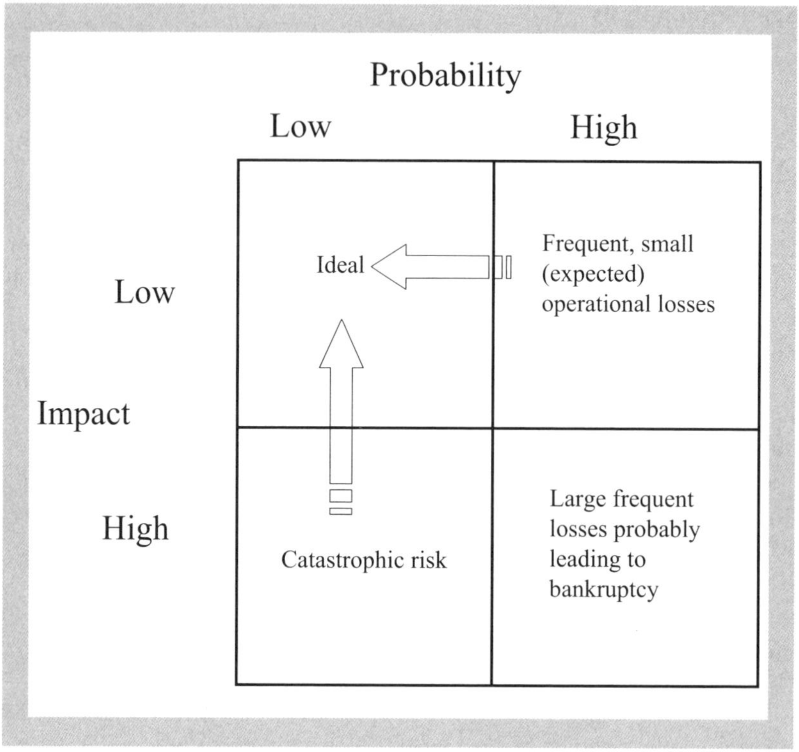

Figure 3.4 Impact probability matrix

Risk assessments

Risk assessments identify and analyse the sources of risk, as well as highlighting those events and drivers that result in losses. They then assess the likelihood of this occurring (and any offsetting sources of risks). This information can then be used to derive more complex models and approaches to modelling risk. When applied in an operational risk framework this approach is usually used in addition to process analysis, which analyses any failings in the processes (or workflow) as data flows through the organization. The aim of any risk assessment is to obtain a thorough understanding of the risks, the magnitude of those risks, how they may be addressed and the priority in which they should be mitigated. The main difference between risk assessments and scenario analysis is that the aim of a risk assessment is to derive those scenarios that will result in significant losses. Risk assessments are most effectively performed when involving the staff responsible for the sources of risk being assessed. Checklists, scorecards, questionnaires, structured interviews, workshops and risk narratives can all be used to facilitate this process.

Key risk indicators and changes in key indicators

A key risk indicator (KRI) is a simple and easy-to-implement measure based on some observable data that acts as a proxy for actual risk levels. It may build on the outputs of any of the previous approaches or be based simply on an internally or externally observed metric. Data analysis and pattern recognition techniques can be used to identify the reoccurrence of correlated event patterns, which in the past have led to high levels of loss. Approaches such as chaos theory can also be used to identify when periods of chaotic behaviour in external events may occur and act as early warning indicators of increasing uncertainty. These approaches are often empirical in nature and, unless there is a theoretically sound causal link between certain events and the occurrence of associated losses, it is difficult to use this approach as more than an initial warning indicator of changes in the level of risk. Other techniques should then be used to further investigate the possibility and likelihood of losses.

Benchmark comparisons

Benchmarking involves comparing risk indicators in one organization with those in a comparable organization. This technique can be applied across all the risk classes, for example in market risk this may be the calculation of relative VaR, where the VaR figure for a portfolio or organization is compared against that of benchmark portfolios or other organizations. In operational risk, the impact on equity price of operational losses (removing effects of market and specific risk arising from balance sheet composition and leverage) can be used to derive an estimate of operational risk capital compared with similar organizations. Risk is therefore quantified not as absolute loss but as underperformance relative to that benchmark.

Catastrophic impact analysis

Catastrophic impact analysis requires the analysis of certain sources of risk to determine:

- whether large losses are likely
- any internal drivers which increase the likelihood of these losses occurring
- changes in KRIs that could act as early warning indicators
- the contingency measures in place and
- what can be done to mitigate this risk.

This analysis is reasonably easy to perform but, as with all approaches to low probability, high impact events, it can be difficult to determine the likelihood of the events actually occurring.

Catastrophic impact analysis is closely related to stress testing, but the aim is to deduce those risk events which are likely to result in significant losses, rather than investigate the losses arising from low probability events. As a result, it tends to be a much more subjective approach to risk analysis.

ASSET CLASS SPECIFIC RISK MANAGEMENT

Market Risk Measurement

Market risk arises from unexpected changes in the value of positions in financial instruments due to changes in external market variables. These risks are usually broken down into the following different types of asset classes:

- Commodity risk (including FX risk)
- Equity risk
- Interest rate risk.

The key risk management requirements on the trading desk are to understand how risk may be mitigated by trading in instruments with offsetting risk profiles and also by understanding the impact of changes in market prices and variables on portfolio returns.

Interest rate versus other assets

Interest rate risk tends to dominate the trading in different asset classes because it dictates the returns and costs achieved in lending and borrowing money. These returns and costs will vary depending on the timescales involved, resulting in a *yield curve* that indicates how yield varies with the period of lending or borrowing (otherwise known as the maturity of the instrument). The yields achieved by different interest rate instruments will vary depending on other factors such as:

- Liquidity
- Tax and regulatory issues
- Credit risk implications (including counterparty risk)
- Other risks such as operational risk, model risk, reinvestment or prepayment risk (where assumptions are made concerning the prepayment rate of a loan or the future rate cash may be invested at).

As a result, the achieved return or *yield* from an interest rate instrument will increase as the risk associated with the above also increases. This leads to many different types of interest rate instrument trading as a *spread* or yield increment over the price of other more liquid or less risky instruments.

The major interest rate markets are composed of the fixed income, money and swap markets or instruments derived or based on the interest rates in these markets (the so called interest rate derivative instruments). Fixed income instruments pay an agreed interest rate over the life of the instrument on an agreed notional amount (the amount lent or used in any interest rate calculation). The interest rate swap market also provides interest rate exposure based on the exchanging of fixed and floating (or benchmark) interest rate payments, where the floating rate periodically resets to the current market benchmark rate.

When analysing total returns across the portfolio or organization, it is important to modify any yields into price behaviour, looking at the sensitivity of price to yield. The interrelationship between price and yield in fixed income instruments exhibits non-linearity in that, depending on the level of the yield, the same change in yield will have different impacts on the price. This is referred to as convexity, and can significantly complicate some risk calculations, as assumptions concerning the linear interrelationship of yield and price will only be valid for small changes.

Monitoring market risk

On the trading desk, traders will focus on likely (high probability) market movements and the instruments they will use to hedge against such events. This breaks down risks into the following types of measures:

- *Delta type risk* arising from price changes
- *Gamma type risk* arising from non-linear changes in prices
- *Vega type risk* arising from changes in the volatility of prices.

When trading fixed income instruments such as bonds, those main market moves will be parallel shifts and tilts in the yield curve. As a result the trader will often view interest rate risk in terms of instrument duration, futures or other equivalent hedge positions[3] that provide market-specific definitions of risk sensitivities to key market changes. These risk metrics reflect the trader's understanding of what drives the value of an instrument, how this risk can be hedged and any residual risk that is left. It is important to note that there are often many different ways to measure that sensitivity of returns to various events, based on different assumptions concerning market behaviour. As a result, when obtaining this information from other systems outside the scope of the risk management solution, it is important to fully specify the units and definition of the risk metrics provided and ensure that these risk metrics can be transformed into a common risk model. Within the continuum of possible risk models (Chapter 1), traders will typically be concerned with managing and hedging risk arising from external events or changes in market variables and hence will concentrate on the exposure-based risk metric. Higher up the risk hierarchy the focus changes to one of risk control, and monitoring the expected distribution of returns and possible losses given the current risk profile. Aggregate-level risk mitigation using trader type tools and analysis may also be applied in order to allow reduction or modification of the risk profile at the macro or organizational level.

Credit risk measurement

For investment banks, credit risk management is concerned with realized or unrealized losses arising from credit events. It arises in a number of ways:

- Through traditional banking book activities such as loans and letters of credit
- Counterparty exposures in OTC derivative transactions
- Settlement risk
- Issuer or underlying name risk in trading equities, corporate bonds, credit derivatives and so on.

Credit risk is inherently embedded in many different types of trading. To fully understand the credit exposure to any specific credit event will therefore require the aggregating of information from across the entire organization; this will include bond, equity and derivative trading information, as well as the usual sources of credit risk such as loans.

The credit quality of a company is monitored by internal credit departments as well as ratings agencies such as Moody's and Standard & Poor's. This credit quality is indicated by a code that indicates the likelihood of a company defaulting on its obligations over various different timescales.

The nature of credit events is that they occur suddenly and often without any pre-warning. This means that any solution must be able to quickly indicate the exposure of the organization to that credit event occurring, using up to date and complete information.

Probabilistic approaches to credit risk require the determination of the likelihood of a credit/default event occurring and then the expected loss/exposure that would follow. Typically this information is determined from current market data, historical data or analysing the quality of a particular company's balance sheet. The metrics used to quantify credit exposure include:

Exposure in the event of default

- Percentage of actual or notional amounts affected by the credit event less any likely amount recovered (expressed as the recovery rate)

- Replacement or market value, reflecting the value of the credit exposure prior to any event occurring. This will vary over the life of the exposure. An additional 'add on' may be included to reflect future credit exposure that differs from any current exposure.

Change in market value of a financial transaction due to a change in the credit quality of a company
Reduction in the market value of a financial transaction due to changes in the market's perception of any credit risk in the transaction. This may arise from a perceived increase in the likelihood of default or a reduction in likely recovery rates should a default occur.

Loss distributions
VaR type approaches that include the diversification effects and correlation issues between different types of credit defaults. The exposures at the portfolio level are often determined through simulations of market and credit events or analytical approximations to this.

Credit models for pricing credit risk are typically based on one of two main approaches:

- structural models such as those introduced by Merton,[4] which use balance sheet information to quantify the likelihood of default and level of recovery
- reduced form models which do not refer to the capital structure of the underlying company but instead model the probability of default and resultant loss, the enhancement in return due to credit risk or the probability of a change in credit quality.[5] This information may be derived from current market prices for instruments containing credit risk by determining the amount of additional yield or return that can be attributed to credit risk in the instrument, by using historical default or credit transition information or calibration.

Internal ratings-based approaches

The internal ratings-based approach to modelling credit uses a list of credit drivers that influence the credit quality of a company and assigns a weighting to each of these reflecting the importance of that driver in assessing the credit quality of the company. These drivers will range from quantitative information such as financial ratios to qualitative information such as the quality of the management, industry attractiveness (barriers to entry, growth and so on). The relevant drivers and weights will differ depending on the type of company, its industry and so on. To generate an internal rating for a specific company, each driver is assigned a score, which is then multiplied by the weighting and summed across all the relevant drivers to give a total score for the company. This total score is then mapped to an internal rating.

Counterparty risk

Just as pricing risk is constantly monitored by traders, total counterparty credit exposure arising from entry into certain financial transactions should also be constantly monitored. This exposure will vary with changes in external market and other pricing variables that impact the value of collateral and the value of ongoing OTC or unsettled transactions with that counterparty. Credit exposure is normally controlled through a credit limit monitoring process. If these credit limits are divided up across the organization then being able to rapidly obtain any clearance prior to executing the transaction is unlikely to be a problem; the business unit should be aware of the current credit exposure to each counterparty due to transactions it itself has originated. This however means that any counterparty must deal with each business unit as if it was a separate operation, which is not always desirable for the client. If a single global limit is required across all business lines then performing a limit check will require the aggregation of counterparty risk globally across all business lines, taking into account portfolio effects, economic offsets and correlations, as well as netting (if the transaction is supported by a valid netting agreement). This can be a challenging requirement to address in a timely manner. Because of the timeliness with which this information is required, these checks are often performed retrospectively or only performed before execution of transactions that result in a significant level of credit risk. If they are performed retrospectively, any resulting limit breaches will not be noticed or resolved until after the transaction has been executed.

Customer limits are usually set according to the following factors:

- Quantitative factor: the 'size' of the company, for example, the market capitalization or net asset value of the company
- Qualitative factor: the rating of the company

- Length of deal
- The inherent credit risk and level of recovery that may be achieved in the event of a default event.

Calculating the recovery rate that may be achieved in the event of default can be exceptionally difficult, depending on the seniority of any claim, the existence of any guarantees or covenants and the amount of collateral available.

Traders should also consider the cost of providing credit to a counterparty by taking account of the total cost of the transaction. Depending on this cost they should modify any mark-up of a financial transaction to cover both the expected loss resulting from a default of the counterparty, as well as the cost of capital required to cover any unexpected losses. This 'cost of credit' will vary depending on the details of the counterparty, and may even be negative if the deal has some risk-offsetting features.

Operational risk measurement

Whereas credit and market risk are reasonably well understood, operational risk measurement is still a new area of risk management. Prior to regulatory pressure to measure and manage operational risk, the precise definitions of the types of operational loss or event and the data on which to base statistical approaches were neither plentiful nor consistent across or within organizations. Even with the Basel 2 Accord, it is likely that the models, data and definitions will evolve over time. As a result, operational risk losses tend to be difficult to predict, covering a wide range of drivers and sources of risk such as fraud, errors arising from loss of key personnel, systems failure, multiple data entry, excessive trading volumes, poor vendor or project management, terrorist activity and so on. Any organization is an open socio-technical system, which can fail in many different ways. The complexity of human behaviour makes it extremely difficult to model and risk manage these systems in a quantitative manner, and these behaviours and motivations can change unpredictably over time. As a result, many of the approaches to operational risk management tend to have a subjective element to them and take a reasonably simplistic approach to modelling operational risk. Alternatively they may take a reactionary approach, ensuring that any potential problems are identified and resolved as early as possible before they result in significant losses. Subjective methods can provide a more holistic approach than detailed quantitative analysis, especially when the underlying model and data are likely to be very poorly specified or understood. This complexity tends to lead to many differing approaches, such as the use of KRIs, risk assessments and more qualitative modelling approaches in order to obtain a more complete and robust approach to operational risk management.

Operational risk should be of key importance to an organization because it can produce the most devastating losses (as witnessed by events such as those instigated by Nick Leeson at Barings,[6] and the failure of the Globex electronic exchange in 2003).[7] Also, when an extreme event does occur, there is likely to be a high level of correlation with other extreme events and an accompanying element of what can go wrong will go wrong – and all at the same time.

Loss databases

The implementation of the Basel 2 Accord by many local regulators will demand the maintaining of a loss database to record all losses above a given size. They may also record near misses, or losses that almost did or could have occurred.

The recording of operational losses should distinguish between those that were expected (dealt with through pricing) and those that were not. As with all historical data, they are a weak signpost; useful for reducing cognitive biases when reviewing historical events, backtesting and validating models but of limited use in predicting future losses. This is especially true when internal processes and other sources of operational risk have evolved over time. Associated with each recorded event should be a full risk assessment, including severity, impact and control assessment, making the loss database more of a comprehensive incident management system. It should associate a cause with each loss event that can be analysed and mitigated if necessary.

The main barrier to collecting this type of data is that operational risk information is not always transparent – it is not posted on publicly accessible locations in the same way as market or credit risk. It relies on a risk-aware culture to always ensure the information is highlighted and recorded (rather than a culture of fear where managers worry about the information being used to monitor their performance). It will also require adequate budgets to be allocated in order to implement the data collection process in a robust and non-onerous manner.

Basel 2 and operational risk

The use of a key risk indicator as a proxy for the level of operational activity within the organization or at the business level, multiplied by an appropriate factor, is the basis of the basic indicator approach and standardized approach in the new Basel Accord. The advanced measurement approaches extend these simple techniques by considering more probabilistic methodologies for the likelihood of loss and the magnitude of that loss when it occurs, with the operational risk broken down by business line and decomposed into various risk categories (see Chapter 2). These approaches range from using causal type models linking events and losses, to deducing the probability distribution for a loss of a given type occurring over time and the probability distribution of the magnitude of loss when it occurs, scaled by some exposure level indicator.

The main problem with operational loss databases is that by definition, in order to observe an event, it must occur with reasonably high probability. This means that loss databases are ideal for recording the high probability, frequent events with a high level of statistical accuracy, but provide little information concerning low probability events. The distributions of loss events also tend to vary dramatically based on the severity of the loss. Instead, these low probability parts of the distribution are usually defined using:

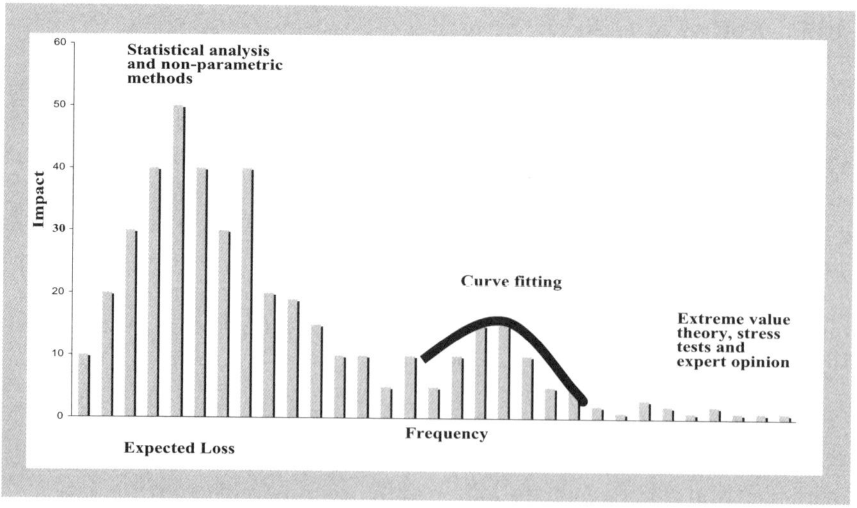

Figure 3.5 Approaches to determining the operational risk probability distribution for the magnitude of loss when an event occurs

- Subjective informed opinion
- Extreme event theory to estimate the likelihood of unlikely but significant loss events[8]
- Scenario analysis ('what if' type questions)
- External loss data to increase the universe of available data in order to obtain greater statistical significance.

External loss databases can provide a wider range of data, including low probability, high-impact events. The quality and reliability of this data should however be analysed to ensure it is unbiased and complete. It may also not be representative of operational losses within any given organization and so will need to be adjusted in order to be directly applicable. It can however be used as the basis for developing operational risk scenarios, as well as acting as a benchmark with which to compare the organization.

These individual loss distributions are combined under various assumptions concerning the correlation and interrelation of different types of events and the magnitude of loss to give a combined loss distribution for the organization or business unit. Obtaining this multivariate loss distribution can be a complex process if the assumed or deduced distributions are unusual or the interaction of events highly complex.

Although determining the probability/loss distribution indicates the magnitude of the problem, unless it is possible to model the actual processes that resulted in those losses, it will not be possible to determine the sources generating those risks and how risk can be mitigated within the organization.

VaR APPROACHES

VaR is commonly used to assess the likelihood that certain levels of loss will occur within a portfolio. Whereas exposure sensitivity approaches benefit from the linearity of the differentiation operation, this is no longer true when considering a more probabilistic approach. The CAPM highlights the issue when analysing the statistical variance in returns of an equity portfolio. As discussed in Chapter 1, statistical measures look at the distribution of returns and typically the width or variance of that distribution. Looking at the variance (or volatility) of a number of equity positions, the variance of the total position is no longer a linear combination of the variances of the individual position, due to the non-linearity of the variance operator. This non-linearity arises from the benefits of diversification (the 'portfolio effect') and imperfect correlations between different positions. This can dramatically complicate the process for determining statistical measures for the aggregate corporate portfolio distributed across multiple trading systems and geographical locations. When looking at the variance of two possible random losses, A and B:[9]

$$\mathrm{var}(A + B) = \mathrm{var}(A) + \mathrm{var}(B) + 2\ \mathrm{covar}\ (A,B)$$

Whereas variance is a measure of how 'wide' a probability distribution is, covariance is a measure of how changes in one variable are related to changes in another. As a result, the total risk of the combined position may be less than the risk of each position individually; in fact if one position is a hedge for the other, the covariance term will be negative, indicating a reduction in the combined risk. The three main approaches to calculating VaR are described below.

Variance/Covariance approach

This approach uses the sensitivities of the positions within a portfolio to various risk factors or buckets together with the covariance matrix for all these risk factors, in order to derive the expected variance of the overall distribution of returns. It is assumed within this approach that changes in return due to certain events occurring remain the same for different states of the external and internal risk drivers. This may be valid for low levels of event volatility or short time periods but is likely to break down in more extreme markets or over long time horizons with non-linear instruments.

Under the assumption that the resulting distribution is statistically normal, it is possible to determine what percentage of the distribution is below a certain level by using normal distribution tables (showing the cumulative probability) or by using a polynomial equation that approximates the cumulative normal distribution. Fortunately, this calculation can be simplified through the use of linear algebra operations which are supported by many third party libraries.

Monte Carlo simulation

In Monte Carlo simulations, sequences of pseudo random variables are generated with the required distributions and correlations. The term *Monte Carlo simulation* comes from the similarity between games of chance and the generation of a sequence of random numbers. The only requirement for this approach is that it is possible to define the multivariate probability distribution for the risk factors or buckets.

This approach is often used to model and price complex financial instruments whose price depends on the random evolution of a number of pricing variables. As a result, this technique has applications in market, credit and operational risk analysis. The derived market covariance matrix (between the different risk factors) is used to convert the generated independent random numbers into a sequence of correlated events that model the expected real world behaviour. From this, hypothetical distributions of P&L can be determined, which are then used to deduce the required VaR order statistic (for example the level of losses below which five per cent of the final distribution of P&L lies).

Historical simulation

Historical simulation involves the calculation of portfolio returns when past historical events are replayed. It provides a sanity check against more complex modelling approaches such as Monte Carlo based VaR, and is an extremely robust approach that is easy to interpret and understand.

Summary

As can be seen from Table 3.1, the most appropriate approach for any particular organization will depend on the types of instruments traded, the skill level of risk management staff and the future strategy of the organization, together with the cost and complexity of implementing each approach. For example, there is little point in implementing Monte Carlo VaR for a financial institution that only trades cash equity; the linear risk profile and availability of market data for these instruments imply that historical simulation or a variance/covariance approach would be much more appropriate. However, if the organization trades illiquid instruments (such as emerging market debt), the lack of available time series data for these instruments will make historical simulation difficult. Historical-based approaches also assume stationarity of market data (that is, the future is the same as the past) and so are not appropriate where step changes have occurred in the markets. For non-linear risk profiles, where the level of risk does not change linearly with changes in event levels (such as those with inherent optionality), this non-linear

Table 3.1 Advantages and disadvantages of VaR approaches

	Approach		
	Variance/ Covariance	**Historical simulation**	**Monte Carlo simulation**
Difficulty to implement	Medium	Low	High
Computational complexity	Low	Medium	High
Accuracy (non-linear portfolios)	Low	Medium	High
Accuracy (linear portfolios)	Medium	Medium	Medium
Handling new instruments	Medium	Low	Medium
Handling structured products	Low	High	High
Assumed market data distribution	Yes	No	Yes
Intuitiveness of results	Medium	High	Medium
Market data processing requirements	Medium	Low	High

nature of returns makes the risk/return profile slightly more complicated. The impact of this non-linearity will also depend on the expected size of any change, and therefore on the time horizon and daily volatility level (that is, longer time horizons and more volatile markets require more complex approaches to the analysis of non-linear instruments).

As no single approach is able to address all the possible issues, it is not uncommon for a combination of approaches to be implemented. This avoids the possibility of results that are unidentified artefacts of the approach, rather than being truly due to the underlying risk positions. For example, variance/covariance and Monte Carlo approaches often assume that the individual underlying distributions of the risk factors are *normally* distributed. This assumption dramatically simplifies the processing of these models, but it is known that most financial distributions exhibit skew and kurtosis (that is, the distribution is not symmetrical about the mean and the edges or tails of the distribution tend to predict a greater probability to low probability events).

THE RISK ANALYSIS PROCESS

The risk analysis process requires sources of risk to be analysed and investigated in the context of current internal and external events (Figure 3.6). Some of the data used in the risk analysis process may not be available for all data points or its quality may be questionable. As a result, various mathematical models or techniques will be needed to deduce all the required data points based on curve fitting, interpolation or extrapolation of data, or more complex approaches such as pattern recognition or neural networks.

Statistical approaches may extend the sensitivity approaches by associating probabilities against various events that result in possible losses, as indicated by calculated sensitivities. These events may be market price moves when calculating market VaR or internal operational events for operational VaR.

All VaR approaches require the use of event data either directly or as the source of information to calibrate to. There are many choices in how this data may be analysed and cleaned which are beyond the scope of this book. The data cleaning will consist of comparing disparities between different data sources, handling missing data, deciding the time

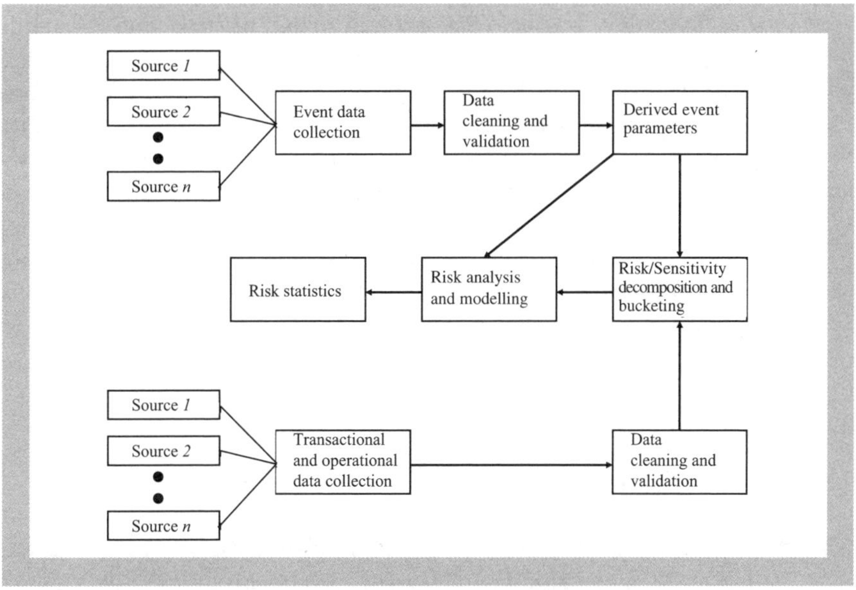

Figure 3.6 Statistical risk analysis process

period of data to use in deriving model parameters, frequency of data (intra-day and close-of-day data can vary significantly), and the weighting to be placed on data from different points in the past (typically some form of exponential weighting is used to give more 'weight' to more recent data and events). Market data may also be distorted by market anomalies or changes in the way in which certain financial instruments are traded, which will result in the past behaviour being very different from that currently seen.

A trader will inherently always try to exploit market or internal mispricings or risk. As a result, the risk manager should always be monitoring trading activity to ensure traders are not exploiting deficiencies in the data or modelling approach and how it determines risk.

One of the key requirements for risk monitoring is to compare changes in the risk profile over time. These changes will arise from changes in:

- Sources of risk
- Occurrence of actual events
- An increase in the likelihood of certain events that modifies the risk associated with a given source; for example an increase in interest rate levels will increase credit risk.

Distinguishing between risks arising from changes in the sources of risk, as a result of business activity and risk mitigation, and those due to changes in the likelihood or impact of internal and external events is a major challenge for the risk manager. This is especially true when viewing statistical measures; the derivation and use of new covariance matrices or historical data will result in a change in the level of risk associated with a given portfolio. This occurs purely from a reassessment of risks due to changes in events. In addition, risk will also change due to various new sources of risk and the results of risk mitigation. If event data is only periodically updated, the change due to this should be understood before investigating changes in the underlying sources.

CHANGES IN RISK WITH EVENT LEVELS AND TIME

When simulating or modelling the evolution of risk events over time, it is important to understand how the risk exposure arising from each source of risk changes as event levels and time change. For some sources of risk this may be constant over time and vary linearly with event levels. For many sources however, a more complex relationship will exist. As a result, when calculating aggregate risks using a Monte Carlo VaR type approach, stress testing or analysing various scenarios, it may be necessary to recalculate individual risks or sensitivities as events evolve. There are several approaches to this problem, each with differing integration, functionality and processing requirements. The recalculation of risk can be obtained by:

Full recalculation through time and as modelled event levels change
This approach is highly accurate but adds a high level of computational complexity and requires either access to the models that can recalculate the individual risks or the ability to pass and receive the required information.

Sensitivities ladder approaches
This provides a ladder of current risk sensitivities with different event levels, but does not indicate how this may vary over time, which can lead to problems with path-dependent risk over long time periods.

Calculated grids of risk over time and with differing event level
These grids are used to indicate the individual risks at various points in time and at different event levels. This can be computationally complex but decouples the calculation of these sensitivities (which may be performed in front office systems that are difficult to access) from later risk calculations. This approach does not however include path-dependent evolutions of events into the calculation.

RISK ANALYSIS AND REPORTING

It is not unusual for the P&L and risk to be driven by a relatively small number of sources of risk. To understand whether this is the result of multiple sources throughout the organization or a concentrated source within one part of the business, it is important to retain the detail of where each source is located. A single VaR figure has limited benefit when risk managing the organization or a given portfolio. What is important is how this figure varies with time and how it relates to other risk analyses (such as scenario testing).

As a result, risk analysis requires many different views on risk within the organization, with the ability to decompose this risk into a number of different dimensions. Once the risk context has been set, the organization can decide whether any risks should be mitigated and the most effective manner in which this can be achieved. The volume of information that is likely to be presented to the risk manager will require the use of graphical methods and analytical analysis tools in order to prevent information overload.

Risk reports should be timely and accurate, highlighting excessive risk concentrations where the level of risk is above a defined acceptable level. In order to ensure they are used, any reports should also be concise and add a commentary to highlight key details within the report, with the ability to provide more detailed analysis where required. The risk analysis process may require 'what if' analyses to be performed. This can occur in one of two ways:

1. What happens if a given risk event occurs?
2. How does the risk profile of the organization alter if certain changes are made to it?

This analysis should identify potential future risks or failure in the risk management process. This may vary from plotting the P&L impact of various changes in events, highlighting situations that may prove difficult to hedge in the future, or breaking down risk by trading strategy to ensure that the strategy is indeed being followed.

This risk analysis and reporting process should:

- Identify risks and be automated where possible
- Assign responsibility and investigate any unexpected losses
- Resolve any issues
- Monitor and analyse and assess why losses or gains occurred.

These analyses are vital to understanding and mitigating risk within the organization.

Risk breakdown

Risk information has many dimensions along which it can be broken down and visualized. One of the major problems for the risk manager will be in handling the inherent information overload from dealing with the high volume of information. Customized reports and visualizations will enable the risk manager to identify unacceptable areas of risk and reduce information overload. Often this will necessitate the ability to generate customized reports and graphs to further investigate certain sources of risk, along with the ability to 'drill down' and understand the data that comprises each risk. There are many ways that the sources of risk within the organization can be decomposed but it is likely to consist of at least:

- Originating area or trade grouping (business unit, trader, region, trading strategy, trading book and so on)
- Magnitude of risk
- Risk metric used
- Type of risk/risk drivers
- Source of risk.

Just as decomposing the risks into different groupings can highlight the major contributing sources of any risk, aggregating this information can show excessive risk concentrations. For example, credit risk is likely to occur throughout the trading environment. This risk may combine in undesirable ways that can be highlighted by:

- Grouping of related entities into legal and economic structures
- Global exposure to companies in the same industry
- Global exposure to entities domiciled in a given country.

This can place significant demands on the ability of static data in the organization to represent these complex credit relationships between counterparties and issuers.

The non-linearity of the VaR of individual portfolios, which will not sum to produce the VaR for the total combined portfolio, highlights how individual sources of risk add to the total risk. Marginal risk for a number of sources of risk is defined as the difference between the risk with and without those sources being included, and highlights the amount of risk arising from adding that specific source to the portfolio. Low marginal risk highlights sources that are acting as hedges to other risks and can be used to indicate the effectiveness of any hedging transactions. Sources that have high levels of marginal risk will be major contributors to the total risk, not being offset by other risks within the organization. A similar concept to highlight the level required to hedge a source of risk is incremental risk, which indicates the change in total risk when the source weighting is increased. Inherently all these incremental and marginal calculations indicate the diversification benefit from introducing additional sources of risk into to the organization.

The diversification benefit between different business units is often split between them, reducing their individual economic capital requirements, so that the total economic capital employed does actually equal that allocated across all the business units. This approach should ideally be used within the business decision process to facilitate the optimal pricing and selection of transactions. For example, a trader should be encouraged to undertake (and price accordingly) certain transactions which reduce the total organizational risk. Even if this cannot be performed across the entire organization, it should at least be performed within the business unit. So for example, a trader should more competitively price a swap transaction which hedges an existing risk, or results in the least increase in marginal risk due to portfolio diversification or risk offsetting effects.

Data granularity and source

When aggregating data within the organization, decisions must be made on the granularity of data required in the risk management process. Just as with a map, users require different scales and levels of details, depending on the use to which they are going to put the information; a street map is unlikely to be of use for someone trying to travel from London to Paris, just as an atlas covering Europe is unlikely to help someone find a street with a given shop on it. At the trading level, full granularity and detailed information are required for the in depth management of a subset of the organization's portfolio. Further up the risk hierarchy, a much more aggregated and generic view is required. The complication comes in that those higher up the risk hierarchy may need to be able to see the detail at the individual portfolio level when the aggregate view is not as expected.

As a result, rather than the problem being similar to users who travel in a plane at different heights, looking at different levels of detail, what is often required is a solution similar to a helicopter that can vary its height, descending to bring into focus the required detail where necessary.

Notes

1 J. C. Hull, *Options, Futures and other Derivatives* (Prentice Hall, 1997)

2 M. Cruz, *Modeling, Measuring and Hedging Operational Risk: A Quantitive Approach* (John Wiley and Sons, 2002)
3 See note 1
4 R. Merton, 'On the pricing of corporate debt: The risk structure of interest rates', *Journal of Finance,* **29** (May 1974) 449–70
5 D. Duffie and K. Singleton, *Credit Risk: Pricing, Measurement, and Management* (Princeton University Press, 2003)
6 J. Rawnsley, *Total Risk, Nick Leeson and the Fall of Barings Bank* (HarperCollins, 1995)
7 Finextra, 'Traders head for the pits as Globex falls over' (Finextra.com, 2 May 2003)
8 See note 2
9 G. Grimmet and D. Stirzaker, *Probability and Random Processes* (Clarendon Press, 1982)

PART II

Risk Management Technology

CHAPTER 4

The software development lifecycle

The software development lifecycle describes the process whereby requirements are transformed into a set of computer instructions or software that results in a system that addresses those requirements. The process can be broken down into a number of key stages (Figure 4.1):

- *Requirements:* the gathering of the requirements for the new system
- *Analysis:* the creation of an analysis model that specifies what functionality the system will provide in order to address the requirements
- *Design:* takes the analysis model and refines it into something that can be implemented
- *Implementation:* the execution of the design in terms of specific technologies such as programming languages, databases and so on. The result of an implementation is software code, together with supporting data, scripts and configuration information that provide a working system
- *Testing:* validation of the implementation to ensure that it meets the requirements for the system. Once the system has been tested and validated, it may then be deployed to the end users.

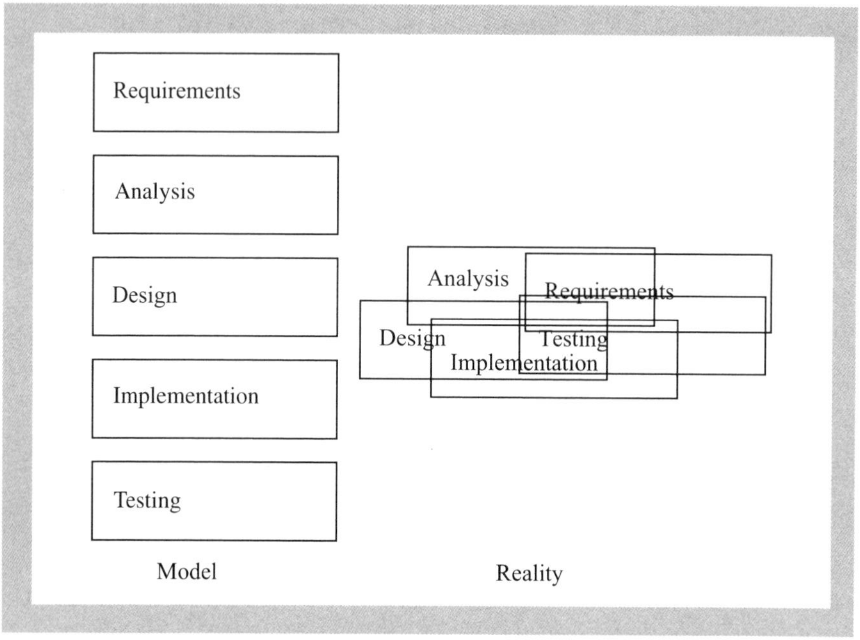

Figure 4.1 The reality of the software development cycle

There will be varying levels of iteration both within and between these stages, which will continue throughout the life of the software. For example, although a specific requirement has been provided, this may be exceptionally expensive to implement, whereas a solution with similar functionality could also address this need but much more easily and cheaply.

There are many different models for implementing the software development lifecycle, each of which indicates a different sequence, level of iteration, interaction and overlap between the stages of the software development lifecycle shown in Figure 4.1. The most common are:

Waterfall
In the waterfall model, the stages of analysis, design, implementation and testing are treated as sequential steps, with the completed outputs of each stage leading into the next, like a cascade of waterfalls (Figure 4.2). It does not reflect the reality of most modern software development, especially within financial organizations where requirements are often highly complex and fluid due to ongoing changes in the business model, external markets or regulatory environment. Often changes or

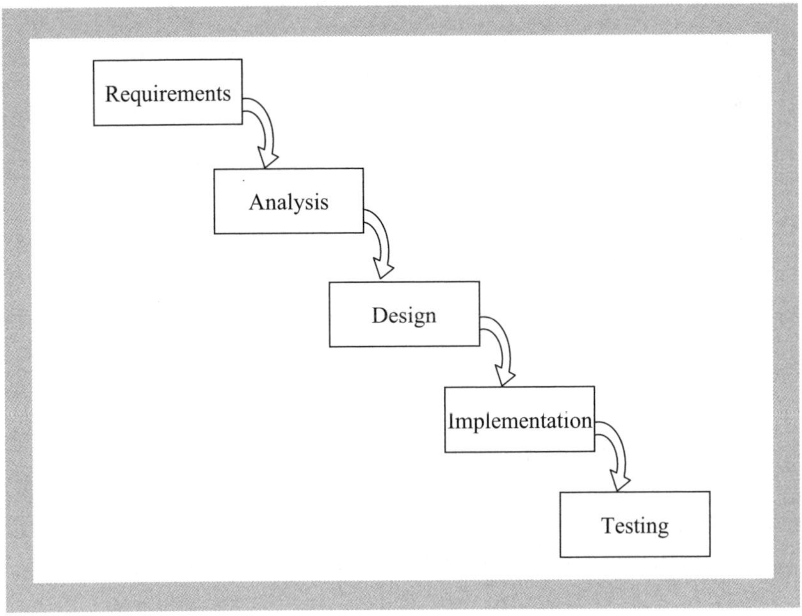

Figure 4.2 The waterfall lifecycle model

clarification of requirements lower down in the development process need to be fed back up the waterfall. Alternatively, changes may need to be introduced into the requirements because of limitations discovered elsewhere within the organization. The waterfall model can be effectively applied if the risk management problem is well specified and where the requirements are clear and concise, and will not change during the development process. However, even when the development process is more iterative, the waterfall model can still provide a framework for managing the development process within each iteration or enhancement.

V

The V model contains similar stages to the waterfall model, the differences being that the outputs of each stage of analysis and development are linked to different types of testing (Figure 4.3). The output from the requirements specification drives the acceptance and system tests, the output from design drives integration testing, and the output from coding individual sections of code drives unit testing. The precise details of testing will be discussed further in Chapter 8.

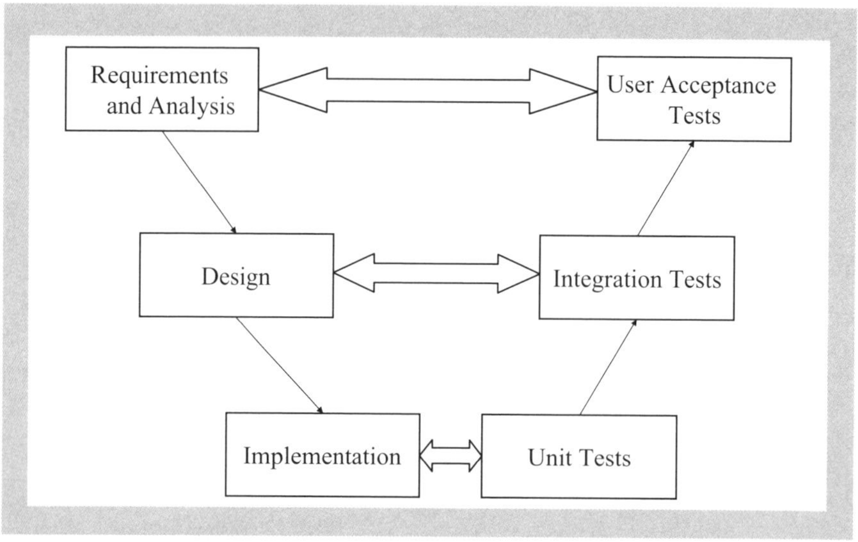

Figure 4.3 The V model for software development

Iterative spiral

The iterative spiral model encapsulates the recursive reality of software development by modelling the software lifecycle (including integration) as a continuous loop of requirements capture, analysis, design, implementation, testing and deployment. The problem should be analysed using enough time to understand the problem domain in its entirety, but without wasting further time on defining all the details; these will be further specified, refined and modified through further iterations. This approach works well in turbulent or fast moving environments, where requirements constantly change or misunderstandings are likely and time to delivery is key. As a result, it is often used in the development of front office trading systems and provides continuous evidence of progress. Iterative development is at the heart of the Rational Unified Process® (RUP®),[1] which is a methodology based on ideas and experiences from a large number of software projects and which is used by a large number of financial institutions.

Continuous Integration

Continuous integration takes the iterative spiral to the extreme of constant ongoing integration, building and testing of the system. This process should occur many times a day and be fully automated and reproducible.

Continuous integration addresses the problem of combining the efforts of many developers. Having integrated all the development effort within the project, any issues or bugs are immediately evident and can be quickly tracked down to the small amount of code that has recently been integrated. Frequent integration also helps prevent conflicts between different developers working on the same area of code.

Extreme Programming (XP)
XP is a lightweight methodology that addresses the needs of small development teams faced with vague and changing requirements. It includes many of the ideas from iterative development and continuous integration and highlights the need to write tests prior to producing any code. Controversially, it also challenges some of the more formal allocations of roles to specific individuals, preferring all team members to participate in all aspects of the development process.

The precise level of formalism, the lifecycle model implemented and other attributes of a project will depend on the context of the problem and the constraints imposed by the organization. This section of the book will be focused on each of the key stages of the software delivery lifecycle. It should be accepted that the precise order and interaction between each of these stages may be more confused and complex than may be implied by linearly reading this book!

There are many interested parties in a new system, many of whom may not be direct users of the system. For example, a corporate risk management system will be used directly by the risk management group, provide reports to traders and senior management and enable the organization to meet its regulatory requirements. Because many of those with an interest in the system (the board, regulators, traders) are not direct users, the term *stakeholder* will be used to indicate any group that has an interest in the system.

A RISK BASED APPROACH TO THE SOFTWARE DELIVERY PROCESS

The risk management techniques discussed in Part I apply not only to managing risks arising from the daily operations of the organization but equally to all the activities it engages in. This includes the software development process. It is important not only to develop risk management systems that meet the specified requirements, but also to perform this in a manner that provides the greatest benefit for a given level of risk.

The software development process should aim to reduce risk (subject to cost constraints) wherever this is possible. These risks may arise from:

Operational failure
The risk of losses arising from failure of the system.

Project failure
The risk of project failure leading to either no system, or an incorrect one, being developed and delivered.

Integration and surrounding process failure
The risk that surrounding systems or processes will fail as a result of changes in infrastructure, the failure to integrate the new system with other systems or changes in workflow. The term *workflow* is commonly used when analysing technical systems and describes the way in which people and systems interact in order to complete a task.

Strategic failure
The inability of the system to be able to be efficiently enhanced to support the strategic direction of the organization as a result of poor code structure or inflexible software engineering.

MODELLING THE PROCESS OF IMPLEMENTING A SYSTEM

In the software development lifecycle, requirements are analysed and generate a logical or conceptual design that is converted into a physical or actual implementation using specific technologies (Figure 4.4). The chosen technology should add value to the project and support the delivery of the project requirements. Moving down each level moves the system closer to physical reality, while moving up the hierarchy shown in Figure 4.4, results in a model that abstracts away from the specific details of how the requirements will be implemented. At the highest level, the requirements model will detail the functional behaviour of the system from the perspective of a user or external system. The requirements model considers the system as a black box, to be interacted with and does not consider the inner workings of the system or how the system may be implemented. The analysis model will convert these requirements into a robust and flexible framework detailing how the proposed system will address these requirements in terms of the structure of data and processing. The design model refines the

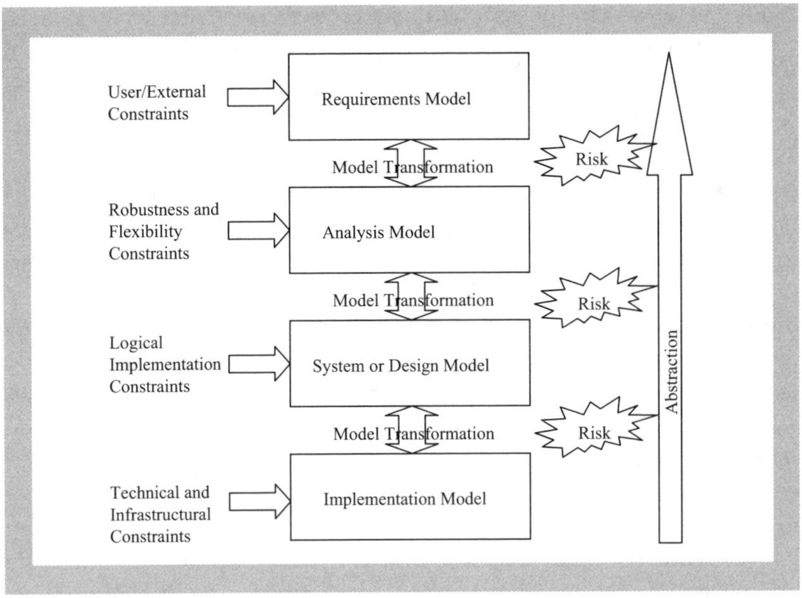

Figure 4.4 The models used in the development lifecycle

analysis model into a structure that can be implemented, considering how the system and functionality can be decomposed into system units or blocks and the physical representation of any data. Finally, the system is implemented, deployed and optimized to be used on a specific technology and integrated to work with other systems.

These models highlight the difference between physical and logical models. Logical models are concerned with what the system does, often at a conceptual or abstract level. Physical models are concerned with how this is achieved, who performs particular operations and where processes and systems will be deployed. The key challenges are to ensure that:

- Each level is adequately decoupled to aid maintainability, so that changes in one level do not dramatically impact other levels. Changes in technology are constantly occurring and it is important that any project is not tied into obsolete or unsupportable implementation technologies. For example, it should be possible to change the underlying middleware (Chapter 6) without enforcing changes in the requirements. Similarly, business requirements are constantly evolving, so any implementation must be able to adapt to enable these changes to be met.

- Each level should consider and map on to the model at the next level. This should mean that the partitioning of business functionality and data in the design model should enable the design to exploit features of the proposed technical implementation.

Each level of this hierarchy will be subject to various constraints. The implementation may be subject to various organizational standards, have to integrate with existing technology used to build surrounding systems or the availability of key skills to support the chosen technology. Using innovative new technology that requires non-existent skills or breaks any technology constraints specified in the requirements process will quickly lead to project failure. The greatest risk of project failure often arises when information is transformed from one model representation and reinterpreted in another. Each model should be validated and tested for completeness to ensure that the derivation of further models does not result in a flawed design or implementation. The risk in transforming between different models can be reduced by using a coherent underlying approach throughout all the models to simplify this transformation. However, because this transformation is often a one-to-many transformation (that is, requirements may be implemented in many different ways), there is inherently a problem when requirements change and what was once the optimal transformation will need to change.

PROTOTYPING

Often the precise requirements and technical challenges of a project can be difficult to clarify. In these situations, a prototype can be developed which is used to highlight, investigate or clarify key functionality or technical issues that the project will have to address. It can serve as an efficient means to communicate requirements between the project team and the end users through a limited demonstration of actual functionality; for example by building screen prototypes to clarify how the user could interact with the system. The focus is on being able to rapidly modify the prototype rather than on robustness, performance or long-term maintainability. Prototypes differ from iterative development in that they will often only address certain aspects of the project that are viewed as being uncertain or sources of project risk. Once this task has been completed and any issues or risks clarified, the prototype should be discarded and replaced with a fully engineered solution. Much of the bad reputation that rapid prototyping has gained has been because the role of prototyping in the development process has not been fully explained. Instead it has been treated more like iterative development resulting in a deliverable solution.

BUY VERSUS BUILD

System delivery is often thought of in terms of the two extremes of either building everything or, alternatively, buying a pre-existing package solution (Figure 4.5). Neither approach is particularly appealing, with each suffering fairly major deficiencies, as outlined in Table 4.1.

One of the major problems with the product or package solution is when the system is viewed as being of strategic importance to the organization, with unique requirements that differ from those of their competitors. By purchasing a product solution, strategic control is given up to the product vendor in return for a generic offering that anyone can purchase. As a result, it is unlikely that the system will provide any clear competitive advantage to the organization.

The significant costs in migrating data and processes from one system to another can also act as a barrier to change, resulting in 'vendor tie in' where enhancements are dictated by the vendor's upgrade schedule. Once a vendor solution has been implemented it is often difficult to

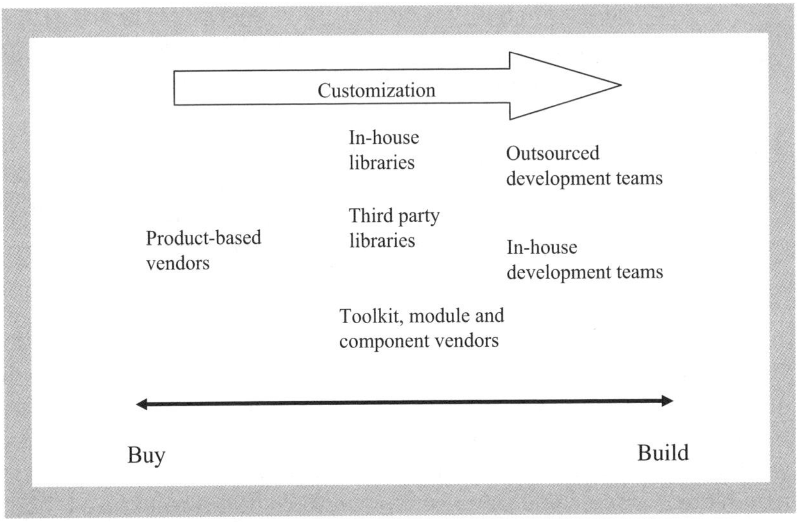

Figure 4.5 Buy versus build continuum

Table 4.1 Comparison of buy versus build

Approach	Advantages	Disadvantages
Build	■ Tailored to exact requirements ■ Incremental delivery and phased migration ■ Interoperability and integration with existing systems ■ Can be customized to meet future requirements ■ Strategic control of evolution of system	■ Resource constraints if developed in house ■ Long lead times ■ High levels of delivery risk ■ Low levels of reuse unless there is an in-house reuse strategy ■ Reduced return on investment; everything may need to be built ■ Ongoing support burden ■ Unproven solution until implemented
Buy	■ Rapid delivery of core functionality ■ Vendor support and maintenance ■ High levels of reuse and likely lower cost of purchase ■ Proven in other deployments ■ Ability to review existing deployments of the system ■ Limited resourcing requirements compared to a build approach	■ Proprietary to the vendor ■ Generic functionality and approach which may not adequately meet requirements ■ Customization can be costly or difficult ■ Support dependency ■ Integration can be difficult and time consuming ■ Vendor tie in ■ Difficult to perform a phased migration to new solution ■ Upgrades may not meet future requirements

justify the cost and risk of moving away from the product. This can result in strategic drift for the organization, with organizational capabilities constrained by inappropriate technology and functionality. Taking the product's current code base and modifying it to match any precise requirements can enable some vendor products to be customized. This, however, means that the system will diverge from that developed by the vendor, removing any benefits from future bug fixes and enhancements, unless any changes applied to the customized version of the system are reapplied to the future releases. If these changes are not trivial or localized, this option can be an expensive and high-risk strategy. This risk can be reduced by using well-defined public interfaces to the vendor system, which support certain types of customization. If stable public interfaces are not used, or available, these system customizations are unlikely to continue to work as expected with future versions of the software. Even if the above can be achieved, the ability to make these modifications also relies on the product being well designed and documented so that it is possible to make these changes easily and effectively.

Despite all these disadvantages, if proven functionality is required which is generic and standardized, or if the requirements of the organization are not well defined and there are no issues with modifying processes and workflows to fit with the product, then a product approach can provide a cost-effective solution. Because it is possible to view an existing demonstrable solution, perceived risk can be reduced and limited to issues concerning integration, rather than functionality. Integration costs should not however be underestimated, especially for risk management solutions.

The main problem with building systems from scratch has been the long lead times and costs associated with such approaches. The technology industry has constantly been trying to discover more efficient development processes and approaches that enable greater levels of reuse to be obtained, reducing both delivery times and development and maintenance costs. Although the move to an object-orientated software engineering paradigm[2] was believed to be a major step towards this goal, with its separation of implementation and functionality/interface, it has not delivered all the benefits that had been hoped for. Typically reuse has only been achieved through:

- Small fine-grained objects or routines, encapsulated in software libraries
- Technical toolkits or infrastructure software used to develop full-scale solutions (for example graphical interface toolkits, databases or system connectivity tools)
- Centralization of functionality in large monolithic or silo applications
- Reuse of common algorithms, models and approaches
- Reuse of common design, analysis and architectural approaches through the use of patterns.

Some of the greatest levels of reuse have come through the use of patterns. These patterns found in design, architecture and analysis have evolved over time into catalogues of simple and elegant approaches to solving recurring themes inherent in certain types of problems. The solution patterns aren't always obvious but reflect the experience of analysts,[3] software designers[4] and system architects[5] gained over long periods of time as they have worked towards greater levels of flexibility and reuse within their solutions.

What has been absent has been the ability to achieve large levels of reuse and the sharing of implemented common business functionality that addresses actual organizational requirements in a mix and match approach. The ideal would be to use common packaged functionality (where the functional requirements permit this) so that resources can be concentrated on what is unique to the organization rather than what is generic. Products are increasingly being broken down into separate modules with well-defined published interfaces so that data flows and functionality can be customized and modified if required. From the other end of the continuum, the use of component-based development (CBD) approaches is also resulting in systems that are built using standalone, reusable components or services that can be shared or redeployed in multiple systems.

CBD encourages a divide and conquer approach to software development where the problem domain is broken down into a number of functional (component) areas. Components are independently deployable units of functionality that have explicit context dependencies and well-defined interfaces and ways of interacting with other systems and components that will not change.[6]

This middle ground between buy and build, of providing building blocks for producing customized solutions, removes many of the disadvantages of a build solution but helps retain most of the advantages. This results in solutions that can:

- Be delivered rapidly
- Have high levels of code reuse or utilize third party implemented functionality
- Provide customized solutions
- Reduce project risk due to the greater use of prewritten and tested functionality
- Give significant productivity gains due to the high levels of reuse
- Be designed to integrate and work with existing systems

- Be easier to maintain/evolve due to the breakdown of the system into a number of independent units.

These solutions can be designed to meet changing requirements through the property of *replaceability* (where existing functional components can be replaced by new functional components provided that the interfaces and contextual dependencies are maintained). Replaceability removes the need to completely upgrade or replace systems when requirements change. This approach also enables the trade-off between reuse and customization to be assessed for each block of functionality, with greater levels of customization reducing likely levels of reuse.

THE NEED FOR FORMALIZING PROCESSES

Given the chaotic and interrelated appearance of the software lifecycle, one would be forgiven for asking why or whether this process should or can be formalized. In his book on the economics of software engineering,[7] Boehm illustrates the relative cost of fixing errors arising or discovered at each stage of the software development lifecycle. Although the specific costs depend on the nature and complexity of the system, Boehm found that costs increased significantly through the stages of the cycle, with an error discovered at the implementation phase costing between 10 and 100 times what it would have cost if it was uncovered at the analysis stage.

The aim must therefore be to implement a software process that reduces the number and magnitude of the expensive errors discovered later on in the process, but without adding so much overhead that the additional process results in time delays and costs that would outweigh these benefits. Again, this is a matter of risk and return; putting in place enough process to reduce project risk, but not so much that it stifles innovation and overly increases delivery times. The degree of process formalization required will depend on the calibre of staff, the nature of the problem and a number of other factors; capable, high quality, experienced staff will be able to make up for process deficiencies. The difficulty is in deciding where this level is (Figure 4.6). Some general characteristics should be included in any software process that will:

- Increase communication throughout the development team and with the stakeholders
- Provide a common language, approaches and techniques through which all communication will occur

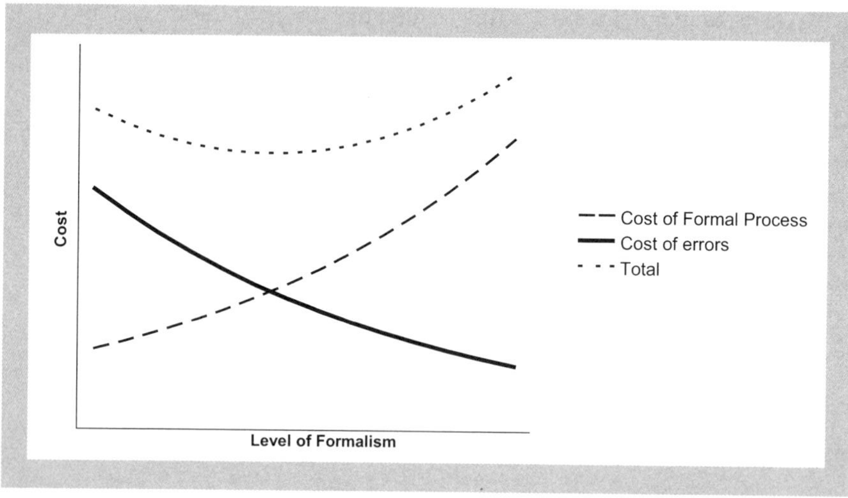

Figure 4.6 Trade-off between cost of process and cost of correcting defects

- Clearly set out expectations and a process road map in order to manage expectations and involvement
- Provide clear controls to manage and mitigate risk within the development process
- Increase the completeness and efficiency of the entire process, preventing ad hoc approaches to development and requirements gathering
- Manage change and problems throughout the software development lifecycle.

The capability maturity model (or CMM) has emerged as an industry-standard set of guidelines for evaluating and improving an organization's software development process.[8] CMM is a general descriptive framework, which does not provide any specific guidance for implementation. Instead it provides a set of characteristics for different levels of maturity in the software process which the organization should focus on in order to elevate its software processes to that maturity level. CMM defines five levels of maturity:

1. *Initial*

   Ad hoc development processes relying on key individuals for successful project completion.

2. *Repeatable*
   Repeatable ability to plan, document and manage projects as well as effectively track progress.

3. *Defined*
   The development and management processes are documented, standardized and integrated, with all projects using this approved process.

4. *Managed*
   More detailed and complex measurement and management of the software process.

5. *Optimizing*
   Continuous process improvement aimed at improving software quality.

The aim of CMM is to advance the software process within an organization from one that is characterized by a lower CMM level towards one with a higher CMM level. This will lead to a process that is repeatable, managed and measured, improving software quality and reducing software development costs. Independent assessment can be used to validate and maintain a software process that meets a certain CMM level. Organizations that have implemented CMM have seen dramatic cost reductions and shorter times to delivery resulting from reduced reworking and correction of software defects.[9]

The result of using formalized approaches should be a clearly defined process, which will drive the software lifecycle and assist in the provision of accurate time and effort estimates for project planning. A summary and comparison of many of the different commercial methods for analysing systems can be found in Tudor and Tudor's work.[10] The precise methodology chosen will be context dependent, with each methodology having its own strengths and weaknesses in dealing with different types of problems; simple problems or small team sizes will not be able to bear the burden of an excessively formal process, just as more complex problems or larger teams will need some level of formalism if the process is to be controlled.

AGILE METHODOLOGIES

Agile software methodologies are a hot topic in improving software quality. They include methodologies such as XP,[11] Scrum[12] and Feature Driven Development.[13] Agile methodologies emphasize the importance and role of people in the development process, highlighting their importance over relying purely on process and tools. The benefits of group problem-solving techniques and approaches have been well known for some time, but the productivity and software quality benefits of collaborative approaches such as *pair programming*[14] can be amazingly significant. In pair programming, two developers sit next to each other, one writing the code and thinking tactically about implementing the piece of functionality while the other considers how this fits in strategically with the overall design and reviews the code as it is written. Jensen[15] found an increase of over 100 per cent in the number of lines written and a decrease in the error rate of three orders of magnitude.

Although these approaches have been most successfully applied in ill-specified high risk projects where iterative approaches compensate for ill-specified or changing requirements, rather than more formalized well-defined traditional types of project, some of the concepts are transferable to other types of project. The approach of agile methodologies can be summed up in the agile methodology manifesto:

Manifesto for Agile Software Development

We are uncovering better ways of developing software by doing it and helping others do it. Through this work we have come to value:

Individuals and interactions over processes and tools

Working software over comprehensive documentation

Customer collaboration over contract negotiation

Responding to change over following a plan

That is, while there is value in the items on the right, we value the items on the left more.

Kent Beck	James Grenning	Robert C. Martin
Mike Beedle	Jim Highsmith	Steve Mellor
Arie van Bennekum	Andrew Hunt	Ken Schwaber
Alistair Cockburn	Ron Jeffries	Jeff Sutherland
Ward Cunningham	Jon Kern	Dave Thomas
Martin Fowler	Brian Marick	

Source: http://www.agilemanifesto.org/. © 2001, the above authors.

Agile methodologies remind us that there is little point in blindly enforcing procedures and documentation unless there are clearly defined and achievable benefits. It again highlights the importance of context and balance in any approach.

WHY SOFTWARE NEEDS TO BE REPLACED

Any system should be periodically reviewed to ensure that it is effectively supporting business operations and not introducing unacceptable levels of operational risk into the organization. If the system is not adequately addressing the users' needs, modifications should be made so that any new requirements are met. Ideally, the process of augmenting functionality onto existing systems would result in ongoing enhancements that could carry on for ever. Unfortunately, the process of modifying software tends to add complexity to it as it is forced to operate in a manner that it was not initially designed to do. This *software entropy* or software disorder[16] results in more and more complex code which is more difficult and costly to maintain. It is also more likely to be incorrectly modified and therefore more likely to fail, increasing operational risk.

Any developed system will have an initial level of entropy, which will increase over its lifetime as changes are made. Eventually, the level of entropy will be such that any further changes are too risky or expensive to perform, requiring significant re-engineering of the software. The aim of good software engineering is both to reduce the initial level of entropy within the system and also to minimize the increase in entropy arising from ongoing enhancements. This will increase the lifespan of the software as well as reduce operational risk. The key question for the software designer and developer is to determine any resultant savings and to compare these against the costs of adding additional structure and forward engineering in order to reduce both the initial entropy level and the incremental increase from ongoing maintenance. CBD and other modular approaches to software development address many of the issues of software entropy by dividing systems up into smaller units that can be individually re-engineered when required rather than requiring the entire system to be re-engineered.

KEY ROLES IN THE SOFTWARE PROCESS

Within any project there are a number of key roles that should be filled, each with its own unique responsibilities:

Sponsor: The end user(s) or some approved representative of the end user(s). This person defines, prioritizes and owns the relevant user needs and requirements. They will also play a key role in validating that the implementation meets the requirements.

Business analyst (BA): Responsible for interpreting, documenting and representing the sponsor's requirements to the rest of the development team and mapping these into a requirements and analysis model. They will be a key resource for transferring business knowledge and interpretation of requirements to the developers as well as facilitating any communication between them and the stakeholders. BAs should have some knowledge of the proposed system design, so that they can clarify any requirements, that may prove difficult or costly to implement. They will also work with the test team to define functional tests.

Developer: Responsible for implementing the functional requirements. This role will typically be performed by a number of different individuals with the requisite skills to implement the defined functionality. This may need expertise in graphical user interface (GUI) development, prototyping, databases or third party packages. More senior developers will assist other developers in understanding and completing individual tasks. They will also act as a key control in the development process, and may provide additional estimation expertise for input into the project plan as well as ensuring unit tests are implemented and code reviews are performed.

Project manager (PM): Responsible for ensuring the overall aims of the project are met. They will maintain the project plan, tracking and managing progress (including taking remedial action), co-ordinate documentation and its review, and most importantly, report status to a programme office or the key stakeholders of the project. The project manager also has a key leadership role in instilling confidence, collaborative spirit and discipline in the team.

Architect: Designs and oversees the overall system and application architecture and reviews design of all sections of the application to ensure that they fit into any overall architectural strategy for the project and/or organization.

Development lead: Manages and directs the entire development team. He or she will also play a key role in resourcing and task scheduling, as well as co-ordinating any review and quality control activities, such as enforcing relevant standards and guidelines. The development lead will also work with the test team to co-ordinate any work required to repair tests or sections of code, based on any test failures.

Configuration engineer: Manages the source code repository, the build process and releases of the system (Chapter 9), as well as any supporting tools used in the software development process.

System support staff: Maintain the non-people related resources for the project.

Quality assurance lead (QA lead): Responsible for overall quality assurance, not just quality assessment or testing, as well as managing the quality aspects of the development process and ensuring adherence to any defined development process. The QA lead will work with other roles in the project to ensure that an adequate testing framework is put in place to support these aims.

Test designer: Responsible for ensuring that adequate testing is performed on any builds and releases of the system. If the testing process is not automated, the test designer may also be supported by testers who perform these tests.

At the overall project or programme office level there may be senior representatives from the roles outlined above who will perform co-ordination activities in addition to the overall programme manager who will co-ordinate all the individual project plans. A help system designer, technical author or other documentation provider may also be needed. Outside the project there may also be similar roles for co-ordinating reuse, development process and architectural standards across the organization.

Many of these roles may be performed by a single individual or shared among a number of individuals, depending on the size and complexity of the project. Conflicts of interest in performing multiple roles should be avoided, such as a developer also having responsibility for quality assurance. The transparency, communication and workload implications of the distribution of these roles across the team should be carefully monitored and managed through the project plan and project management process. Absence of any of these roles, however, will indicate an incomplete software development process, increasing the likelihood of project failure.

Although experience and specialist knowledge are important requirements for certain tasks, within any project it is important that these resources are used as partners and expert helpers rather than key individuals vital to the success of any project. Viewing individuals as key to project success will only end up in them becoming bottlenecks to the development and review process.

TEAM-BASED DEVELOPMENT

Communication is key to ensuring that there are no misunderstandings in the implementation of functionality. If project members with different skills operate independently of each other, only communicating on an occasional basis, there will be a tendency for barriers to build between them. The aim must be to break down these barriers in order to bring people from different functional silos into an integrated process. Constant ongoing communication and sharing of information will resolve the many interrelated issues that will arise in implementing risk management functionality. The classic approach of having one functional group 'throw' work over the wall to the next downstream group (Figure 4.7) can give everyone a false impression of progress; the former group will appear to have done their work (and will probably have started working on new tasks) while the next group appear to take

Figure 4.7 Avoiding the barriers to team communication

longer to complete their tasks because they have to resolve issues or inconsistencies arising from the received information. Without adequate *contracts* between teams, for example, between BAs and developers in the form of properly structured documentation and frequent review meetings, developers will, at best, be chasing requirements whilst the details are finalized. At worst, significant delays to the deliverables of any tasks may occur.

Cross-functional teams address this communication issue and comprise staff covering all the roles mentioned above. Each multi-skilled team comes into being for the sole purpose of carrying out the assigned body of work. Once that work is completed the team can disband and be made available for other work. By including representatives from all the different roles, the process becomes much more transparent, and easier to manage, especially as the drivers and sources of project risk are likely to be distributed across the different functional areas. This will ensure that the causes of risk and the realization of those risks are combined into a single manageable unit. Communication also becomes much more robust and durable, which helps to ensure that what is implemented is what was requested and for this to be achieved on the first attempt at delivering the functionality. Cross-functional teams do however add different risks to a project in terms of co-ordination and resource management.

As well as being cross-functional, teams may also be distributed in multiple locations. This may be because of constraints on resource availability or in order to provide improved (global) around the clock support and development. Ensuring a local presence to the users of a system will also help to guarantee that adequate front line support is maintained and any user relationships are more effectively managed.

Resource constraints can arise from the location of key skills within the organization or, alternatively, be due to the cost and availability of skills in the external employment market. This has led to a major drive towards outsourcing development to regions such as India or China where there is a large, low cost, highly skilled technical skill pool. Productivity can also be enhanced by performing sequential tasks on a constant global basis. For example, a daily testing and validation process run in Asia can follow development in Europe, with this information available for the development team on the following day. Global teams also tend to involve people from more diverse backgrounds ensuring balanced teams that have fewer cognitive biases and a lower danger of 'group think' where all the members of a team convince themselves they are correct rather than questioning their assumptions.[17]

The soft or people aspects of software development require some level of face-to-face communication and interaction in order to build trust and rapport between team members. This can be an issue with global teams and takes significant amounts of time to develop using less interactive approaches such as email; the more interactive the medium the better. A common approach to improving team communication and coherence is to arrange a project kick-off meeting in a single location. This enables the team to form and develop as a group as early as possible, ensuring the entire team is involved. It also provides a sense of ownership of the project from the outset. Good communication is key in any project and the informal meetings that improve information flow, which may occur by the coffee machine in single site projects, will be more difficult to achieve on global projects. Ensuring that frequent discussions occur, are documented, agreed and any outcomes are distributed to the project team will address this deficiency. Some of the key requirements for team performance are:

Trust

Both the stakeholders and project team must trust and empower each other in achieving a common well-defined goal. Developers must trust and be willing to help one another in every way possible to achieve that goal. The management team must trust that each developer is a skilled professional who will perform to the best of his or her ability and make the best decision given the information available.

Courage

The team must not be afraid to restructure or redevelop aspects of the system when the situation clearly warrants it. This decision must be made carefully with input from all relevant parties. In the long run, brave decisions will dramatically reduce issues later in the project that other team members may have had to address. There is always a tendency, when the time pressure is on, to attempt a quick fix that can increase code complexity and reduce maintainability.

Confidence

To know what is right and implement it with conviction. Many issues arise from uncertainty and indecision in implementing functionality. Incorrect decisions can always be resolved later. Procrastinating will achieve nothing.

Discipline

Any defined process and related tasks, such as testing or maintaining documentation, must be performed, even if the modifications are only a 'one line change'. Failure to be disciplined will remove the benefits of any defined approach.

Focus
Time should not be wasted on functionality that is not required. The '20/80 rule'[18] tells us that 80 per cent of the useful functionality of a system comes from 20 per cent of the total effort of a project; this is where any focus should be.

Truthfulness
To ensure effective communication and enable the project to be effectively managed, correct information on progress and project status must always be provided by all team members.

DOCUMENTATION OF THE PROJECT

Documentation provides a lasting record of the development of the system and forces the development team to make explicit all implicit assumptions. This can then be used as a checkpoint in the team's understanding of the project that is formally 'signed off' and agreed by all interested parties. Ensuring that there is an effective requirements management process and that the entire process is documented is a key requirement in achieving CMM level 2. Sign-off procedures also formalize and ensure responsibility and accountability for producing documentation that is correct. This is important at the requirements gathering stage, as the functionality of the developed system will depend on the specified requirements, which should have been validated against the actual requirements.

The documentation of a project will range from requirements to actual implemented code and test cases. It may also include emails, notes, and recordings of conversations that provide the context for information or changes. Ideally, any documentation process will have the ability to link design, code or test cases back to specific requirements (and vice versa) and even back to individual conversations and decisions. This ability to recall the history of any project output (or *artefact*) in the project is known as *traceability*. Traceability provides a context for any decision to be fully understood at a later date, as well as ensuring that the full impact of any change on previous decisions is completely understood before being made. This can be vital for large projects or systems that are likely to undergo major enhancement throughout their life.

Requirements and documentation will change through time. The concept of the requirements being frozen as of some point and remaining frozen does not match reality and can only lead to the successful delivery of the wrong solution. Traceability requires us to be able to track changes in documentation over time, linked to the new information that caused that change to occur. It should also be possible to view the documentation as of some defined point (the baselines or snapshots which will be the basis of the requirements for the system being built at that moment in time) along with the changes that occur between each snapshot. The evolutionary nature of information gathering also means that it will be necessary to associate various states against all the artefacts produced by the software process. This will typically include initial release, under review, reviewed and final, with these states being iterated over as changes impact the system. Keeping these artefacts consistent and synchronized between different versions is a major challenge for the development process and can introduce a significant burden on the project. Significant risks may, however, arise if consistency is not maintained, leading to tests or code not reflecting current requirements.

Ideally, documentation should be based on standard templates, used across all projects so that there is:

- An element of familiarity when using any of the documentation, with a common consistency, look and feel
- A focus on content rather than layout when the document is authored
- A checklist of content laid out by the template that must be filled in.

Care should also be taken to avoid combining too much information into a single document. Conflicts and problems can arise when multiple people work on the same document, which can introduce unwanted dependencies into the process. Often a project workbook is created,[19] which acts as a repository for all this information. This document provides a list of all the output from the project, in effect, a project-specific customization of the general process, outlining precisely what is to be delivered within the project. The project team members should agree on the types of artefacts that are needed based on the nature of the work being carried out. The project workbook can also be used to maintain the project contact list, billing and timesheet codes, and the like. If all artefacts are hosted online, the project workbook can be used as a portal homepage, using hyperlinks to point to the relevant artefacts. The use of a document management system can help automate and remove many of the problems associated with tracking changes, versioning documentation, managing state change and improving traceability. The following section highlights the range of potential documentation.

Project proposal

This will be concise, non-technical and authored by the project stakeholders. It defines the scope and purpose of the project and should also clearly articulate the business reasons and benefits from performing this project.

Requirements

Authored by the BA, this will define the precise requirements for the system and form the basis of a requirements model, which should provide enough detail for the test team to develop various system and acceptance tests. This requirements model may detail specific business, customer and operational models that have been proposed or need to be supported.

Functional analysis

This document takes the requirements and transforms them into an analysis model that will meet these requirements. This model should be defined in enough detail for the development team to be able to respond with a corresponding technical design and implementation strategy.

Design, implementation and architecture documents

Authored by the development team (architects, developers), these documents describe the design and implementation details, derived from the results of any analysis. They will describe how the system, other systems and units of software will interact to satisfy the requirements and how various infrastructure issues will be addressed. These documents should also detail the relevant physical data and process flows and how these relate to the physical infrastructure.

Test documentation

The test documentation should consist of:

Test plan
This will set out the plan, objectives and approach for testing the system. It will also define the testing environments and resources that will be required, the test results review process and how this information will be used throughout the rest of the project.

Test cases
This will define the types and range of testing that will be performed, deriving individual test cases from the functional requirements, analysis and implementation documentation, depending on the type of testing to be performed. These should be fully traceable back to the artefact that resulted in the test case.

Test procedures
Details of how and when the tests will be performed and any tools that will be required.

Test results
Record of the results of testing and how this information will be reported to the project team.

Standards, project procedures and style guides

The processes and tools to be used within the project should be fully documented. This should also cover all procedures to be implemented with the project, including tasks that should be performed at various stages of the development process concerning quality assurance, estimation approaches, risk assessment, management and so on. When a number of developers work on or are likely to maintain pieces of code, it is important to define screen layout, coding standards and style guides that any work should adhere to. Unless this is achieved, the look and feel, structure and usability of the application are likely to be inconsistent. The international deployment of risk management solutions also means that the code should be 'internationalized' requiring the GUI to be customized to the locale it is used in. This documentation should also highlight any reoccurring design patterns that should be standardized and defined as part of any design standards.

Project plan and project process

The project plan will define all the detailed tasks, resources, pending issues required to deliver the system, together with estimated and actual task completion dates. The skeleton outline should be common to all projects and, in effect, document the process in terms of predefined tasks, deliverables, task orderings and completion milestones (Chapter 7). The plan should always reflect and maintain current estimated and actual completion times for each task.

Change control plan and requests

The procedure for dealing with and prioritizing changes to the requirements must be agreed with all the project stakeholders and the process documented. Because these requests will change the requirements of the system, they must be fully documented and traceable to changes in the requirements document.

User and support documentation

Depending on the requirements of the users, various amounts of documentation or training materials and courses may be required. The type of information to be provided will depend on the characteristics of the user group. Traders are unlikely to attend extensive training courses or read manuals and will instead require targeted individual tuition. Risk managers will be more amenable to group training and training manuals.

User documentation may also include installation notes, support notes, release documentation, checklists, sign-off forms and other material relating to the installation or use of the system.

Notes

1 P. Krutchen, *The Rational Unified Process: an Introduction* (Addison-Wesley, 1999)
2 I. Jacobson *Object-orientated Software Engineering – A Use Case Driven Approach* (Addison-Wesley, 1992)
3 M. Fowler, *Analysis Patterns: Reusable Object Models* (Addison-Wesley, 1996)
4 E. Gamma, R. Helm et al. *Design Patterns: Elements of Reusable Object-oriented Software* (Addison-Wesley, 1994)
5 M. Fowler, *Patterns of Enterprise Application Architecture* (Addison Wesley, 2002)
6 C. Szyperski, *Component Software – Beyond Object-orientated Programming* (Addison-Wesley, 1999)
7 B. W. Boehm, *Software Engineering Economics* (Prentice Hall, 1981)
8 P. Jalote, *CMM in Practice: Processes for Software Development at Infosystems* (Addison-Wesley 1999)
9 W. Humphrey, T. Snyder and R. Willis, 'Software process improvement at Hughes Aircraft', *IEEE Software,* **8** (4) July 1991, 11–23
10 D. J. Tudor and I. J. Tudor *System, Analysis and Design – A Comparison of Structured Methods* (Macmillan, 1997)
11 K. Beck, *Extreme Programming Explained* (Addison-Wesley, 2000)
12 M. Beedle and K. Schwaber, *Agile Software Development with Scrum* (Prentice Hall, 2002)
13 S. Palmer and M. Felsing, *Practical Guide to Feature-driven Development,* (Prentice Hall, 2002)
14 See note 11
15 R. Jensen, 'A pair programming experience', *Cross Talk – The Journal of Defence Software Engineering* (March 2003)
16 See note 2
17 G. Salaman and J. Butler, 'Why managers won't learn', in *Managing Learning,* C. Mabey and P. Iles (eds) (Routledge, 1994) 34–42
18 See note 11
19 IBM, Object Orientated Technology Center, *Developing Object-orientated Software – An Experience-based Approach* (Prentice Hall, 1997)

CHAPTER 5

Requirements gathering and analysis

Before the formal start of any requirements gathering and analysis, there should have already been a reasonable amount of informal requirements gathering and problem scoping through the production of a project proposal or business justification statement. This may have even resulted in an initial feasibility study or the building of a prototype. The justification statement will be the basis for all further project work and will provide the high-level objectives to be achieved and the context of the problem to be solved. This statement will have considered both internal and external events and the drivers that are forcing change on the process under discussion.

The project proposal will typically be a descriptive document that highlights the key issue that needs to be addressed. It should not specify how this problem should be solved and may not even clearly define the problem beyond indicating that existing processes and systems are unable to address the organization's needs. Its main purpose is to acknowledge that senior staff within the organization understand that there is a problem to address. This problem may have arisen due to an alarming increase in certain KRIs that highlight an inability to measure and manage risk or potential failures in the workflow or processes such as:

- Poor levels of data consistency

- Transactions not recorded in systems
- Incorrect measurement of risk
- Difficulties in ensuring data quality
- Inability to support the future business strategy, in terms of financial instruments traded, the way in which they are managed or the volumes traded.

Any project proposal should highlight all the evidence that supports its assertions, and any constraints (such as delivery dates or costs) that must be met. The aim of articulating the nature of the problem and why it must be addressed helps to ensure that the stated assumptions are in agreement with organizational strategy.

In order for the project to occur, this initial assessment must have been able at least to show that further analysis should be performed. This will enable any issues to be more precisely specified and determined, as well as leading to a list of possible options and requirements for a system to resolve these issues. Once the problem is better understood, some level of cost and risk can be associated with each proposed solution, and any additional or specific benefits that will result. The organization can then make an informed decision whether to proceed with the project and what the scope of the project should be.

The importance of some level of initial project proposal or business justification cannot be overstated. Its absence will often indicate a project that has no clear sponsor, no allocated budget and which may not be aligned with the organization's strategic needs. This will make the project likely to fail, becoming either incapable of addressing the organization's true needs or unachievable within it. When defining the requirements for any solution, the best approach to obtaining these will be highly context specific, depending on the unique nature of any organizational issues and the attitude and influence of various groups involved.

RE-ENGINEERING WORKFLOW AND TECHNOLOGY

There are very few 'green field' sites where the business analyst simply needs to specify a new solution that meets the users' requirements, which can be implemented using whatever is the most appropriate technology. Dependencies on existing systems and workflows greatly complicate this process. Instead, a constrained, ill-specified optimization problem often arises; existing workflows and technology must be enhanced so as to meet the new requirements within the context of organizational standards and competing demands for resources. Understanding the existing technology and the users' interaction with it is key to bridging the functionality gap and implementing any new required functionality and workflows (Figure 5.1). Only by understanding the existing functionality, its associated workflows and technology, as well as future requirements is it possible to:

- Ensure that any new system enhances rather than subtracts from existing functionality
- Minimize project risk by fully understanding current and future requirements, the gap between them that must be bridged and why this must be achieved
- Provide enough contextual information for the development team to be able to assess the most efficient approach, given the risk appetite for the project. Any new implementation should work with rather than against, or ignoring, existing processes and technology.

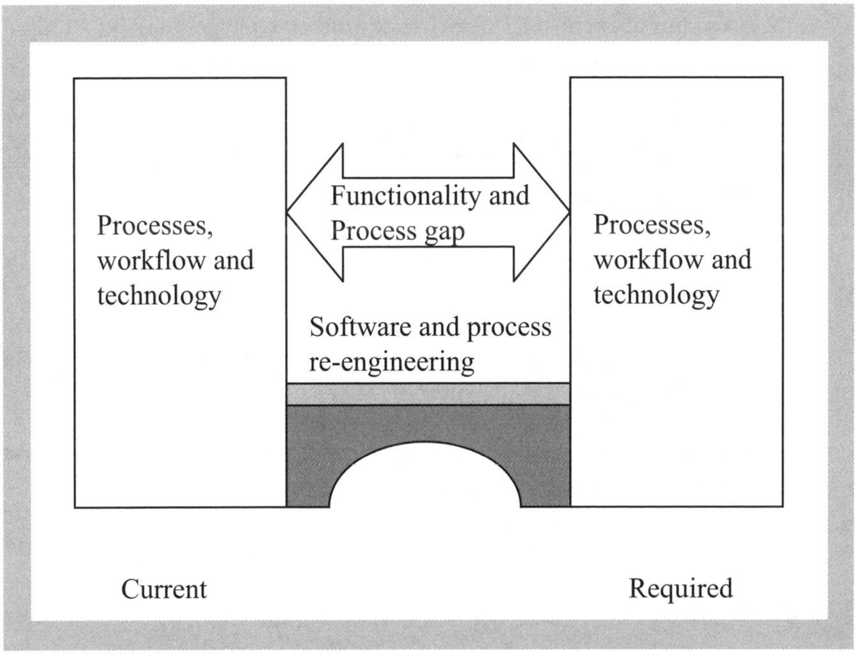

Figure 5.1 Software bridging the functionality gap

This is a very similar problem to using a map to plan travel between two locations. Although the destination may be known, without being aware of where you currently are it is impossible to know the most appropriate manner in which to reach it.

It is rare for the implementation of any new system only to require technological changes within the organization. Often requirements have much wider reaching implications, necessitating the re-engineering of workflows and other systems that interact or are outside the proposed scope of the project; not all problems can be solved through technology alone or can be localized to a single piece of functionality! These organizational and operational changes are as important as the new functionality being delivered. If they are not implemented, any proposed solution will not integrate with the surrounding processes and technology. As a result the project is likely to fail.

Process change can be difficult to achieve. It requires a holistic perspective that challenges the current way work is performed. It may even impact the culture of the organization and the way certain behaviours are rewarded. Such changes can be exceptionally difficult to implement and must be clearly communicated to the sponsors of any project.

The business analyst should not only be gathering requirements from the users but also considering what additional changes may be required in surrounding processes and systems. To achieve this, the analyst must look for deficiencies in and implications of existing and proposed processes. These deficiencies may impact the quality of risk information, increase operational risk or reduce operational efficiency within the organization. Any proposed solution should aim to:

- Enhance existing workflow and processes – automate rather than obliterate

- Manage the trade-off between functional requirements and cost in terms of money and time – nothing is for free

- Produce solutions that are designed to automate and integrate – end error-prone multiple data entry and excessively manual tasks

- Standardize models and approaches through shared functionality and approaches – solve the reconciliation nightmare.

REQUIREMENTS GATHERING

The aim of requirements gathering is to obtain an agreed understanding between the stakeholders and the project team of what any proposed project should achieve. This should define the functionality that will be provided, but not necessarily how this will be achieved. Constant ongoing communication and confirmation of the requirements with these stakeholders is vital to the success of any project.

The requirements document is key to defining the rest of the work to be performed in the project. In particular it will define what will be implemented and how it will be tested, together with the defined sign-off criteria. Any errors or misunderstandings at this stage will therefore propagate throughout the rest of the project.

In order to ensure the success of this stage of the project and the commitment of all those involved in this process, it is advisable to have some type of 'kick off' meeting. This should be attended by the sponsor and clearly articulate the:

- Reason for this work
- Benefits the project will bring
- Influence those attending the meeting can have on the project and why their involvement is important.

One of the key challenges for the analyst is to avoid thinking in terms of a concrete implementation. This is also true for the users of the proposed system, who may be more comfortable thinking in terms of specific physical implementations of systems that they are familiar with or how any solution could be implemented in a spreadsheet. Instead, all discussions must be in terms of requirements that can be converted into logical or conceptual processes that address these requirements. The system architect and lead developer then decide how these logical processes should be implemented to deliver both the functional and the behavioural characteristics of the system.

The process of requirements gathering can be broken down into a number of distinct stages (Figure 5.2):

Problem discovery

Ensuring the problem is well specified and understood at a conceptual level. The underlying causes of the problem must also be well under-

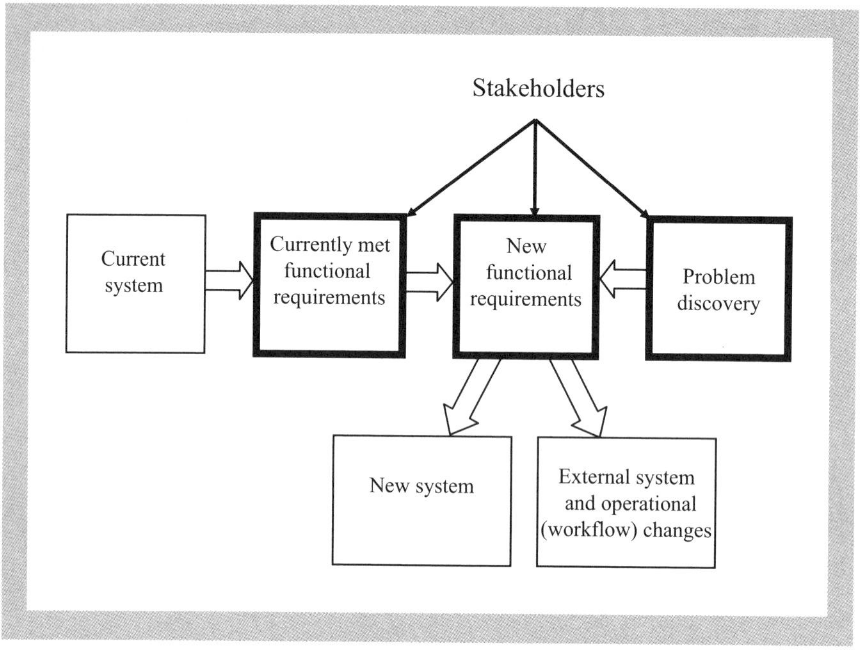

Figure 5.2 Process for system change and requirements gathering

stood so that any solution will address these and be able to cope with likely short-term changes.

Analysing the current context of the problem
Understanding the existing workflow, technology and processes as well as why and where they are deficient. This will also drive the strategy for delivering and deploying any solution.

Specifying new requirements
Specifying and prioritizing the new requirements in sufficient detail to fully address the needs of the business and define the completion criteria for the project.

The requirements gathering process should be fully documented and cover not only functional issues but also any other project-related constraints. These constraints may include available budget, delivery deadlines and other organizational or technical limitations and assumptions. By making these explicit as early on in the process as possible, major misunderstandings can be prevented.

Politics and budgets

Before gathering any information concerning the requirements, awareness and commitment to the project must be obtained. This should include identifying the key users, roles and responsibilities of all those who will be affected or will have influence on this project. This will cover all users:

- Involved in the workflow to be modified
- Who support current processes or system
- Who operate in related areas that produce or consume information related to the processes to be modified
- Who comprise groups involved in the setting, defining or implementation of standards or controls, such as architecture groups or internal audit.

One vital outcome of this process is to identify the key sponsor of the project. This user must be influential enough to ensure commitment from all the parties involved in the process and will also have ownership of the budget allocated to the project. Within any organization resources are, to varying degrees, always constrained and opinion and commitment of various stakeholders may not always be as supportive as hoped for. Many projects will be competing for these scarce resources both in terms of budget and key staff, and those who have influence over these must be convinced that this project is worth supporting. Unfortunately this process is not a completely rational one. At best it is subjectively rational,[1] that is, rational to the decision makers given their experiences and available information, even if these decisions appear irrational to others. At worst, personal agendas and political relationships may result in sub-optimal (to the organization) decision making. It is therefore important that any project manager is prepared and armed to deal with this and that:

- The goals and solution are clearly articulated
- Details and benefits of the proposed solution are clearly communicated
- Any goals agree with the company strategy and the personal goals of the key decision makers
- The project works within and adheres to any constraints imposed by the organization or those involved in the decision process.

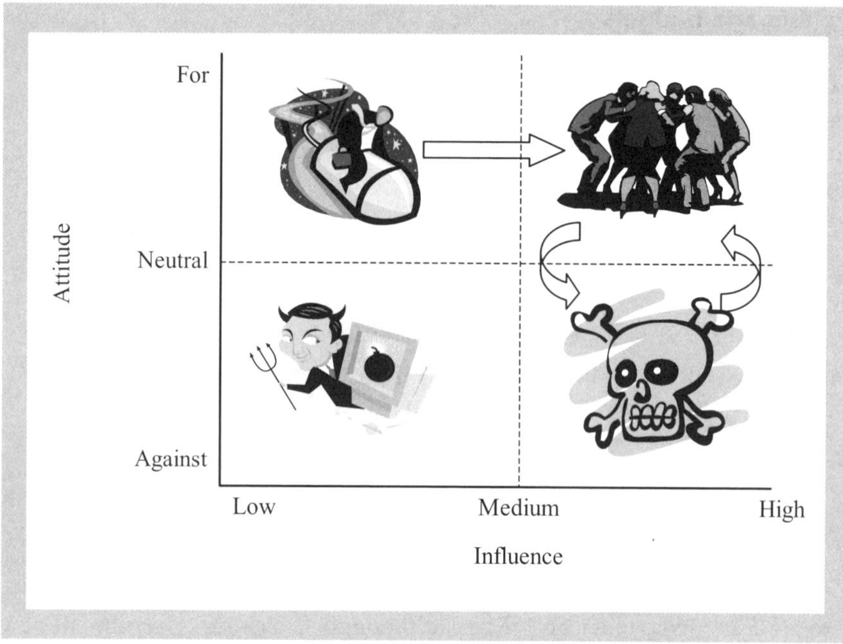

Figure 5.3 The attitude and influence matrix of those involved in a project

People, as well as financial organizations, have different risk tolerances, approaches for comparing risk (of project failure) versus return (benefit from project) and timescales (short-term career benefit versus long-term organizational survival). The participants and stakeholders in any project (whether at the proposal, ongoing development, or maintenance stage) can be broken down into different groups depending on their influence and attitude to the project (Figure 5.3). The influence that someone has is typically broken down into a number of categories that will include:

Decision maker

This is the person or group that will fundamentally make the decision and allocate budget. As a result these people have a high level of influence on whether the project goes ahead or continues.

Influencer

This group does not have decision-making powers but can influence those with them.

Recommender
This group does not make or assess project decisions but can increase the visibility of a project to those with greater influence.

Specialist/Evaluator
Specialists have one-sided influence in that they can only reject proposals, setting a bar above which all projects must be able to climb. Their ability to influence is based on their knowledge of the underlying technical or business details. It is therefore important that those in this group are adequately informed. They may also be influencers, based on their expert knowledge and opinion.

Gatekeeper
Gatekeepers control access to other groups, restricting and controlling information flow. They can even distort information, resulting in an incorrect representation of the project to others.

End user
This is the group who will use any proposed system and will drive certain aspects of the requirements process.

Resource or budget allocator
This group controls the allocation of resources and budget to the project or decision maker. As a result, these people have the option of withholding or removing resources, preventing the project from starting or effectively continuing.

One of the key challenges is mapping out those involved in the process onto the influence and attitude matrix (Figure 5.3). It is then important to inform, influence and argue the benefits of the project so that those with high levels of influence do not become negative to the project and those that are against the project come to support it. The relative importance and role of these users will change over time and it is important to remap the matrix during the different stages of any project. Influence diagrams can also be used to map the complicated interdependence and influence of different groups within this process in order to understand how views and decisions can be changed.

It may be possible to modify those involved in the project, so that groups who were perceived to have low influence and support the project increase their influence. For example, internal auditors can become key influencers in a project when informed of the unsatisfactory alternatives. They can become strong allies to projects that will deliver key controls within the organization, as well as support the required risk management functionality.

Problem discovery

Often the root cause of a problem is not clear and its precise nature needs to be determined. Each interested party will have a unique, but incomplete perspective on the problem, in the same way that a group of people using binoculars to look at an object have. They each see the detail within their field of view but often cannot grasp the context and wider problem represented by the entire object being viewed. This is the essence of problem discovery and the role of the analyst in producing a coherent model that represents all these requirements. Fortunately there is a wide range of creative techniques that can be applied in order to discover the true underlying nature of a problem.[2]

At the heart of problem discovery is the use of different thought processes and approaches to thinking about the problem in a divergent and then convergent manner (Figure 5.4). This process is then iterated

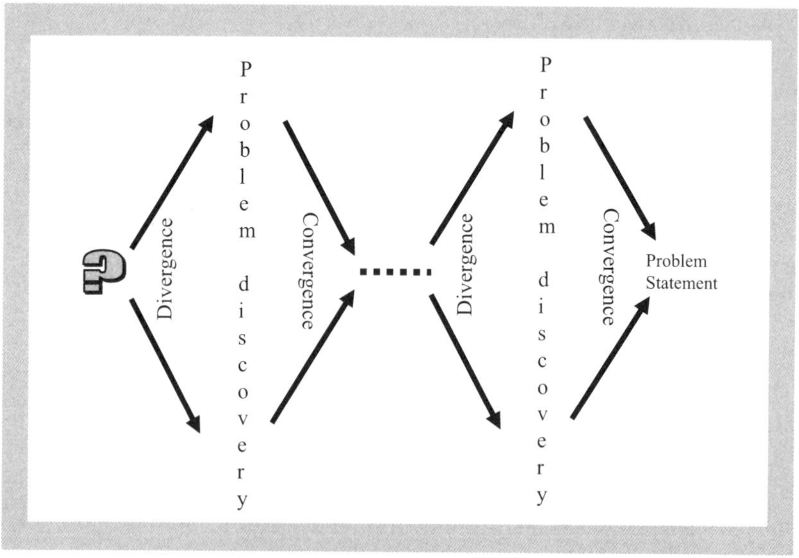

Figure 5.4 Convergent and divergent approaches to problem solving

until the problem is well understood. Divergent approaches encourage many different perspectives on the problem, encouraging people to 'think outside the box', challenge accepted understandings and consider different requirements to address any issues. This process is important if the problem is to be well understood and to ensure the quality of the proposed requirements of any solution.

On their own, divergent approaches do not follow through into concrete proposals, but instead lead to a list of possibilities. As a result, every divergent phase must be associated with a convergent phase, where different requirements that address the problem are evaluated and the best approach selected.

Current processes

Analysing the current processes and technology requires the analyst to perform the reverse operation of the typical development process. That is, to derive the logical model for the system from its current physical implementation (Figure 5.5). This requires deriving the design model

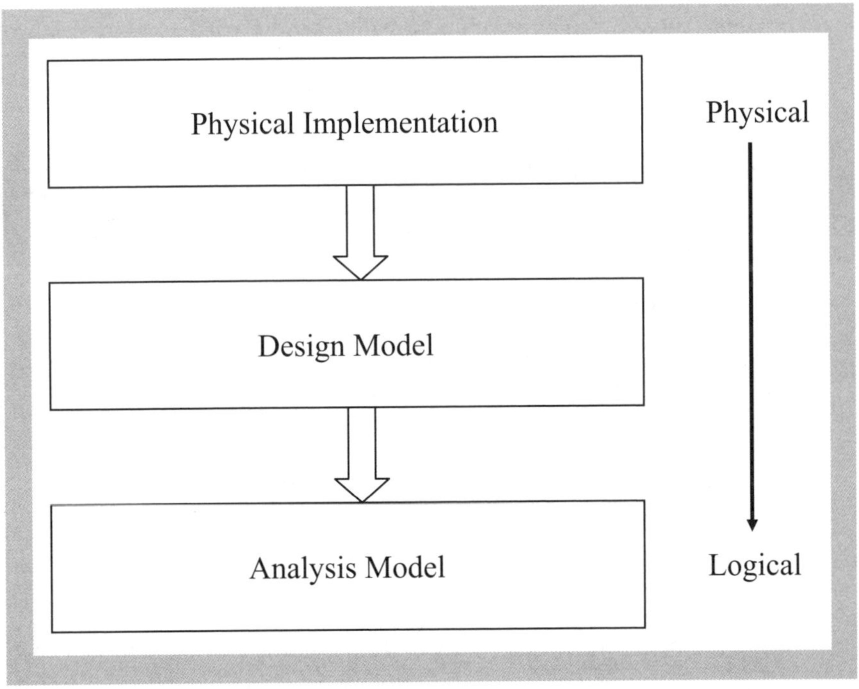

Figure 5.5 The system reverse engineering process

from the physical implementation, and from that, deriving the analysis model. Unless the system is well documented, this can be a time-consuming process. It is also one that should not dominate the time and budget assigned to the entire project! Once a physical model representing the implemented processes, work and data flows has been derived, it can be validated against the current implementation through discussion with the users and current workflows. The logical model will not be as easy to validate. It will require the removal of certain implementation details such as data replication, regrouping of processes and the paring down of data flows and data representations to those that are relevant to a given aspect of the supported functionality being analysed.

Determining requirements

The process of gathering requirements needs an understanding of the problem domain and the performing of various preparatory work before engaging in any information gathering, as previously discussed. Gathering requirements is an iterative process (Figure 5.6), repeated until a consistent and agreed understanding is achieved with all the stakeholders. There are many techniques that can be used to extract infor-

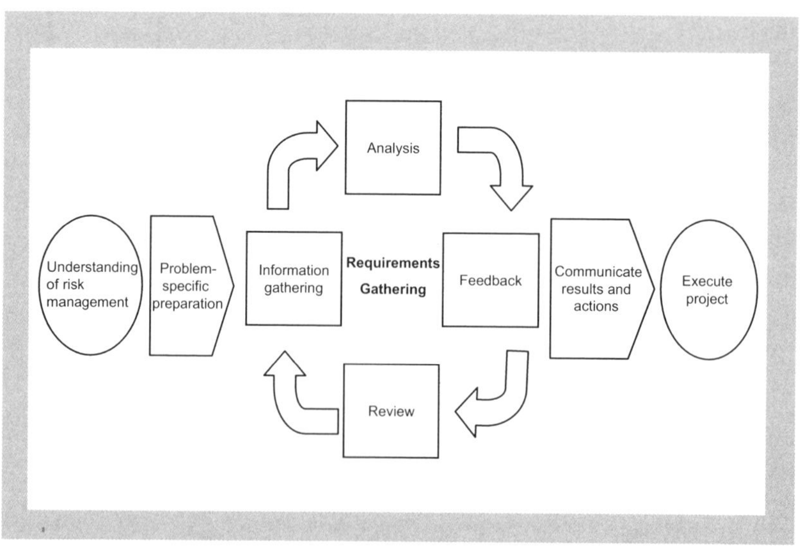

Figure 5.6 User interaction for requirements gathering

mation concerning the requirements, each with its own time demands and efficiency characteristics. The most common approaches are:

Review of any current documentation relevant to the project
This may include any standards documents, regulatory documentation, existing system or process documentation, loss database information or audit reports highlighting system deficiencies.

Interviews or workshops
Interviews can be held on either a one to one or a group basis depending on the likely level of input from the interviewee(s). The key stakeholders to be interviewed will be the sponsor and other major or influential users (either directly or indirectly) of the system. The sponsor will be able to give a strategic view of the organization's current status, constraints, priorities and strategy. In a contextual sense, the sponsor should also be aware of any specific issues relating to areas or individuals to be interviewed. The proposed users of the system will then be able to provide a link between the sponsor's vision and their knowledge of the capabilities and constraints of their own business areas and skill sets. These users may also recommend others who should be interviewed or involved in process shadowing. In order to encourage consistency and pragmatism, these interviews may be in groups with a key stakeholder also attending to ensure commitment to the process.

Process shadowing
Watching and documenting the existing process to ensure all major issues and requirements have been highlighted and correctly defined.

Questionnaires
These are often used in collaboration with interviews or process shadowing. When business analysts are trying to uncover as much information concerning the requirements as possible they should use 'open' questions. These are questions that invite additional clarification and comment from the user (rather than a yes or no response). When defining or trying to limit scope later on within the process, 'closed' questions inviting yes or no answers may be used.

The requirements gathering process highlights the communication gap between users and the project team. Users will often state requirements verbally in face-to-face interviews and process descriptions through the above processes. The analyst must interpret and convert these requirements into an unambiguous and sufficiently detailed description of the problem to be addressed that can eventually be implemented. Often no individual user will know the total functionality and detailed requirements of any system. Instead, more detailed specifications and definitions will need to be provided by specialist groups or other users involved in the trading or risk operation.

The goal of gathering requirements is to extract as complete a view of the problem as possible, from as many different perspectives as possible. Care must be taken that this process does not degenerate into a whining session that highlights issues outside the current scope of the project. Although these issues may be important and need to be communicated to other groups within the organization, it is important to retain focus on what the particular project is trying to address. Projects that try to address all potential issues and problems within the organization will result in an endless expanding discussion of scope. This entire requirements gathering process should be managed through the project plan, with clearly defined deliverables and deadlines for completion of the work.

Benchmarking and gap analysis

Any analysis and requirements gathering phase will involve a level of benchmarking or gap analysis. Often benchmarking is performed subconsciously in that users compare current capabilities with their previous experiences or expectations. Formalizing this process and comparing current functionality and processes against those of other successful organizations or systems provided by third party vendors can highlight the deficiencies of the current process. It will indicate what functionality should and should not be included in any proposed solution. This can be taken to its natural conclusion of determining the ideal solution, even if its contradictory requirements or complexity mean that it could never be achieved. It will still act as a benchmark against which to assess possible solutions.

The business analyst can obtain user requirements by phrasing questions in one of two ways, which will require making a comparison with either the current system or some ideal set of functionality:

- What is it that the current system doesn't do, or doesn't do well, that you need to do, or do more efficiently?
- What should the new system be capable of doing?

The danger of basing the requirements on an idealized functionality list is that the requirements can end up being an endless wish list. This list will typically be too time consuming and expensive to implement and as a result will require closer scope control and prioritization. The outcome of the benchmarking process should be a list of requirements that indicate the gap between current and required functionality. Additional information should also be provided that will assist the analyst in categorizing and prioritizing these requirements:

- Required functionality
- Reality of current process
- Gap between requirement and current process
- Benefit from closing this gap
- Cost of closing this gap
- Risks in closing and not closing this gap
- Priority of this requirement
- Dependencies on other projects or internal functionality

Hierarchy of business requirements

Requirements gathering is best performed in a hierarchical top-down fashion. At the highest level will be initial discussions with key stakeholders, setting overall project scope, and at the lowest level, process and calculation definitions of sufficient detail to be transformed into a detailed proposed logical design (Figure 5.7). This design must be able to address all the specified requirements and be sufficiently defined for a development team to unambiguously implement it.

Initial requirements gathering should focus on a high-level description and overview of the functionality that must be provided by any solution. It should define what requirements are in scope and which are out of scope. Any potential requirements that are noted as being neither in nor out of scope will add uncertainty and risk into the project. They should be clarified as early in the process as possible, and should lead to the analyst being able to draw a context diagram for the proposed project.[3] This context diagram will indicate which desired high-level functionality or current systems are within the scope of the project and which are not. Functionality and systems that are outside

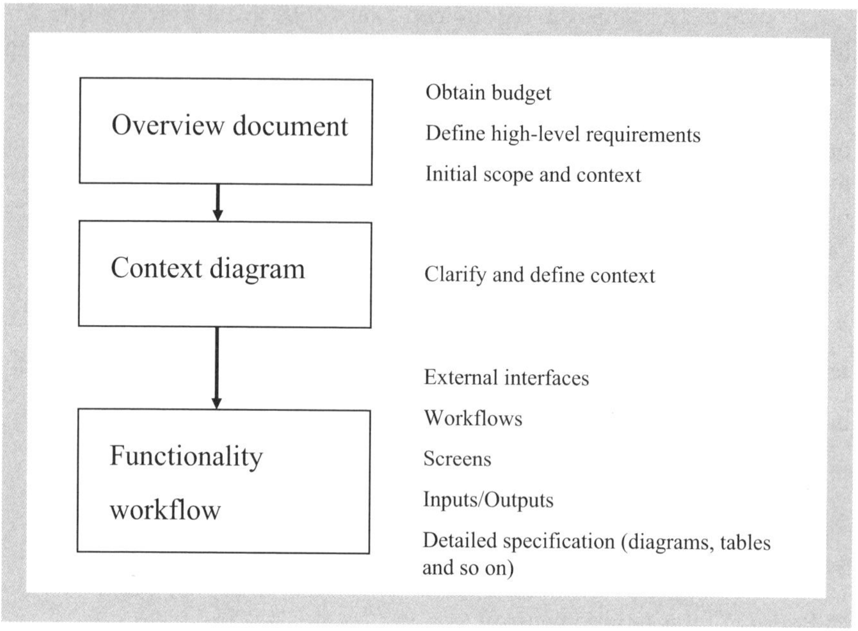

Figure 5.7 Hierarchy of requirements gathering

the scope of the project will need to be integrated with, whereas existing system functionality within the context diagram may need to be replaced, enhanced or utilized in a different manner.

The requirements gathering process will need to produce a precise definition of external interfaces, screens and any calculations or data transformations that need to be performed. It is only by specifying these requirements to a sufficient level of detail that the scope of the project can be controlled. The outcome of this process should be sufficient information for a detailed analysis and project plan, with reasonably precise estimates, to be produced.

The phrase that a picture paints a thousand words should not be underestimated. Although it is appropriate to use high-level written descriptions for overall requirements, many problems arise from verbose textual descriptions of detailed required functionality (Table 5.1). Language is inherently imprecise and ambiguous and so the analyst should always aim to reduce these detailed requirements down to easy-to-understand diagrammatic or tabular representations. The process of listing behaviour in response to user inputs or other system

Table 5.1 Comparison of textual and diagrammatical descriptions of requirements

Document	Diagrammatic
Cross-referring issues	Easier and clearer to understand
Difficult to read	Clearly shows workflow and process/data flow
Difficult to follow process	More concise
Can be ambiguous and ill defined	Easier to walk through and understand underlying issues
Can be difficult to describe the complexity involved	Can provide a holistic view

events also helps to ensure completeness of defined behaviour. It is much easier to note a missing condition in a table or list than in the middle of a page of text. Textual descriptions also make it difficult to determine how requirements have evolved over time. Comparing the differences between pieces of text not only shows changes in the underlying semantics of the text but also syntactic changes arising from grammatical restructuring.

Because the requirements gathering process is concerned with defining what issues any proposed solution must address, rather than how this may be achieved, it should focus on external interactions with the proposed system. This will cover any interfaces to other systems as well as user interaction through GUIs. These interactions are usually broken down into what information should be persisted, what aspects of the functionality should be defaulted and how any interaction should occur (Figure 5.8). More precisely the aim is to define, for the system as a whole addressing some required user workflow or external system interaction, the:

Goal of the interaction

- What is the purpose or aim of this workflow or interaction? Why is the task being performed?
- What calculations or data transformations are performed? How are they defined?

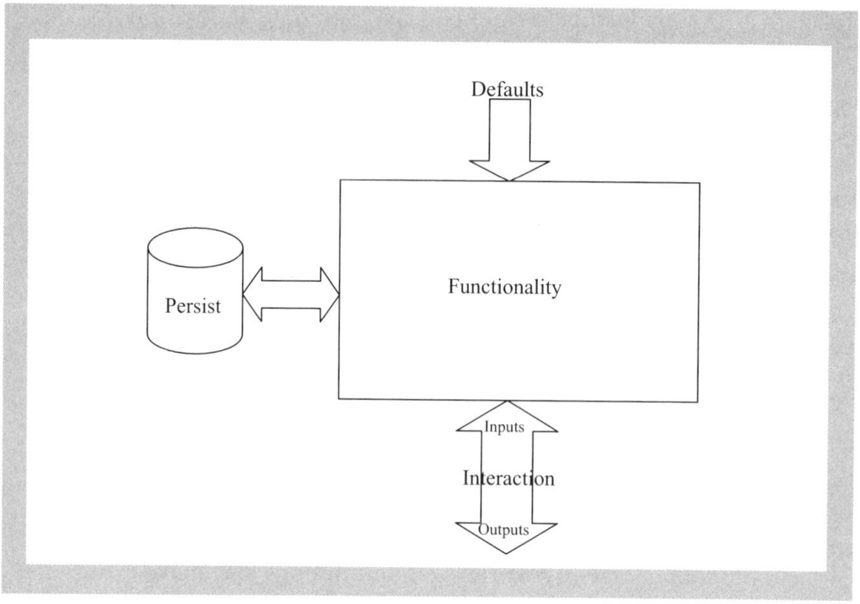

Figure 5.8 Viewing the functionality of a system

- Is this performed as part of a larger process? What are the data and processing interdependencies?

Nature of any interaction

- *Inputs:* What data is required? Where is it obtained? What synchronization events occur?
- *Outputs:* What outputs are required? Why and by whom? Where should this information be sent and who has permission to see it? Should this information be persisted?
- *Screen interaction:* How are these screens and their functionality defined? What are the roles being performed? Who has permission to perform this operation, who hasn't? How is responsibility transferred to other groups of users or locations?

Defaults
What information is defaulted? How are these defaults defined? How are they modified?

The interaction of the external environment with the system is often specified through *use cases*. Use cases are stories or cases describing how external actors (which may be other systems or users) interact with this system in order to complete some task or action.[4] These stories then specify the system's requirements through its defined behaviour under various conditions. A key advantage of the use case approach is that it encourages a walk-through of the proposed workflow with the end users, often including example screen layouts. This process can highlight ill-specified interactions, and incorrect sequencing of operations, and as a result ensures that the requirements are validated.

Prioritizing requirements

The result of gathering requirements from a diverse group of users is often a long list of sometimes contradictory requirements. From this, the requirements must be clarified and prioritized so that any project constraints such as available resources, budget and time can be met. The natural tendency is for the stakeholders of any project to push for as much functionality as possible to be delivered within the project. This should not be permitted if it will result in a plan that contravenes any project constraints, including exceeding the project's risk appetite. Including tasks that cannot be met within the project constraints will only lead to even greater issues and possible project failure later on in the project. This will result in an associated loss of stakeholder confidence in the project when ongoing commitment is crucial for the survival of the project. Fundamentally the issue is one of finding balance within the *delivery continuum* (Figure 5.9). Delivery must be achieved within budget and on time, but what is delivered must add value to the stakeholders and act as a platform for ongoing enhancements. If this balance cannot be achieved, it is far better to be honest and upfront about any such issues. The stakeholders can then assess whether more time or budget should be assigned to the work. This also sets the expectation of open and honest communication between the project team and the stakeholders from the very start of the project.

Given the requirements of a diverse set of stakeholders, there are two main ways in which requirements can be prioritized:[5]

1. *Maximizing the benefits from the proposed functionality*
   Functionality is prioritized so that the maximum benefit is obtained for the organization as a whole (rather than any benefit arising to any

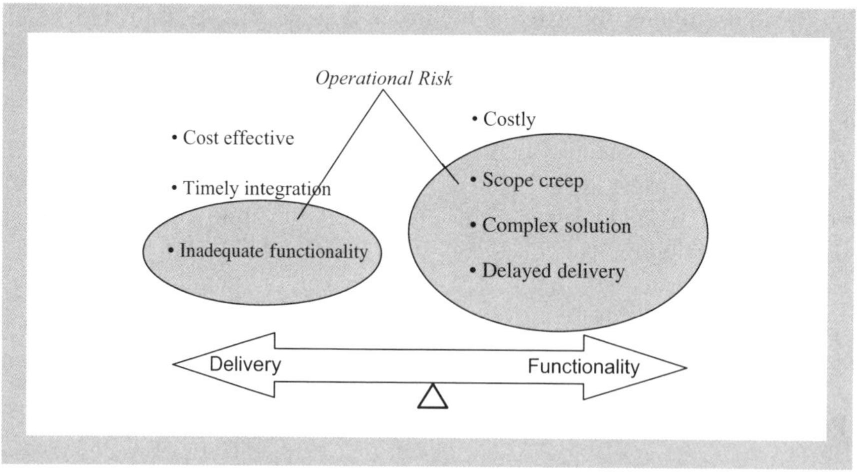

Figure 5.9 The delivery continuum

particular stakeholder). However, this approach to prioritizing requirements fails to take into account the problems of precisely defining what this benefit actually is. Typically the ambiguity of many goals, the subjective nature in which resulting benefits may be measured, as well as the relative influence and different requirements of various groups involved in the process, make this an impossible task.

2. *Satisficing the requirements of the stakeholders*
   Satisficing is the process of providing acceptable levels of functionality to all of the stakeholders.

Related to the concept of satisficing is the general rule that the project team should adopt an approach of 'good is good enough'. Rather than trying to solve every problem with the perfect solution, it must be accepted that there is a law of diminishing returns. Once an adequate solution has been determined, subsequent effort will result in ever-reducing improvements in that solution. As a result, the decision of when a solution is 'good enough' must be taken so that scarce resources can be assigned elsewhere. Failure to do this will result in the project never fully addressing all its requirements, just some of them with exceptionally high quality solutions.

Validating requirements and defining key success criteria

The requirements of a system must be specified in a way that can be understood and verified by the stakeholders of the project. Once the requirements have been well specified, it must be possible to define the criteria against which project success or failure will be measured. In order to ensure that these requirements and success criteria are adequately reviewed and agreed, a sign-off and review process should be implemented. By formalizing this process, responsibility is clearly assigned for ensuring sign-off occurs. The requirements document is then used to specify and agree the scope of a project, defining what constitutes minimum functional requirements. Any changes and enhancements to these agreed requirements must then be accepted as being likely to have an impact on the project.

Defining success criteria is also vital when dealing with external parties who may be involved in the delivery of a system or modules of functionality. These criteria should be used as the driver for payments and for defining when any final completion payment should be made. In order to ensure that the external party remains focused on delivery of any specified requirements, it is important that payment is aligned with the acceptance of any deliverables. As a result, it may include other issues beyond purely functional ones such as code handover, or provision of service level agreements.

ANALYSIS

Whereas requirement gathering is concerned with the external behaviour and functionality that the proposed solution must address, along with any constraints on the implementation, system analysis and the later stages of the software lifecycle are concerned with the internal design and workings of the system. Once the initial requirements have been gathered, they must be understood and mapped on to a consistent analysis model and interpreted in terms of what they mean for the proposed design. This is the point at which analysis, design and development become intricately entwined (Figure 5.10).

The systems analysis stage is concerned with addressing the requirements with a logical analysis model. To simplify this process, physical issues and assumptions of how this will be achieved are omitted. This process will inherently require additional assumptions and constraints concerning what data is required, how it can be structured and the calcu-

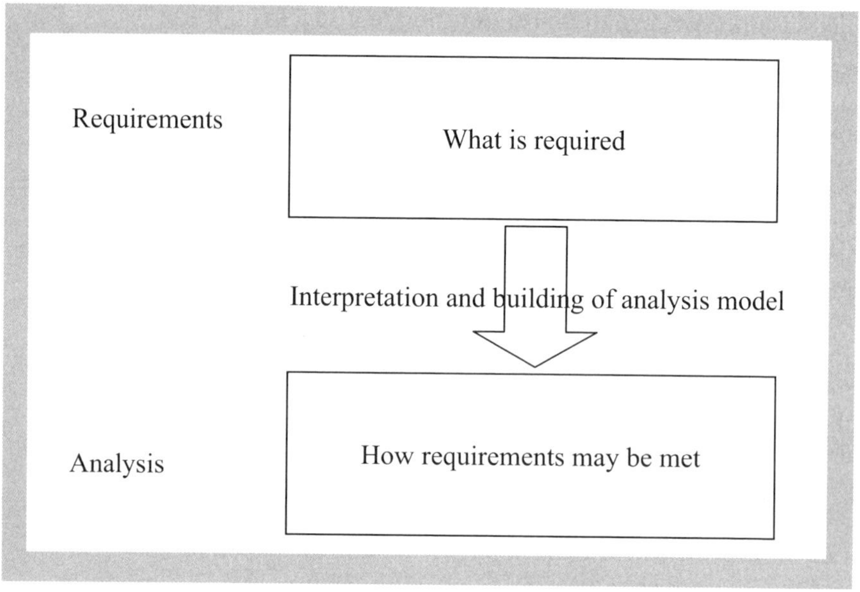

Figure 5.10 The transformation of requirements into an analysis model

lations performed on it. As a result, the outputs from the analysis process should be discussed with the end users to ensure that the proposed logical model will meet their current and future requirements.

The problem discovery approaches used during the requirements gathering stage will also be useful during this subsequent analysis. Different perspectives will be required to group, regroup and reconsider the interpretation of the requirements in terms of the provision of system specific functionality.

The results of any analysis should be a logical model describing functionality for:

- Handling external interfaces and the presentation of information to the users
- Representing and handling information within the system
- Providing other required behaviour.

This leads to a number of different views of the proposed system covering:

Behavioural view
How the system reacts to various internal and external events, the sequencing of those events and how sections of the system interact and collaborate, passing data and control.

Data view
The static relationships between information within the system.

Functional view
The calculation and algorithms that must be supported within the system.

These views are validated through robustness analysis.[6] This ensures that the specified requirements are reasonable and can be supported, that the requirements fully specify all possible behaviours and that the analysis model is complete and able to support these requirements.

Many analysis methodologies utilize diagrammatic approaches to provide the above views and support the validation process. Just as in the requirements gathering process, they enable key issues to be clearly understood and explained using standard representations of that information. These diagrams may be broken down into *static* or *dynamic representations* of the logical system. Static views tend to focus on the structure of data, processes or decisions, highlighting dependencies and relationships, but omit the dynamic interactions that will occur within the system. Dynamic representations highlight how different parts of a system interact and collaborate. They are especially important for determining and validating system concurrency or process interaction issues.

Building an analysis model is an iterative process. It is likely that the first attempt to build a consistent and complete model addressing the requirements will highlight inconsistencies in the different views within the analysis model. Each iteration should address the deficiencies of the previous iteration until the model is sufficiently well specified and can be clearly shown to address the requirements. This will typically be when each iteration is addressing and exploring ever more detailed and subtle issues concerning the system. It is important to understand the interplay between static and dynamic representations of the analysis model. Static views of the system are acted upon through dynamic behaviour. They can therefore only be verified by investigating this behaviour. Similarly, dynamic behaviour requires some structure within which to occur. The analyst will therefore need to iterate between these two views until they converge into a consistent and acceptable solution.

Some of the more popular methods used in many analysis approaches will be considered below.

Data modelling diagrams

Many approaches to analysing system requirements concentrate purely on the flow of data and the details of the processing to be performed. However, if the data is both to be persisted and to satisfy the '4Cs' of data quality, it is important for the analyst to investigate the interrelationship of any data that will be required by the system. There are many approaches to data modelling, the most common of which is the entity relationship diagram (ERD) or model, which defines the main *entities*, their attributes and relationships between each other (Figure 5.11). Entities are conceptually separate groupings of data attributes. Relationships between entities indicate a business connection between them, together with the multiplicity of any relationship. For example, a system may contain two entities, financial transactions and counterparties; a financial transaction will involve a specific counterparty and a counterparty may be involved in many transactions.

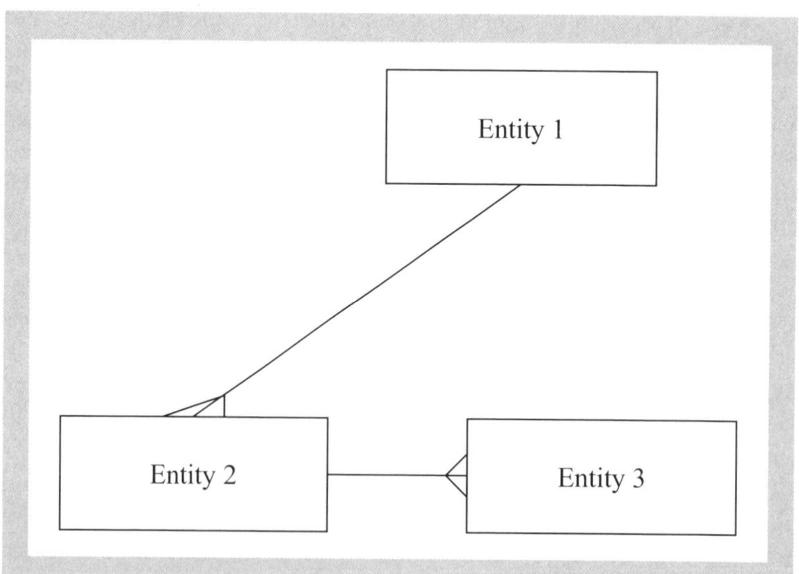

Figure 5.11 Example of an entity relationship diagram linking 3 entities

An ERD is a non-technical representation of data that can be used to clarify the analyst's understanding with end users, as well as to represent a physical data model. The ERD can be further refined through relational data analysis to remove redundant data attributes and partition entities into a form that enhances the analyst's understanding and validation of the data model. This is a process known as *data normalization*.[7]

If an object-orientated approach[8] is taken to data modelling, techniques such as class diagrams that provide a richer representation of class relationships (including data inheritance, aggregation and delegation) can be used.

Data flow and collaboration diagrams

Data flow and collaboration diagrams graphically describe a static view of what parts of the system interact in order to address some functional requirement. Data flow diagrams show the processes that are carried out on the data and how this data flows between functional modules within the system. Collaboration diagrams focus more on the interactions that can occur between different processes. Data flow diagrams can be applied to both physical and logical models, indicating both the conceptual flow of information within the system as well as the actual implemented flow both within the system as well as to and from external systems and users. Data flow and collaboration diagrams should be validated against any data model to ensure that they support a consistent view of the system.

Although not strictly data flow diagrams, the highest level data flow diagram would be a context diagram (produced as part of the requirements gathering phase) that shows the system as a single process with all the data flows to and from external systems and users. It indicates the interfaces that will need to be supported and the integration issues in delivering the system. Context diagrams are decomposed into a series of internal data flows and processes. These processes may be further refined during the analysis stage, providing finer granularity of information as processes are further decomposed (Figure 5.12). Data flow diagrams can identify incompleteness in the requirements gathering and analysis process, by highlighting data flows that are not processed, data that is not utilized or persisted data that has no source.

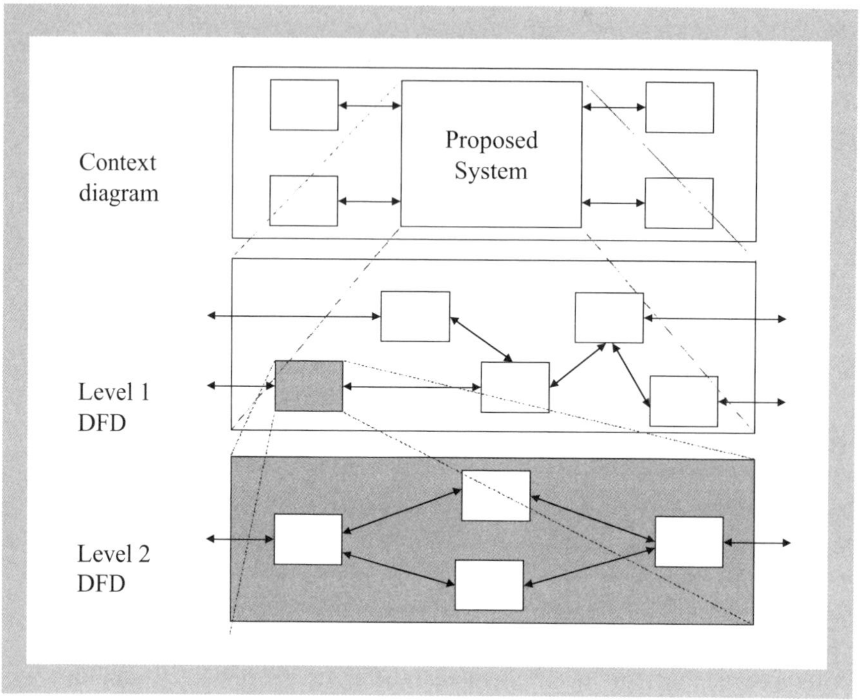

Figure 5.12 Hierarchy of data flow diagrams

State diagrams

State diagrams model behaviour that can be represented as a finite number of states. Each state can lead to different system behaviour with changes in state occurring based on some defined event (Figure 5.13).

Interaction, dependency and processing/flow chart diagrams

These diagrams cover a wide number of ways for viewing how processes or workflows are broken down into a sequence of individual tasks. They can also include dynamic information concerning how different roles or processes interact over time. These diagrams cover:

- *Flow charts* that illustrate the sequence of processing and decisions that must be made in order to implement a given algorithm or piece

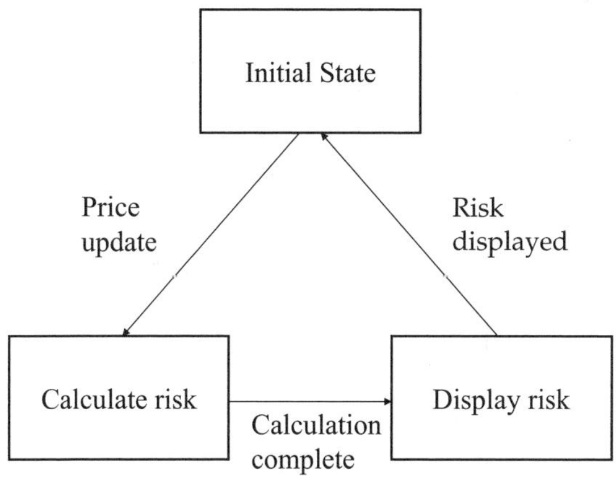

Figure 5.13 Simple state transition diagram for displaying the market risk associated with a market price change

of functionality. They can be used to highlight how different decisions result in the execution of different code paths. Unlike a state diagram, a flow chart will usually have defined starting and end points, with progression through the flow chart depending on completion of certain actions or decisions, as well as the occurrence of certain events.

- *Activity* and *swim lane diagrams* that extend the flow chart concept to indicate how different tasks are distributed across various user roles or parts of a system (Figure 5.14). They highlight any interactions that may occur and the flow of information, control and events. Swim lane and activity diagrams can be used to highlight when certain tasks can be performed concurrently and identify inefficiencies or likely failure points in the way in which the system will be utilized. They can also highlight which roles should be allocated to different users in order to enforce various controls within the process.
- *Interaction* or *sequence diagrams* that indicate how different processes interact over time. They usually extend collaboration diagrams to describe the sequencing and timing of any interactions.

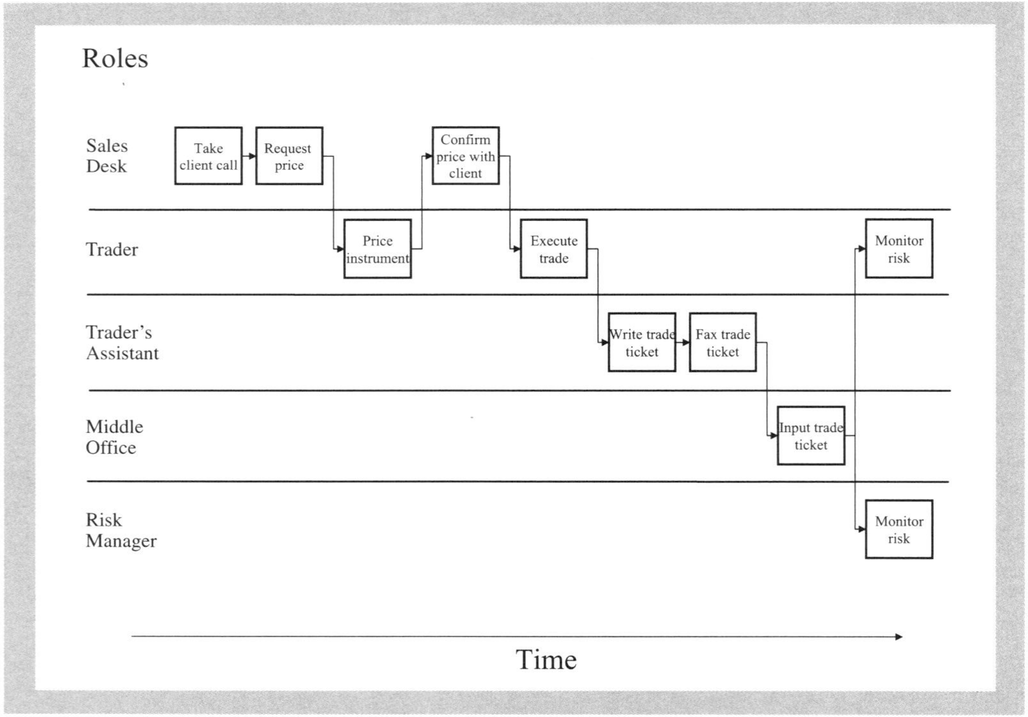

Figure 5.14 Example of a swim lane diagram for entering into a financial transaction and monitoring risk

- *Dependency* and *procedural diagrams* that show how modules depend on each other or show how the flow of control passes to different routines within a procedural application where tasks are executed in a sequential manner.

Diagrams that highlight process interactions are important for showing the flow of control between processes and identifying potential 'race' conditions where the relative timing and ordering of the arrival of events or data are unpredictable or cannot be guaranteed.

Decision trees

A decision tree is a simple diagrammatic representation of the branching structure resulting from the answer to a sequence of questions (Figure 5.15). The process starts at the root of the tree and proceeds (left to right) through a number of decision nodes to any number of outcomes represented by the tree's leaves. Decision trees are often used to represent and model behaviour under various scenarios and simulations.

Tables and lists

Although not strictly a diagram, tables and lists are used to describe details of the analysis model. This may range from:

Attribute lists
List the attributes of various entities, along with the type of that attribute (for example a number or textual string)

Data dictionaries and catalogues
Describes design decisions and data constraints

Function/Entity matrices
Describes the way in which processing and data are interrelated. It is a powerful technique for indicating how certain events or user functions cause defined actions to be applied to the data within the system. This is set out as a simple matrix with defined functionality in one dimension and data entities in the other. The matrix then consists of all the actions that must be applied to the data entities within it in response to that function.

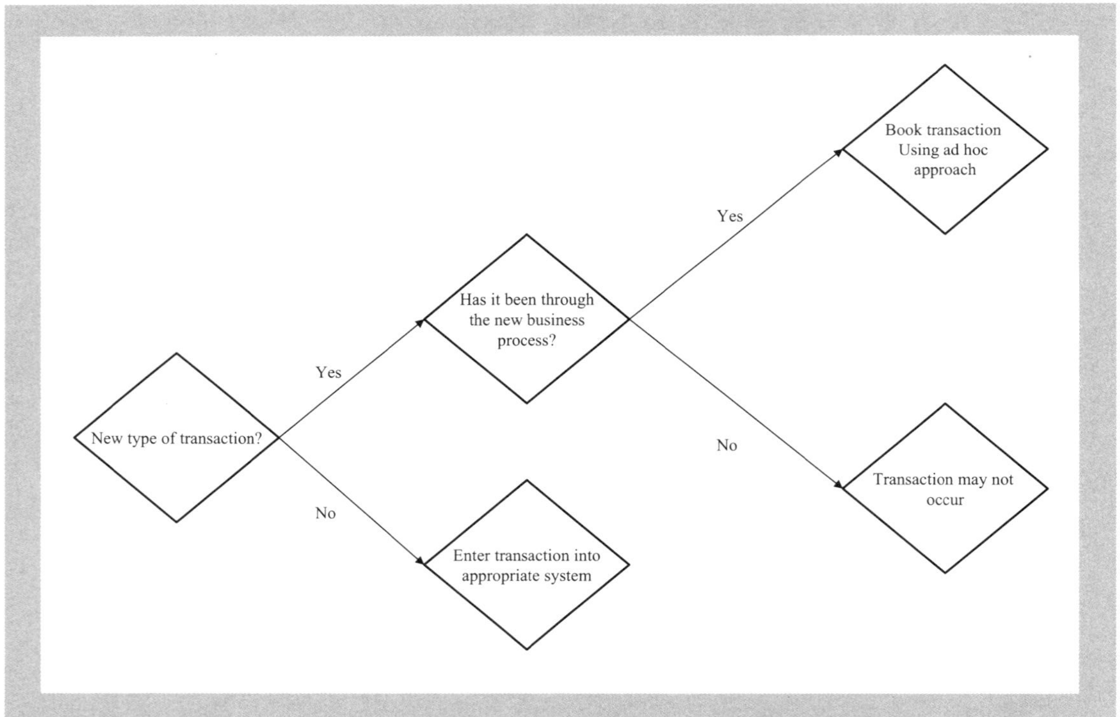

Figure 5.15 Example decision tree for trading a financial instrument

THE DATA REQUIREMENTS FOR A RISK MANAGEMENT SYSTEM

The aim of any risk management solution is to manage the data collection, processing and tracking of risk management information in a robust and scalable framework. The key requirements to building any risk management solution are to:

Collate the data
In order to be able to perform any risk analysis, the relevant information must be obtained in a manner that has minimal impact on the operational systems within the organization. This process should ensure the integrity and security of any systems it obtains data from. This is also the point at which data must be validated and cleansed in order to ensure data quality within the management system.

Enrich the data
This will involve the addition of further information and performing of various risk calculations to augment the data before further analysis.

Archiving and aggregation
Different types of storage media can be used that are appropriate to the frequency and speed of access required. The process, known as hierarchical storage management (HSM), defines how data should be archived in order to use available storage devices as economically as possible and without the user needing to be aware of when data is being retrieved from archive storage media. Typically recent data is the most important as it reflects the current risk environment. It needs a high level of granularity and will be frequently accessed. Other data may be transformed or summarized into more aggregated forms in order to limit any potential data explosion and reduce storage requirements. There will also be a point at which the usefulness of the data decreases rapidly with time and it should then be archived out of the system. This process should ensure that the information is still available if necessary (but with slower access times). It enables resources to be freed to maintain the ongoing operation of the system and performance requirements.

The requirement to summarize data is often driven by a desire to maximize resource allocation. The more summarized the data, the easier and quicker it is to access both from a processing and a human resource perspective. It may not, however, always be possible to replace detailed data by summarized data due to legal or regulatory reasons.

Deliver information

Once information has been extracted from the data it must be packaged into a form that is convenient for consumption and distributed to the relevant consumers. This information can then be used to manage and mitigate risk within the organization. The effectiveness of any risk management system is therefore only as good as the delivery mechanism used. This mechanism should ensure that frequent reports or real time data analysis is automated as much as possible, but also enable one-off ad hoc queries to be efficiently implemented.

Manage meta-data

Meta-data is information about data. It maintains the flexibility of any risk management solution and typically contains information concerning the source and type of any data received. It is especially important in systems that aggregate risk information because of the importance of transforming, controlling and interpreting a varying set of data sources. It contains information about the different sources of risk data, its composition, transformation, validation rules, summarizing rules and so on. Coding any raw or source data transformation rules into meta-data can achieve enhanced flexibility. Changes to the feeder system interfaces then only require modifications to this meta-data rather than to the software code.

Notes

1 H. Simon, *Administrative Behavior: A Study of Decision-making Processes in Administrative Organizations* (Simon & Schuster, 1997)
2 J. Henry (ed.), *Creative Management*, (Sage, 1991)
3 D. J. Tudor and I. J. Tudor, *System Analysis and Design – A Comparison of Structured Methods* (Macmillan, 1997)
4 A. Cockburn, *Writing Effective Use Cases* (Addison-Wesley, 2000)
5 H. Simon, 'Rational decision making in business organizations', *American Economic Review*, **69** (4) September 1979, 493–513
6 D. Rosenberg and K. Scott, *Use Case Driven Object Modeling with UML, A Practical Approach* (Addison-Wesley, 1999)
7 R. Elmasri and S. Navathe, *Fundamentals of Database Systems*, (Addison-Wesley, 1989)
8 I. Jacobson, *Object-orientated Software Engineering – A Use Case Driven Approach* (Addison-Wesley, 1992)

CHAPTER 6

System design and implementation

Having produced an analysis model that addresses the requirements, the design phase takes this model and refines it to a logical format that can be implemented and deployed. This will require the grouping of functionality into components and subsystems that can then be realized as a specific physical implementation using a given technology.

Ideally, any approach that is used to specify requirements should support any subsequent analysis and design. The Unified Modelling Language (UML),[1] which has become the de facto industry standard for analysing and designing software systems, is an example of such an approach. UML also encompasses the use case approach that is often used as part of any requirements gathering phase of a project. A consistent approach that links across the different stages of the software development lifecycle can help to reduce the likelihood that requirements will be omitted from the analysis, design and subsequent implementation. It also aids traceability within the process.

PHYSICAL ARCHITECTURAL AND IMPLEMENTATION REQUIREMENTS

Building enterprise applications is much more complex than building standalone applications or desktop solutions. Risk management solutions typically fall into the enterprise applications category, as they must deal with multiple events, have superior performance and support multi-user access. The physical architecture onto which any enterprise system must be deployed can be assessed in a number of dimensions:

Scalability

Scalability concerns the ability to attain any performance requirements as the processing demand increases. Scalable architectures are achieved in one of two fundamental ways:

Vertical (scale-up)

This comes from adding additional resources to existing computers (such as memory and processors) in order to provide initial scalability. It is usually cheaper than horizontal scaling, since most computer architectures are designed to utilize several processors. It can however prove to be very expensive if significant scalability is required, since it is fundamentally limited by the underlying hardware performance characteristics of the computer, such as memory, communication and processor speeds, which can be expensive to increase.

Horizontal (scale-out)

- Scalability can be achieved by *clustering* additional computers into the architecture so that they appear as a single computing resource. A common implementation of this is the also called 'pizza box' approach, whereby additional computer units are stacked like pizza boxes on top of each other in a rack system. This approach can be further refined with *blade* technology which removes the complex cabling to each unit and increases processor packing densities. This is achieved by removing the individual printed circuit boards from each unit and vertically slotting them next to each other into a common cabling back plane.
- *Distributed computing* describes the situation when computing resources, rather than being located in a single location, may be distributed across the organization and connected using a network. The most common distributed computing environment occurs with users having PCs on their desk, which utilize shared computers or servers that provide certain services such as a centralized filing system or database.

- *Grid computing* is an extension of the concept of distributed computing that utilizes any of the independent computing resources within the organization, depending on their availability. These can be dynamically allocated tasks depending on their spare computing capacity, capability, performance and any reliability considerations. Grid computing can provide highly cost-effective horizontal scalability but reliability and availability can be an issue, depending on the location and usage of the resources; PCs on a user's desk are likely to be in a less reliable environment than servers located in a secure computer room.

Maintainability

Maintainability refers to how easy and cost effective it is to fix, modify or extend existing functionality or increase capacity requirements. Ideally, changes in one part of a system should have minimal impact on existing functionality. Component-based approaches tend to lend themselves to more maintainable solutions, purely because component-based design tends to segregate functionality into separate well-defined components which interact through clearly determined and maintainable interfaces. Maintainability is especially important where the system interacts with users or other external systems, which may radically change over time, even if basic processing requirements do not.

Reliability and fault tolerance

Reliability indicates the ability of the implementation or underlying physical architecture to support any required functionality. Reliability is achieved through fault tolerance, which describes how a computer system or piece of software is designed to act in the event of hardware or software failure. In a fault tolerant system failure will result in a procedure being initiated that ensures there is minimal loss either in the provision of system functionality or of data integrity. Fault tolerance may be implemented within software or hardware, or some combination of the two. Software can be used to reroute processing to other servers or detect system failure, while hardware can provide additional fault tolerance through the use of backup or redundant hardware such as with disk mirroring (duplicate concurrent storage of data on another disk), RAID (redundant array of inexpensive disks), additional processing capability or secondary network connectivity.[2]

Higher levels of reliability have associated higher costs and so must be considered as part of a cost/benefit analysis. This cost/benefit analysis is a business issue as the project sponsors must decide what cost level they are willing to accept in order to achieve a given level of reliability. If real time risk information is critical to the business then a high level of reliability will be required. Higher up the risk hierarchy, the impact of a delay in providing risk information may not be so critical.

When a system fails or is not available, a failover process will be used to transfer processing to other secondary or backup systems. This may be achieved either as a:

Hot failover
Where failover occurs automatically with negligible impact on any users or processing.

Warm failover
Where the user is required to log in to a secondary system which is consistent with the state of the primary system up to the point where system failure occurred.

The degree to which the previous state of a system can be recovered in the event of a failure will depend on the persistence and replication of information that is impacted by it. Transactions and information persistence introduce bottlenecks and can reduce performance but ensure the integrity and consistent state of a system.

Performance

The architecture should ensure that the solution attains any performance requirements in terms of *throughput* and *latency*. Throughput indicates the amount of processing that can be performed in a unit of time, whereas latency indicates the delay or perceived response time between initiating and receiving back any processed information. Any bottlenecks in the architecture will need to be identified, addressed and minimized.

Manageability

Manageability refers to the ability to manage the day-to-day overall availability and performance of the system. Simple architectures that utilize few resources are often easier to manage than more complex systems. Limiting the number of resources utilized may, however, reduce performance and reliability. The emergence and use of component-based frameworks such as J2EE and .NET have dramatically increased the manageability of complex and highly scalable architectures compared with previous frameworks such as the Common Object Request Broker (CORBA) and DCOM.[3]

Security

Security is about ensuring that data is neither modified by or disclosed to unauthorized individuals. Secure systems reduce operational risk but are more complex to specify, costly to develop, and require more data maintenance in setting up and maintaining security hierarchies and privileges.

Availability

Availability is concerned with managing the access to scarce resources and ensuring the system is available for use when required. Availability is related to reliability, since hardware or software failure in an unreliable architecture will result in the system becoming unavailable. Additionally, some architectures do not scale well as the number of users of a system increases. This can result in a dramatic reduction in performance or even failure to be able to use the system and often occurs when each user accessing a system requires a significant amount of system resources. It is often seen when a large number of users access a shared database; each user requires a large amount of database memory to be allocated to them in order to manage this access. Although adding more memory to the database server can address this problem, the design will have a fundamental user limit based on the available or maximum amount of memory that can be physically installed.

The management of transactions across multiple systems and the managing of access to limited resources can, however, be solved by using transaction processing (TP) monitors. Rather than each user having his or her own personal connection for utilizing functionality or accessing data, TP monitors control access to a limited number of resource-intensive connections and share these across all the users (Figure 6.1). TP monitors can be expensive to manage and implement in a distributed environment and should only be used when they

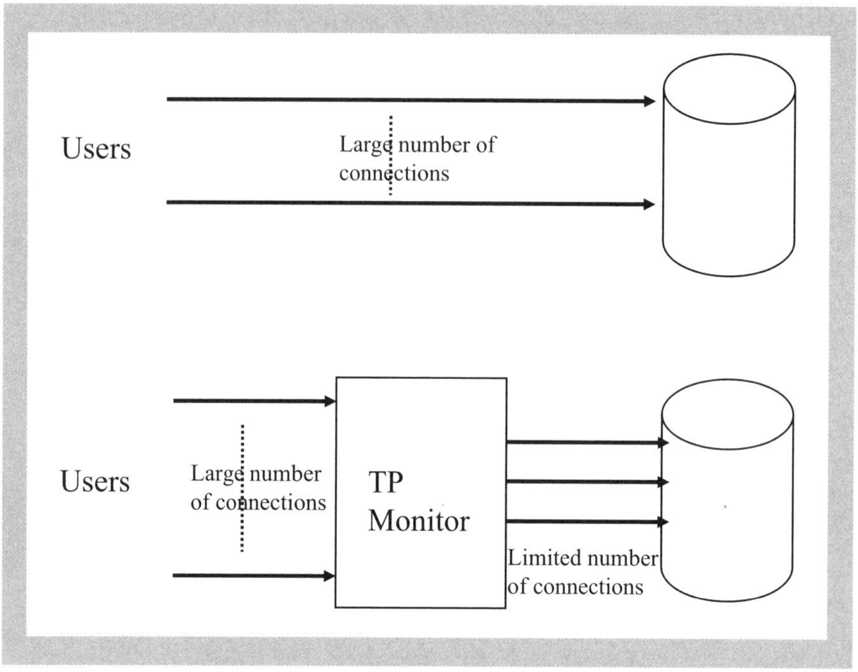

Figure 6.1 Using TP monitors to manage the use of scarce resources

are required. They do, however, address a key issue in managing distributed transactions and controlling access to limited or centralized resources.

ACHIEVING CONCURRENCY IN PROCESSING

Scalable, high performance, risk management solutions require multiple tasks to be performed concurrently. This permits resources, such as multiple servers or multi-processor machines, that can perform multiple tasks concurrently to be utilized in order to reduce the elapsed time taken to perform computationally intensive tasks. It also ensures that a system remains responsive while it is waiting on other processing to be completed or events to occur. The implications of a lack of concurrency are most evident within GUI applications when an application can appear to 'hang' and not be responsive to user interaction until the required processing is completed or an expected response is received from another system. Concurrent systems or applications are broken down into processes, which are instances of pieces of software running on a computer. The models for concurrent processing are categorized by how memory is used (shared versus distributed) and how communication occurs:

Process concurrency

- *Shared memory:* Each process can access a shared area of memory, but otherwise executes independently.
- *Data parallelism:* A process is able to perform the same operation on a number of pieces of data at the same time, such as being able to add or multiply all the elements of a list by the same number.
- *Message passing:* The system runs as a collection of independent processes, each with its own private local memory. These processes communicate by passing messages between each other. This approach is one of the most popular models for designing concurrent systems. Such systems are easier to debug and are more tractable to mathematical proof and validation.[4] This model is also applicable across a wide range of different hardware platforms, avoiding software and hardware vendor dependencies; message passing can be implemented on most networked computers and multiprocessor machines.

Intra-process concurrency

- *Single-threading:* A process usually has a single 'thread' or path of execution through the software where tasks are performed in a sequential, deterministic manner.
- *Multi-threading:* A multi-threaded process is one where there are multiple threads that are all executing (or appearing to execute) at the same time, performing small units of work and then terminating as required. Multi-threaded processes have the advantage that processing may continue even if one thread is waiting on some external communication or event. There is, however, no general way to predict how the instructions of different threads are interleaved. A change to shared data by one thread can also be seen by the other threads in the process.

Whenever there is concurrent reading and writing access to shared data (such as communication between processes using shared memory or in multi-threaded processes) there is always the potential that, if this access is not *synchronized*, the shared data may be corrupted in some way. Synchronization is provided by constructs such as mutual exclusion locks, condition variables or semaphores.[5]

The forms of concurrency that are utilized and the resulting design of any system must enable the scalability features of the architecture to be exploited. For example, horizontal scalability is really only possible with message-based multi-application architectures since it is not usually possible to directly share memory between a number of different computers. Scalability for multi-threaded applications can only be achieved through vertical scalability, and will require there to be more threads than there are available processors. For a single threaded application the only option is to utilize a higher performance processor to execute the application. This limitation fundamentally constrains the potential scalability and performance of certain designs.

THE DESIGN ARCHITECTURE

System architectures have evolved over time in order to provide more scalable and distributed architectures. The degree to which processing can be distributed has been indicated by the number of *tiers* or logically separate levels in the architecture. Historically the approach to building a risk management system has evolved from single tier to multi-tier architectures.

Single tier architectures

Single tier architectures are also known as *monolithic* architectures. These systems consist of a single application that stores data, implements business logic and performs data visualization and user interaction. They may only be vertically scaled since the solution consists of a single application that will run on a single server. There are therefore inherent limits on their scalability depending on the level of threading within the software and the physical scalability limits of the server.

Two-tier architectures

Two-tier architectures, otherwise known as *client–server applications*, separate data visualization and user interaction (the client) from transaction management and data storage (the server).

The client application can either be *fat* or *thin*. In a fat client application, the client application would, in addition to handling data visualization and user interaction, also perform a large amount of processing and, as a result, typically have a large amount of embedded business logic and functionality. In a thin client application, the business logic and functionality would be implemented on the server, leaving the client purely performing display operations and forwarding user interaction information on to the server. In two-tier architectures, the client and server would typically be deployed on different machines connected via a network for transferring data between the two.

N-tier architectures

N-tier architectures (which are typically three tier) extend the two-tier architecture so that data visualization and interaction, business logic/functionality and data persistence are logically separated. The logical design of this architecture may result in either single or multiple numbers of business or other functional layers that interact. These additional layers result in additional tiers to the logical architecture, giving rise to the term N-tier.

THE INTEGRATED SERVICE-ORIENTATED APPLICATION ARCHITECTURE

The concept of multi-tier architectures has evolved into the concept of an integrated application architecture or service-orientated architecture.[6] This is now seen as a valid alternative to the silo application approach that currently tends to dominate in financial organizations and is aimed at providing a consistent and scalable solution to system design. This architecture provides a generic view of the services and concepts that need to be provided in a multi-tier architecture (Figure 6.2). Functionality is broken down into:

Transactional services
Data quality is key to both trading and risk management systems, irrespective of system or processing failure. Transactions are units of processing that must pass the ACID test:

- Atomic: changes within a transaction are either all successfully applied or none at all are (in the event of a failure or other error)

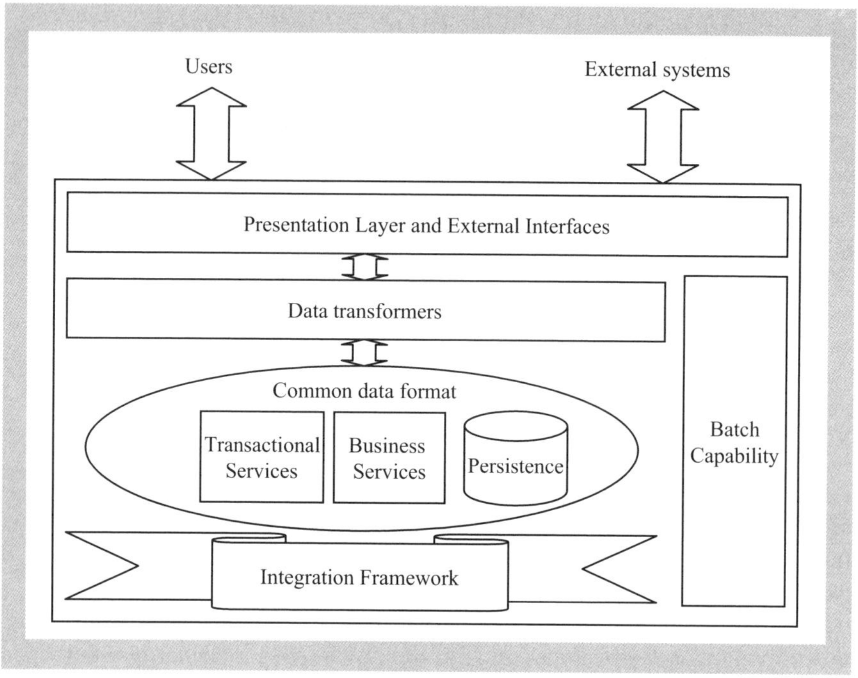

Figure 6.2 The integrated application architecture for risk management

- Consistent: transactions change data from one consistent and valid state to another
- Isolated: changes to data within a transaction are not visible outside the transaction until it is complete
- Durable: once a transaction is complete the changes are permanent and do not suddenly disappear for some unknown reason.

Transaction support is usually supported by some form of *locking* model that prevents the simultaneous modification of data. This locking may be optimistic (where a transaction may fail if any of the data has been modified since the transaction began) or pessimistic (where no other changes are permitted outside this transaction on the data).

Business Service
This is responsible for the business logic and functionality of the system. Separating business functionality from data and event distribution has

the advantage that calculation algorithms and other business issues are separated from the software engineering issues concerned with how this business functionality should be utilized. It is then possible to support, for example, multiple calculation styles (such as incremental, full, event-based, timer-based, on-demand) depending on the manner in which information is delivered or requested, rather than tying it to the implementation of the calculation or business functionality.

Presentation layers and external interfaces

Multi-tier architectures naturally lend themselves to deployments of data visualization and user interaction over a number of different technologies. Each approach is able to utilize the same common business functionality and data persistence but can choose to display or make this information available in a different manner. Visualization may be via a web browser that provides a thin client interface, responsible only for rendering and displaying information, or it may contain *applets,* which are small client applications that are downloaded to the client machine and run within a browser environment. Alternatively, a GUI client application may be installed that runs on the client machine and typically provides a richer interface than can be provided by web clients or applets, although the gap between these two approaches is reducing.

The advantage of decoupling external interfaces from the underlying functionality is that it is easier to support different types of system interactions without having to replicate any of this functionality in the interface. For example, if validation is performed in a fat client application then, when that data also needs to be received electronically over a network or via a web browser, the validation logic must be duplicated in each interface in order to handle this additional form of interaction. This duplication can easily lead to inconsistent functionality, as modifications must be replicated in multiple points within the system.

Thin client applications can also dramatically decrease testing requirements, as most of the key functionality to be tested is concentrated behind a single interface, which can also be accessed via other routes apart from a GUI. The proliferation of fat interfaces will conversely increase the amount of code to be tested since key pieces of functionality are likely to be duplicated in multiple interfaces.

Data transformers

Data external to the system is likely to be represented using different data models and data representations. Once data has been transformed and mapped into a common representation, it can be processed within the system.

Integration framework
Frameworks should provide support for distributing processing within the system, event notification, data distribution and security. This permits distributed and scalable applications to be easily developed.

Persistence
Some information will need to be persisted or maintained over a long period of time, irrespective of whether the system has had to be restarted or upgraded during that period. This will require the storing of information to a non-volatile storage device such as a filing system or database.

Batch capability
Any system is likely to require some level of *batch* type processing. These are tasks that are performed in a non-interactive manner, perhaps for performance reasons or in order to provide certain types of maintenance or processing which cannot be performed in an interactive real time manner.

The aim of this architecture is to decompose a design into the different types of tasks that will be required, and to provide well-defined interfaces to functionality that can be freely accessed within the architecture using a standardized internal data model. This internal data model should be independent of any data models used outside the system, provided data can be transformed between the two when required. The services-based architecture is the underlying basis of web services. These are a set of modular applications or services with a publicly exposed standard interface that provides access to data and functionality via a network. Although they are an ideal way to provide standardized functionality that can be shared across the organization, they do not address one of the major issues within risk management, which is obtaining the requisite information from existing systems with minimal impact upon them.

INTEGRATION AND MIDDLEWARE

The integration of distributed processes or systems can be achieved through the use of connectivity solutions called *middleware*. Middleware enables functionality to be dynamically 'glued' together with little additional effort or the writing of large amounts of software. Although middleware can be written as part of a project, the expense and knowledge required to implement an efficient, robust and scalable solution should not be underestimated. As a result, it is only appropriate to develop such approaches when the form of interaction is trivial or needs to be highly customized. Even if proprietary third party middleware is used, many are based on common standards and any proprietary interfaces or behaviours can be hidden behind software 'wrappers', reducing vendor tie in.

Middleware

Risk management is a data dominated problem. Efficiently obtaining and transporting this information to where it is required is critical to the success of any risk management solution. The term middleware is associated with a large amount of jargon and many definitions as to what exactly it is, but it can be thought of as any software that allows applications to interact, facilitating this interaction despite differences in underlying business models, operating systems, data representations, development technologies and programming languages. Middleware enables all types of applications, including legacy systems, to interact and is key to any architecture because it brings together disparate heterogeneous systems into a single integrated solution. The main types of middleware are:

Message-orientated middleware (MOM)
Data is converted (or marshalled) into a message and then passed in a one way data exchange with a message type that is used to define where it should be routed, similar to a letter being placed in an envelope which is marked with the delivery address.

Language-based middleware
Data is requested using a special language, such as SQL,[7] which is used to obtain data that meets some specified criteria.

Remote procedure call-based middleware (RPC)
The middleware provides interfaces used to pass a number of parameters to another process, in order to perform a defined operation and return any associated results.

Distributed object-orientated middleware (DOM)
DOM hides the location of objects, permitting methods on remote objects to be invoked in the same manner as those on local objects. CORBA is one of the most frequently used examples of this type of middleware.

Part of the confusion with the term middleware is that it covers products that provide anything from pure data distribution to the ability to support and invoke functionality in different processes, possibly located on different machines. MOM is often viewed as the superset of all middleware because fundamentally all inter-process communication requires the transfer of data, be this to exchange information or to access specific functionality.

At the simplest level, the transfer of information in middleware is between something that is producing the information (the *producer*) and something that requires this information (the *consumer*). The interaction between the producer and consumer may be in a:

Push strategy
Data transfer is initiated by the producer, who 'pushes' this out to the consumer(s). Push strategies can ensure that information is kept current by pushing out updates as they occur. This will however occur even if those data updates are not required.

Pull strategy
Changes to data or calculated results are requested from the producer who returns the data to the requesting consumer. Pull strategies reduce the amount of effort required in distributing information but at the expense of ensuring that the consumer is informed when data becomes out of date or new data is available.

The interaction between the producer and consumer may be:

Synchronous
This approach will expect the thread of execution sending the data to wait until that data has been received and acknowledged by the consumer. This blocking behaviour provides better support for transaction-based messaging, the receipt of data when executing an RPC (in what is known as a request/reply interaction) or the handling of error situations; processing only continues if success or failure has been determined or when any results have been sent back to the consumer. It does however introduce a tighter coupling between the producer and consumer.

Asynchronous
This type of interaction introduces a looser coupling between the producer and consumer; neither the producer nor the consumer are blocked waiting for receipt of data. This can improve performance if communication latency is an issue within the design; processing can continue rather than the process being forced to wait for an acknowledgement.

Asynchronous interactions can introduce timing issues concerning the access of data as the precise point and time at which the data is sent and received cannot always be determined by the other party unless some form of data versioning or time is 'stamped' on the data.

It should be clear that middleware is complex. It is software that implements many different approaches to enable processes to interact. Different types of middleware support different types of programming interfaces. These interfaces may be static and predefined or may be generated for the specific requirements of the interacting processes, using an interface definition language (IDL) to define and generate them. They may also be supported directly by the language or runtime environment, such as with Java's remote method invocation (RMI).[8] The most common logical models for how the producer and consumer of data interact are:

Publish/Subscribe
Publish/Subscribe is the most common push strategy, and is typically used when there are many consumers and many producers. Producers will publish messages to a subject, which are then distributed to all consumers who have subscribed to that subject. The producers need not know who all the consumers are; they will publish the data regardless and the consumers will independently subscribe to receiving it. This approach is commonly used to distribute market prices.

Point-to-point
This is used when there are many producers but only one consumer. Each point-to-point communication is associated with a channel or queue between a named producer and a named consumer with the consumer able to access multiple channels associated with different groups of producers. The nature of this interaction may be unique and customized, leading to a number of unwieldy and difficult to maintain interfaces and process interactions.

Broadcast
This covers a number of approaches to sending data to all potential consumers.

Middleware should always try and ensure that data is not corrupted and is received in the order it is sent. The delivery of data can however be performed to different degrees of reliability. Middleware reliability defines the likelihood that a message reaches its intended destination and is categorized as:

Reliable
In the absence of any system failure, the consumer will receive any data sent to it; no data will be lost in transit. This approach is commonly used for transferring volatile, constantly updating information such as the prices of financial instruments. It is not appropriate for transferring transactional-type information or trades in financial instruments as the possibility of losing that data in the event of a failure is too great.

Certified
The producer is notified of the successful or unsuccessful delivery of data to each consumer.

Transactional
The processing of data transferred using the middleware is utilized in a transaction, which has the ability to be rolled back or undone if part of the process fails.

Guaranteed
Data will always be delivered to the consuming system no matter what the current state of that system. If any aspect of the system is not available or fails after the producer has sent the data, the information will be reliably persisted until the consumer is available.

Each of these delivery methods has different performance implications and physical resource requirements.

When building a risk management solution, various types of middleware are likely to be required. One middleware strategy will be required to obtain risk information from the different producers of risk data within the organization, with another strategy being used for accessing functionality found throughout the organization and distributing processing to obtain improved performance and scalability.

Enterprise application integration (EAI)

Historically systems are built using the technology that is in vogue at the time and then only replaced when there is a clear cost/benefit. This leads to a mix of different technologies in which risk information is likely to reside. As a result, any risk management solution must co-exist with other technology and systems within the organization. Adapters that will permit different technologies and business processes to interact must be built to access existing functionality and data in these legacy systems. EAI covers the plans, methods and tools for enhancing, consolidating and co-ordinating all these systems within the enterprise. It is more than middleware and may also provide data transformation tools and implement business rules to control the flow of data. EAI provides a holistic view of an organization's business, showing how existing applications fit together into the (new) model for the organization, as well as helping to devise a strategy to efficiently reuse existing legacy applications and databases while augmenting it with new applications and data.

Extensible protocols

Risk management requires data to be exchanged between subsystems within a risk management system, with external applications that may be the sources of risk data and even with systems outside the organization that provide information on the external environment (such as market prices or credit assessments of companies). Within an application developed by a single group, there will be significant control over the way parts of the application interact. This interaction will be optimized to ensure that the application meets any performance requirements. As a result, efficient methods for data transfer will be implemented that may result in tighter levels of coupling and dependency between the various producers and consumers within the application. When this level of control decreases and there is a need to interface with other applications outside the group's direct control, which utilize different interfaces and data representations, it may be difficult to agree on the form in which data should be exchanged (Figure 6.3). These systems are also likely to change in a manner beyond the group's control, implying that any coupling should be as loose as possible, ideally not requiring any changes to either system to have to be co-ordinated.

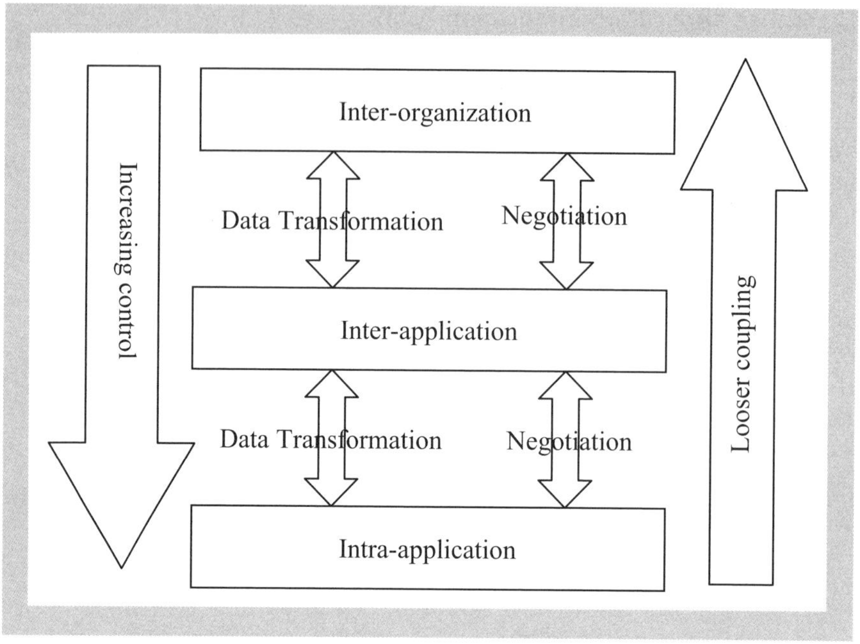

Figure 6.3 Coupling of systems throughout the organization

The latest concepts in data interchange for achieving this loose coupling is to use XML, which is an extensible methodology for encoding data into text. The emphasis with XML is on the message content, not on how that data is sent over various types of middleware. XML has a number of advantages over other approaches to data encoding used in the transfer of data:

- It can be viewed or written using text editors rather than proprietary tools
- It is flexible, being able to represent complex data structures
- It is extensible in that additional data can be added without impacting the interpretation of other data within the message. XML achieves this through the use of tags to link data items with values. Less extensible approaches have relied on field location within a message, which requires co-ordinated changes between the consumer and producer when the message format is modified
- It is technology independent.

XML does not solve the fundamental problem that both the consumers and the producers of data must agree on how that data will be represented (defined by an XML schema), but it does loosen the coupling so that the format can be extended to include further information without having to rely on co-ordinated changes to the consumer and producer interfaces. This makes it ideal for interfacing to external systems that are not under the control of the risk architect or are subject to slower upgrade constraints; additional information can be included in the XML message that can be utilized once it is made available or when the consumer interface is updated to interpret it.

A number of standard protocols such as ORML (operational risk mark-up language) for exchanging operational risk information within the financial services industry and SOAP and WSDL (used in web services) have been derived from XML. They address the issue of agreeing on the schema to be used by providing an accepted and proven industry standard that can be adopted by both the consumer and producer.

XML is, however, a verbose method for transferring data and can have an adverse performance impact on systems and networks if the volume of data transmitted is excessive. This is often acceptable given the flexibility of using such an approach. The performance impact can be an issue when distributing price data within organizations but is typically not a problem when distributing less volatile and less frequently updated information.

APPROACHES TO PARALLELISM IN SOFTWARE

In order to exploit potential process concurrency, the risk management problem must be decomposed into a number of tasks that operate concurrently and interact with each other. This decomposition may be at a fine- or coarse-grained level. Fine-grained parallelism is concerned with the decomposition of small units of processing into concurrent operations whereas coarse-grained parallelism is concerned with the decomposition of the problem into a number of high level concurrent tasks. Developing software which executes in parallel does however introduce a number of new challenges for the developer such as the danger of deadlock (when there is a circular dependency between processes so that none is able to proceed) and non-determinism, where it is not possible to guarantee the order in which certain events or processing will occur.[9]

There are a number of broad classes of approach to decomposing a problem into a number of tasks that can be executed concurrently. For simplicity, only message passing-based approaches to parallelism are considered here. These are the most prevalent and appropriate approaches to developing multi-tier systems:

Event or process farm replication

This is the easiest form of problem decomposition. Each process performs the same function but with a different set of data. All processing is performed independently with the only communication being the receipt of new data or forwarding of results.

Data or geometric parallelism

Each process performs a similar function but only receives a subset of the data. The division of this data is such that the data in any one subset is in some sense related so that, in the main, only local operations are required to process it. Typically a process will have to access non-local data or forward on results to processes responsible for other data sets. Examples of this type of parallelism are seen in linear algebra where operations are applied to large vectors or matrices. The data in these matrices can be broken down into sub-vectors or sub-matrices, whose processing can be distributed over a number of different processes.[10]

Distributed, functional or algorithmic parallelism

This is a more fine-grained form of parallelism, specific to a particular algorithm that breaks down into a number of concurrent processes that interact in solving the problem. The data then flows between the processes in the system, requiring the software to have a fairly elaborate communication and control structure.

Dynamic parallelism

All the previous forms of parallel decomposition have been static, in that the resources allocated to the problem are fixed. The alternative is to migrate or create new processes during the execution of the software, as they are required, in a data-dependent manner, in order to maximize the utilization of processing resources available.

Hybrid decomposition

This is a combination of the above approaches, where the problem exhibits a number of different types of parallelism for different aspects of the problem.

DATA MANAGEMENT, PROCESSING AND PERSISTENCE

Persistence is a problematic area in many designs. The technology used to persist data often changes, and can adversely impact poorly designed systems. As a result, the system should utilize as technology neutral an approach as possible, making the minimum number of assumptions concerning the particular persistence technology used.

One frequent design error is to persist or replicate data that does not need to be persisted or replicated. In real time risk management applications, many pieces of data are extremely volatile, rapidly changing in response to frequent market or trading events (Figure 6.4). Traditional databases find it difficult to keep pace with the typical rates with which data can be updated – if all these changes are to be persisted either before or after they have been processed – and introduce a bottleneck into the system. Instead, the risk management solution could aggregate risk information from various systems, and retain this information in

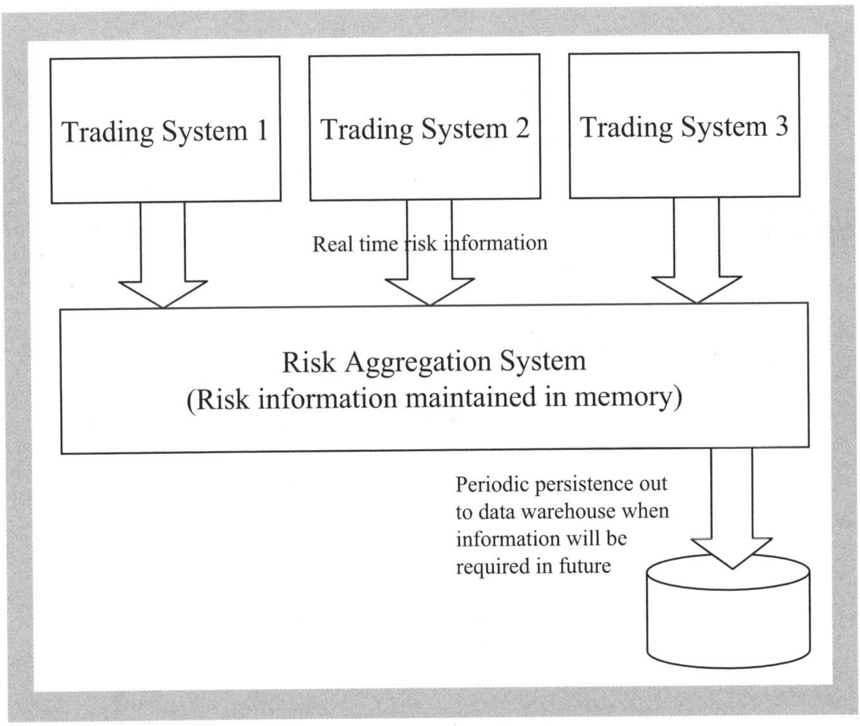

Figure 6.4 In-memory risk aggregation and persistence

memory. Should the risk management system fail, it can reobtain this information from the various source systems. This information should then only be persisted if it will be required again in the future and can no longer be efficiently extracted or recalculated from the source systems responsible for the data.

By decoupling business functionality from persistence, access to the data can be hidden behind interfaces and adaptors that obtain the information from wherever it may reside, be it in memory or in a database (Figure 6.5).

It also decouples the business functionality from implementation issues of how, when and where data is persisted and obtained. All that is required is the ability to uniquely identify data and for some data service to be able to relate this information to a specific location responsible for that data (Figure 6.5). Whether this data is then obtained locally or from a remote location should be immaterial to the consumer of the information.

Not only does this hide issues of when data should be persisted but it can also hide other issues concerning data replication. This has the advantage of aligning the owners and users of that data through a single

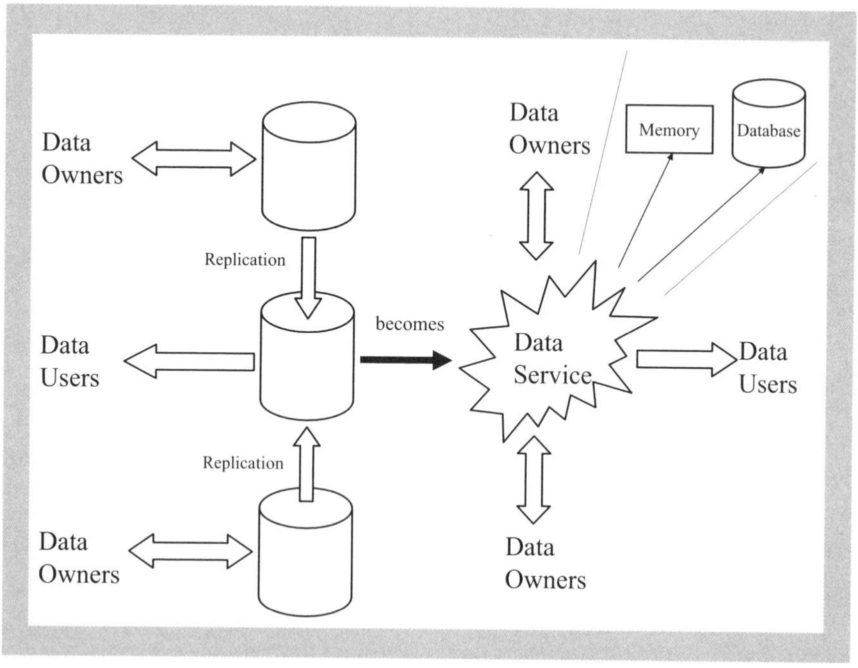

Figure 6.5 Hiding the location and implementation of data persistence

interface or service that manages access to the data, so that it can be shared and updated in a co-ordinated manner. Rather than data owners being concerned with keeping data to themselves and replicating read-only copies to other users, in order to prevent unpleasant side effects from other users accessing their data, a single controlled service is used by everyone which hides these specific implementation details.

When producing the logical application design for managing data, the model will view data as a centralized store in certain parts of the system. By centralizing data, it is easier to monitor and control the dissemination of information. However, this introduces various constraints on the implementation that must be addressed (Table 6.1). The secret of a good implementation is often how the problem and data domain are divided up in order to provide an efficient solution. Centralization of processing and data can reduce the overall amount of processing and replication but increases the volume of data that may need to be transferred if frequent remote access is required. Localizing data and processing will require less data transfer but may result in greater local processing requirements and data replication.

Replicating data should improve access speed since the replicated information will be 'closer' to where it is required. Maintaining multiple local data stores can, however, dramatically reduce manageability since each site will require the skills and resources to manage that data. There may also be additional reconciliation issues. As a result, data should only be replicated when performance demands it and preferably only for stable read-only information.

Table 6.1 Trade-offs for global system design of centralization versus localization of data and processing

Centralization	Localization
Introduces a bottleneck into the implementation	Improved performance and scalability
No synchronization issues	Data consistency and reconciliation issues between source and replicated data
Latency in accessing information for non-local users	More responsive
Single site to manage and deploy system to	Difficulty in managing multiple sites
Data is always consistent and current	Potential replication problems
Single point of control	Replicated data is always out of date

Although data access may be via a common data service, behind this façade the different approaches to the partitioning, sharing and replicating of data may be utilized as seen in Figure 6.6. Data that may be modified by more than one application is either placed in a single location or ownership is taken by one of the applications, to which the other applications must make requests in order to effect changes. Effective management of data whose values can be changed by multiple processes is vital in any concurrent environment. It not only drives data synchronization and copy policies but mutable data will require transactional and locking support in order to ensure data consistency. This can most effectively be provided when a single location is responsible for that data.

The partitioning of data is typically one of deciding data ownership. Whichever application owns the data will be responsible for maintaining and updating it and notifying other processes of any changes to that data; any modifications must be directed at that system, with any associated performance implications. This should result in data being stored locally to where it is entered and modified most frequently. For example, trading positions initiated in New York should be stored locally in New York rather

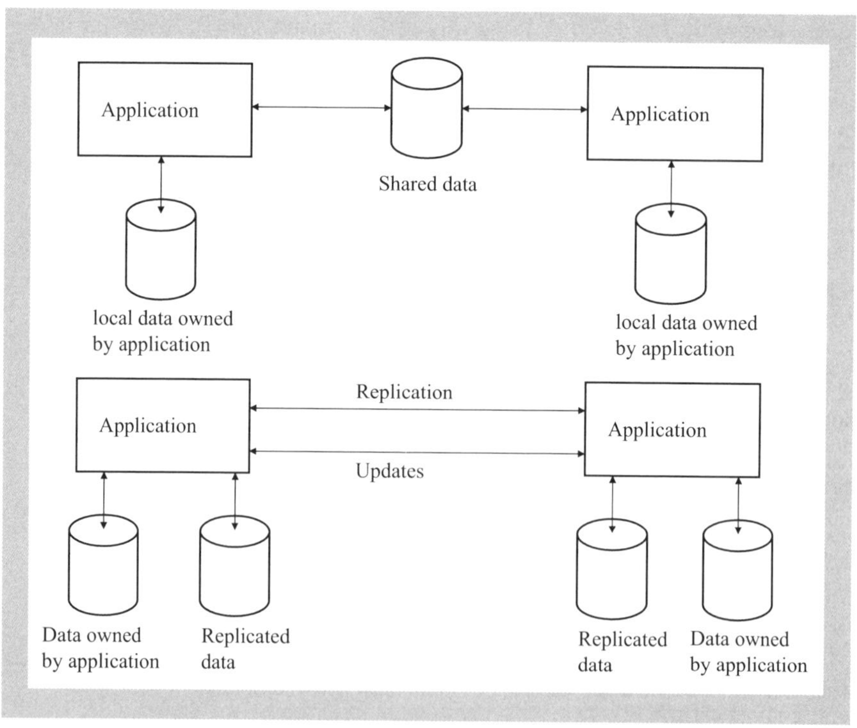

Figure 6.6 Approaches to accessing shared data

than, say, London, where network latency and bandwidth issues would impact any trading in New York. This process can be complicated if a position is traded in multiple locations at different times, and may require ownership of that data to migrate from location to location. This can complicate the collection of risk data, in order to ensure that data is not 'double counted' and will rely on successfully determining which system is responsible for the required data at a given time or being able to uniquely identify replicated data so that duplicate information is clearly indicated.

Although transactions and the ACID test are reasonably easy to enforce when all the affected data is localized into a single location, or if only one user can write the data, when the data in a transaction is distributed over several locations, this can be more complex to manage. Fortunately distributed transactions are supported by the concept of a two-phase commit transaction.[11] If any sub-transaction in the distributed transaction fails, then the whole transaction will fail.

In the same way that data should be owned by a single location or application, business functionality should also be standardized and shared by all interested systems. For example, a standard methodology for calculating the market risk of an instrument should be used throughout the risk management hierarchy. This can be achieved by

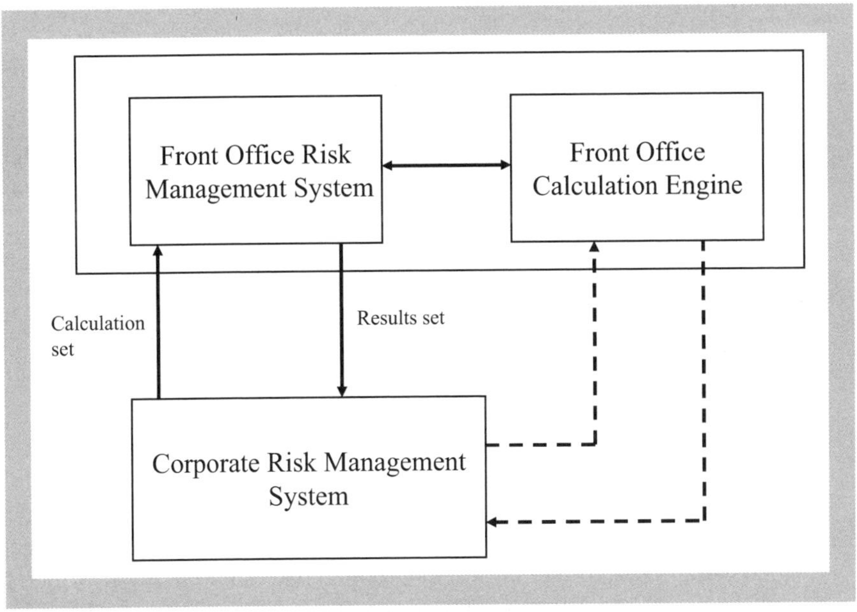

Figure 6.7 Leveraging existing functionality within the organization

leveraging existing functionality in the systems that are viewed as owning that functionality within the organization. Calculation requests can then be passed on to these legacy systems that own the functionality and the associated result sets received back (Figure 6.7). This can also be achieved by extracting the required functionality into a separate scalable service that is directly accessible by all interested applications in a similar manner to the previously described data service.

DATA WAREHOUSES

Higher up the risk management hierarchy there is a need for a more holistic view of risk information, monitoring how this has changed over time and what has caused these changes to occur. Such consistent views of the organization are usually provided by data warehouses or decision support systems. Bill Inmon, one of the key figures in developing the data warehouse concept, defines a data warehouse as a collection of data which supports management decision making which is:[12]

Subject orientated
Many systems have a process or functional orientation. A data warehouse focuses exclusively on data modelling.

Integrated
A data warehouse integrates all data into a common data model, removing any differences in data representation chosen by the designers of the feeding systems.

Non-volatile
Data warehouses only permit data uploading and data access. Updates (in their general sense) are not permitted to data (unless the snapshot of data was loaded incorrectly) and data will remain unchanged until it is either summarized or purged from the system.

Time-variant
All data is accurate as of some specific previous moment in time (rather than being the real time information which is required in an operational environment). As a result, time tends to act as a unique identifier for accessing the data. This versioning of data within a data warehouse

ensures a consistent view of the organization, which will not suddenly change during a complex risk calculation.

The requirements above imply specific design considerations (such as optimizing the database for searching rather than updating or deleting data), which will result in a database model, and design that may be significantly different from that used by online transaction processing (OLTP) systems. It is important not to think of a data warehouse as simply duplicating information in OLTP systems. A correctly implemented data warehouse only maintains the information that is relevant to it and the time horizons of the two systems are very different; data in an operational environment is concerned with up to date, real time data, while a data warehouse is likely to contain data which covers a much greater time horizon. The process of integration also means that the data is likely to have been radically altered as it is imported into the data warehouse. The challenge for the risk system designer is to implement a framework that can leverage common functionality to provide both real time risk management information lower in the risk hierarchy, as well as a more holistic decision support system that monitors this information over time.

One of the major challenges faced by data warehouses is obtaining data when the source systems and data representations may be constantly changing. Jenks[13] noted that the greater the degree of semantic volatility in the source data, the greater the need for data warehouse layering where multiple *data marts,* or reduced scope data warehouses, aggregate data which is then fed into a data warehouse. The development of multi-tiered data warehouses is a common feature described in the data warehouse literature, and is recommended by many data warehouse experts.[14] This approach permits an architecture that can support both flexibility and scalability to achieve short-term tactical as well as long-term strategic goals. Each of the layers in a multi-tiered data warehouse is aimed at solving a different type of problem, supporting different sets of users and the problems posed by different constraints.

One problem with using data warehouses has been that they are optimized for general queries using star or snowflake schemas[15] that represent the multidimensional nature of the data and support its processing using OLAP and data mining tools. Attempting to optimize a data warehouse for specific data queries can be a never-ending task and one that no one data model or design is likely to be able to support. Instead, data warehouses should be used as a read only source of quality

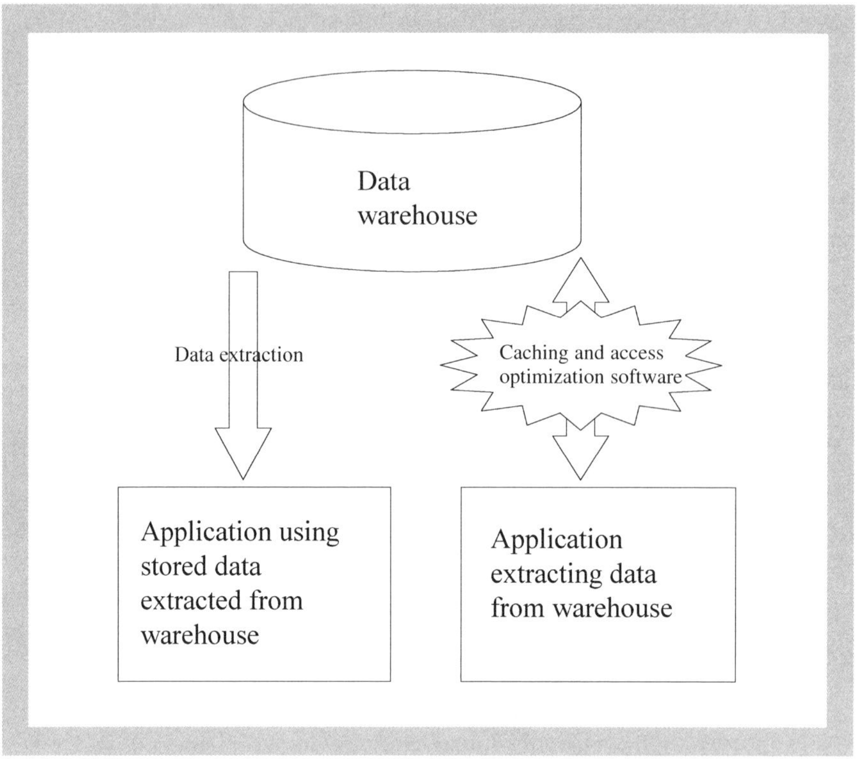

Figure 6.8 Efficiently extracting data from data warehouses

data and information extracted, if required, for processing using external tools and applications which can be optimized for certain frequent types of data access and analysis without adversely impacting the design of the data warehouse (Figure 6.8).

PRODUCING HIGH PERFORMANCE SOLUTIONS

The key to performance tuning is identifying performance hot spots in processing and inter-process communication. Performance is impacted by infrastructure constraints as well as design and implementation decisions such as:

- The manner of decomposition of the system into concurrent processes
- Latency and bandwidth of the network

- Availability and capability of processing resources
- The representation and availability of data and how efficiently it can be accessed
- Performance of the implementation of each process, including any trade-offs in the accuracy and computational complexity of any algorithms used.

The implementation will also have to meet various constraints concerning potential future architectural requirements as well as project constraints limiting the cost and time taken to deliver any solution. Providing a highly performant implementation will prove more costly in development time, which may not be justified if a less efficient solution can produce the required results within an acceptable period.

Performance bottlenecks

The physical architecture, design and implementation will introduce bottlenecks or synchronization points in the system that impact system performance. Obtaining high performance solutions is usually a balance between the duplication and decomposition of various calculations and the communication overhead implied in distributing calculated data.

The decomposition of the system should try to ensure that any calculations that can be shared are centralized where possible, provided the additional latency in accessing this information is not excessive or significantly greater than the time taken to generate it. These calculations can then be performed once and made accessible to all interested parties, concentrating processing resources on performing this task once. Calculations that will only be required by a subset of users can be performed either using centralized resources or locally to the client, depending on the availability of resources and any data bandwidth constraints. Either static or dynamic load balancing of processing requirements over the available resources should then be performed to ensure that all resources are fully utilized and performance bottlenecks minimized.

Bottlenecks in the transfer of data can be removed by reducing the volume of extraneous information that is transferred between processes or ensuring that processes which frequently interact are physically deployed so that the infrastructure is able to support such interaction. The volume of data transferred can be reduced by:

Filtering
Only forwarding the required data between processes. Data that is not required should be discarded instead of being sent or forwarded.

Throttling and aggregation
In real time systems, data should not be updated at a faster rate than it can be processed. Doing so will only result in a backlog of updates that can never be processed in a timely manner and that will overflow buffers or consume resources. Data may be throttled (its update rate reduced) or aggregated and then only released based on a number of mechanisms, ranging from the rate of updates, a defined timer, the magnitude of any change and so on. Typical examples of this are found in trading risk systems, where price changes from the markets occur at too fast a rate to be able to recalculate the risk associated with a given of source of risk within the organization. Provided the change in magnitude of any additional risk arising from these variations is not significant, this is not an issue. Other data such as position updates may be aggregated and then released at defined time intervals. The ability to aggregate data relies on there being no loss of information when that data is netted together.

Incremental data updates
Rather than transmitting a complete copy of the updated information, only the specific changes or deltas are sent.

Caching and data access

Using data caching can further reduce data communication volumes. This involves the local, in-memory storage of commonly accessed information, thereby removing the need to retrieve this from a more remote location. Caching differs from replication in that only information that has been requested and recently accessed is stored. Complex caching techniques can be used to enable data access to this stored information using retrieval based on some unique identifier. In order to ensure efficient access to this cache of information and to limit the memory consumption, eviction policies will also need to be defined, which should be tailored to meet the expected access requirements of different types of data. Although caching can improve performance, it also introduces complexities in ensuring that any cached data is current, if the data contained within the cached data is updated elsewhere in the system.

Data access performance can also be improved by modifying the representation or encoding of data passed within the system. Data models implemented within databases are often *denormalized* in order to achieve this. This involves the duplication or storage of derived data within the database in order to reduce the time taken to perform certain calculations or execute a data query. This increases the speed with which the data may be retrieved. Denormalization does, however, reduce the maintainability of the database, making data consistency and integrity more difficult to ensure.

Precision, throughput and computational complexity

Many risk calculations require the use of numerical methods or highly complex algorithms. Unlike accounting systems, risk management solutions do not require calculations that are 'penny accurate'. The risk manager only requires results that contain all material risks and is willing to trade accuracy against calculation time. As a result, the risk management solution should also be able to sacrifice accuracy for reduced computational complexity. For most numerical methods, this is achieved by a simple change to the required calculation accuracy or number of numerical iterations performed. For other calculation approaches, it may require the replacing of a complex model with a simpler model that approximates the true solution.

Processing throughput can also be increased at the expense of increasing calculation latency, so that the perceived time taken to perform an individual calculation increases, but the volume of calculations performed also increases. This can be achieved by performing batch-type calculations that are able to optimize the performance of a known sequence of similar calculations or the single task of obtaining a large amount of data rather than a large number of requests for small amounts of data.

Notes

1 M. Fowler and K. Scott, *UML Distilled: A Brief Guide to the Standard Object Modeling Language* (Addison-Wesley, 1999)
2 E. Marcus and H. Stern, *Blueprints for High Availability: Designing Resilient Distributed Systems* (John Wiley, 2000)
3 R. Orfali, D. Harkey and J. Edwards, *The Essential Distributed Object Survival Guide* (John Wiley, 1996)

4 C. Hoare, *Communicating Sequential Processes* (Prentice Hall, 1985)
5 M. Walmsley, *Multi-threaded Programming in C++,* (Springer-Verlag, 1999)
6 C. Britton, *IT Architectures and Middleware* (Addison-Wesley, 2001)
7 R. Elmasri and S. Navathe, *Fundamentals of Database Systems* (Addison-Wesley, 1989)
8 C. Horstmann and G. Cornell, *Core Java2 Volume II – Advanced Features* (Prentice Hall, 2001)
9 See note 4
10 I. Foster, *Designing and Building Parallel Programs – Concepts and Tools for Parallel Software Engineering* (Addison-Wesley, 1995)
11 See note 7
12 W. Inmon, *Building the Data Warehouse* (QED, 1996)
13 B. Jenks, 'Tiered data warehouse', *DM Review* (October, 1997) 54–7
14 J. Rawls, 'Multitiered data warehouses', *DM Review* (June, 1977) 26–31
15 W. Giovinazzo, *Object-orientated Data Warehouse Design* (Prentice Hall, 2000)

CHAPTER 7

Project management

The task of the project manager is to maximize the return or benefit from the project, while managing any risk and keeping it within defined risk limits. Basic financial and risk analysis techniques are used in project assessment[1] to quantify the financial benefits and costs of any projects as a set of future cashflows. These cashflows are discounted using a risk-adjusted rate of return appropriate for the project, to give an expected present value of the financial benefit from performing the project.

We can define a simple model for project management that extends the standard project assessment approach in order to try and quantify some of the precise benefits and risks associated with delivering certain functionality. The project manager's role is then to maximize the expected present value of the system. A crude expected value of a project is defined as:

$$Value = \sum_{i} tv_i b_i$$

where tv_i is the (risk adjusted) time value or discount factor for the system delivering the benefit b_i at time t_i in the future. Higher levels of risk will result in a reduction or adjustment to tv_i, as the level of uncertainty in the delivery of any benefit increases. As a result, greater benefits should be achieved if higher levels of risk are to be taken.

Time value in the context of managing projects, as with present value calculations in financial pricing,[2] has the characteristic that if $t_1 < t_2 < ... < t_n$ then $tv_1 > tv_2 > ... > tv_n$ for a given level of risk in delivering the benefits b_i. This decline may not, however, be linear or well behaved, because certain business or regulatory deadlines can dramatically reduce the value of a system benefit if it fails to be delivered by some critical date. The values assigned to benefits and time value in this equation may also be highly subjective, with different stakeholders having very different views on both the benefits and the time value of certain pieces of functionality. From this model it is possible to derive a number of basic lessons for structuring and managing projects:

Incremental delivery
Rather than utilizing a big bang approach, make incremental small releases of functionality that provide benefits to the users. This has the advantage of decreasing the level of discounting and hence increasing the present value of the benefit from the system. It also ensures that the benefits are realized as early as possible, rather than continuing to be part of a subjective expected value calculation and associated with the risk of non-delivery.

Front end projects
When projects are delivered incrementally, deliver as much valuable or key functionality to the users as early on in the project as possible. This increases the present value of benefits from the system by associating them with lower levels of discounting.

Don't decommission existing systems too soon
Only remove existing desirable functionality when it can be adequately replaced by functionality in the new system. The benefit from a system will usually be positive but, if another system is to be replaced with some benefit from existing functionality temporarily being lost or additional work around processes needing to be added, then there may be an initial negative benefit. This will decrease the value of the new system to the users.

Cut your losses
If the project is failing, it is better to restructure it and deliver some functionality than to deliver no functionality at all. Although not desirable, this is better than letting it fail so that there is no return from the project.

Deliver what is required
Increasing the amount of desired functionality delivered increases the benefit from a system even if this is delivered later in the project.

The other side of the equation is to manage risk within the project and ensure that the maximum value is attained for a given level of risk in delivering the benefit b_i at time t_i or earlier. This level of risk or uncertainty is also likely to increase the later in the project the benefit is delivered. As a result, high-risk aspects of a project should be delivered as soon as possible. Ensuring delivery or prototyping functionality that has a high level of risk of non-delivery (possibly due to problems with the associated technology or project skill levels) as early in the project as possible allows remedial action or project redesign to be performed equally early, with minimal impact on other (as yet unimplemented) tasks within the project. This can dramatically reduce overall project risk.

Uncertainty or risk in project delivery will be increased by:

- Using unproven or *bleeding edge* technology, so called because it is so cutting edge that many project managers end up hurting themselves with it!
- The complexity of the solution. The more complex something is, the more likely something will go wrong; a golden rule is to always keep things as simple as possible.
- Not using highly trained and balanced teams that have formed into a cohesive unit. The importance of team dynamics and communication should not be underestimated.[3]
- Using new processes or technology that the team has little experience of without the provision of training, the building of prototypes or allowing the team to adequately climb the learning curve.
- Poor communication or relationships within the project team and with external stakeholders. Good communication has two benefits. Firstly, frequent communication and sharing of ideas and knowledge ensure that misunderstandings within the project are minimized. Secondly, the state of the project needs to be communicated to the stakeholders so that their understanding of the expected value from the project and the actual value that will be realized are kept in close agreement. If the stakeholders' view diverges too significantly in either direction then the project may be cancelled due to the project not meeting their expectations or their expectations being too low to justify the project cost.
- Poor system design, not permitting future benefits to be delivered in shorter periods of time. With good system design future benefits will also be associated with lower levels of risk and therefore lower levels of discounting, increasing the future value of any changes to the system.

- Subjective approaches to project management and cognitive biases (Chapter 1) so that there is more uncertainty and risk associated with the current and future state of the project.

THE PROJECT MANAGEMENT PROCESS

The project management process can be broken down into a number of steps as shown in Figure 7.1. Although the steps are shown as being discrete, it is not uncommon for many of the stages to overlap. For example, rapid start projects may require planning to overlap with resource hiring and the start of some aspects of the project delivery cycle. The decomposition and timing of tasks will also need to match resource availability.

Projects may also be partitioned into a number of sub-projects, each of which can be treated as an individual project, but which roll up in a consistent manner into the final project plan.

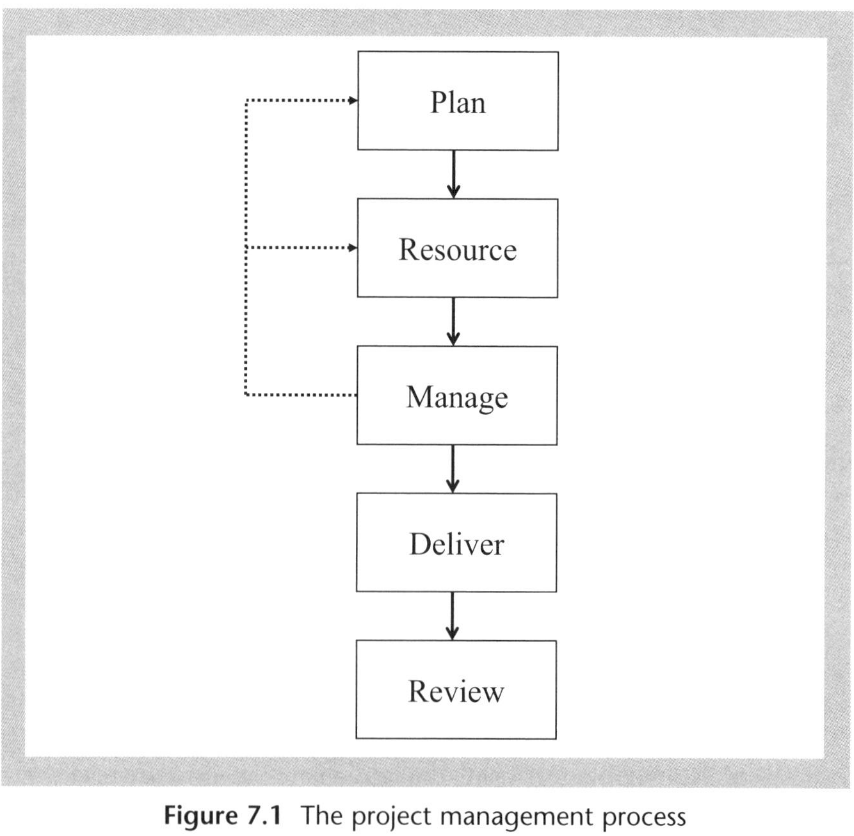

Figure 7.1 The project management process

Plan

The project plan is an estimate or expectation of progress of the project over time. Time estimating is difficult and subject to error. Features and priorities often change and evolve, making the task even more difficult. As with any large problem, it is best partitioned into a number of sub-projects or tasks, each of which can be individually estimated and managed. The project manager should be able to obtain reasonable estimates of effort, either based on personal experiences regarding task effort and the duration of common patterns of design or by utilising and working with more experienced members of the project team who have been involved in similar projects. Involving more people in this estimation process also reduces the impact of any individual's inherent bias or misunderstanding of the project, ensuring a more complete and well-thought out plan. Planning is, however, an iterative and inexact process. It is therefore important to accept that there will be an ongoing need to revise and replan over the life of the project. This expectation should be built into the project from the beginning, and expectations managed accordingly.

The detail to which time estimates should be developed will depend on the size and complexity of the project. Often, it is prudent to plan and schedule the most detailed levels of work just a few weeks in advance because of uncertainties of individual team members' availability, and actual project progress. This avoids significant effort being expended on aspects of the plan that are unlikely to add any further value to the project and will need to be readdressed later.

The individual project tasks should cover the entire project lifecycle, from initial scope and requirements analysis, through to testing and deployment. Associated with these tasks will be resources and expected start and end dates for work on the task. The allocation of resources should clearly identify responsibility and accountability for completion of each task. Completion of either single or multiple independent tasks may also be associated with *milestones*, which define measurable objectives or deliverables that can be used to provide an unbiased assessment of project progress.

A task may depend on the completion of a number of other tasks either internal or external to the project, which should be clearly highlighted. These dependencies will introduce causal relationships that will impact the execution of the project, and hence complicate the risk management of the project. The partitioning of the project should ensure that any tasks are as self-contained as possible with no circular dependencies of one task on another; that is, completion of one task should not depend on another task, which depends on completion of some aspect of the first task. Attempting to manage the interdependency and risk associated with such complex dependencies can be extremely difficult.

One of the key issues of project planning is defining the sequence in which work should be accomplished. At a high level, this sequencing determines the overlap of the major work activities and how resources and skill sets must be deployed, especially if specific skills are required to complete certain tasks. At a lower level, it determines the sequence in which functionality will be produced and integrated within the project.

This sequence should aim to reduce the risk and enhance any value delivered by the project, subject to any project scheduling constraints and tasks dependencies, as discussed previously. The aim of the planning process is to produce a project plan where completion of the highlighted tasks will result in a system which meets all the requirements and which can be completed using the available resources. Once the project plan has been produced it should be discussed and signed off by all the appropriate stakeholders. This will define expected project timescales as well as the required human and physical resources. This plan will then set both the project team and the external stakeholders' expectations.

Resource

The most carefully constructed plans are not sufficient in themselves to guarantee success. Plans do not complete projects – people do. As a result, good team dynamics, open communication, effective organization and man management skills will be crucial for success. Organizing and managing people effectively will pay dividends in terms of increased productivity, quality and likelihood of project success. Once the project plan has been created, there will be an estimate of the resourcing requirements needed to deliver the project in the permitted time. Once these resources have been acquired, they can be assigned to various tasks in the plan. This assignment must enable the ordering and timing of the tasks in the plan to be achieved without overloading any individual resource while still being able to meet any constraints concerning their availability. This process is known as *levelling*. The matching of resources to tasks in the project plan should result in a number of SMART[4] objectives:

Specific

The objective must be specific and clearly explained so that completion of the task is well defined. Specific well-defined tasks will depend on the quality of the requirements gathering and analysis process to remove any ambiguities or inconsistencies.

Measurable

It must be possible to measure progress and decide when the task is complete.

Achievable

The task must be achievable for the assigned person(s) using their existing skill set. If it is not, training must be provided and allowances made for unfamiliarity with the chosen technology or problem domain. The resource(s) will then take responsibility for completion of this task and must therefore be empowered to be able to perform any required work.

Relevant

In order to motivate the team members, tasks must be relevant to them and fit in with their career goals. Keeping goals relevant will require career development planning as well as coaching and counselling.

Timely

The time permitted for the task must be achievable within the project time frame by the person resourced to complete the task.

The organization or external employment conditions are likely to impose a number of constraints on the project manager when resourcing a project; it may need to be staffed using existing staff with training provided if necessary. In order for the project to be properly resourced, it is therefore important that the requirements and tasks are sufficiently well understood to be able to match the right tasks to the right available resources. Any training requirements should also be included within the project plan, as they will impact the timing of when a resource can be assigned productively to a task.

Training for the project should not only ensure that the resources have the right skills to successfully complete the assigned tasks but should also provide project orientation, highlighting any project-specific standards, processes or skills. This is also the point at which effort should be made to put in place communication and project monitoring structures and to start team-building exercises.

Once the plan has been resourced, time and effort estimates should be refined to reflect the actual skill and productivity levels of the resources assigned to each task. At the end of the resourcing stage of the project, all the project infrastructure should be in place, the project team and structure established. All aspects of the plan should be resourced and all team members orientated with a full understanding of the expectations placed on them.

Manage

Project management is essentially the process of communicating, identifying and solving problems in the execution of the project plan (Figure 7.2). Potential and actual problems are identified by measuring and monitoring progress and performance against the project plan. This should be supplemented with qualitative feedback from the individual team members. The project plan will contain a number of sources of risk, which will be impacted by various events both internal and external to the project that will result in an outcome other than that expected. Additional risks will arise as the project evolves and known risks may become greater or significantly different than expected.

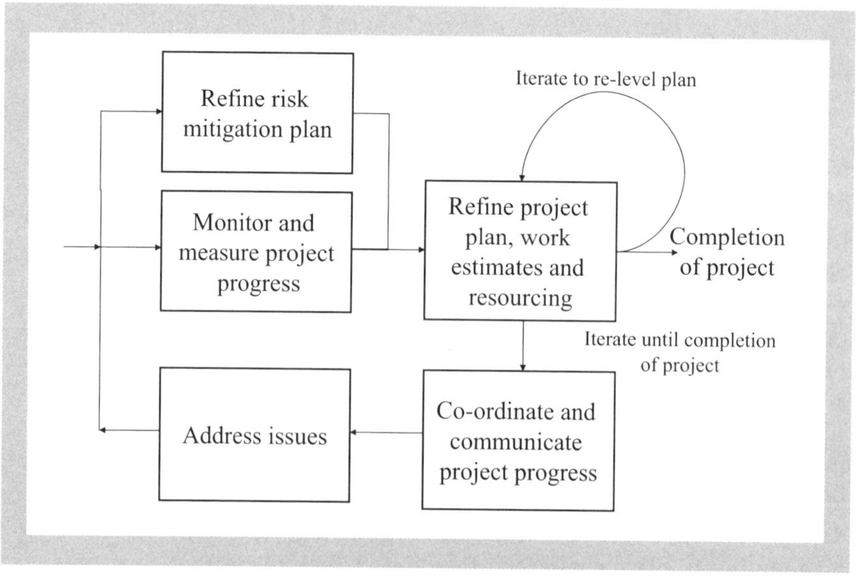

Figure 7.2 The project execution process

The reality of project management is that events and timescales described in the project plan are unlikely to be achieved as expected. What is important is that progress is monitored so that it is known when expectations are not being met and why this has occurred. It will then be possible to take corrective action and reassess the ongoing risk within the project. All this requires a baseline against which actual project progress and requirements can be compared, which is provided by the project plan.

Monitoring Progress and Refining the Project Plan

In order to measure project progress, activities must be monitored to provide an accurate view of what has been achieved. As a result, the process should avoid any cognitive biases and should not permit developers to provide potentially optimistic assessments of progress or percentage of task completed. Progress should instead be measured as objectively as possible and these measures should be defined at the start of the project. The easiest way to achieve this is to ensure that there are objective measures for project progress covering reasonably short time periods, typically defined by milestone events indicating the completion of various tasks. These milestone events may be the provision of functionality that can be validated by defined tests, or may require independent review of the task by other team members. Progress can be defined in a number of different dimensions, each of which will give a different perspective on the project:

Start and completion of tasks and milestones on or before the dates in the project plan
Any differences will require modifications to the plan and any slippage will require corrective action if the project is to meet any timeline dependencies.

Actual effort (in man hours) and resources involved in completing each task
Although achieving milestone dates is important, this may be at the expense of excessive work effort from those involved, which will hide either inaccurate effort estimates or variances in the availability or capability of certain resources. Although such activity may be acceptable in order to address short-term plan slippage or lack of resources, if it is performed over long periods of time it will overload some resources and result in a decrease in their productivity. It is therefore important that this should only occur with the knowledge of the project manager, who should assess the impact on risk within the project and be able to take appropriate action.

Quality of any deliverables from each task
Not only should each task result in the required deliverables, but these should meet specified minimum quality requirements. Quality may be assessed in terms of adherence to coding standards, forward engineering, maintainability of code structure or conciseness and completeness of any documentation. It will typically require more qualitative review techniques involving other project team members.

Having measured project progress, any discrepancy between what was expected and what was achieved will require further investigation and corrective action to be taken. This variance may arise from:

Dependencies on other external projects
The plan should be modified to accommodate any delay in external projects that impact the project. Essentially this task can only minimize rather than remove any impact. Any changes to the plan should be discussed and communicated to all the relevant parties (including the project's stakeholders and team members, as well as the external project team responsible for any delay), so that expectations can be readjusted and any implications clearly understood by all involved.

The way the plan is executed
The development process, or team or individual performance may not be as expected. This may be due to productivity issues, excessive effort in over-engineering aspects of the solution or performing tasks that are not required. Team member evaluations, process reviews and feedback should be used to identify the underlying cause.

The project plan itself
The estimates in terms of the availability of resources, complexity of tasks, or the completeness of the task list may be inaccurate. Incompleteness of the task list can arise from either inadequate requirements gathering or requirements changes and '*scope creep*', where new requirements are added by the stakeholders during the project. Estimates will also change due to unforeseen technical challenges. Any project member should be entitled to initiate changes in the plan estimates, provided there are good reasons to do so. These changes must be communicated as soon as possible, so that the plan can be kept up to date. Any impact on delivery dates, along with the reasons for any change must be clearly communicated in order to manage expectations.

If the initial plan estimates were inaccurate before commencement of the plan, slippage will be a regular occurrence. Estimating is an imperfect science so being able to spot slippage early on and identify the reason for it is crucial. It is important to 'step back' and reassess the entire project plan and take significant corrective action rather than letting the slippage continue, as this will only reduce the quality of information used to evaluate project progress and will increase project risk.

In order to bring a project back into line with the plan, the drivers for a project must be reviewed and addressed (Figure 7.3). These drivers are interrelated in that a change in one will impact the others:

Resources: The skilled people performing the work, their productivity, as well as the things they require such as workspace, PCs, phones and so on. Increasing the number or quality of resources can reduce the time taken to complete the project, enable additional functionality to be included (in order to enhance scope) or improve project quality. Improving resource motivation is also a low cost approach to improving resource productivity.

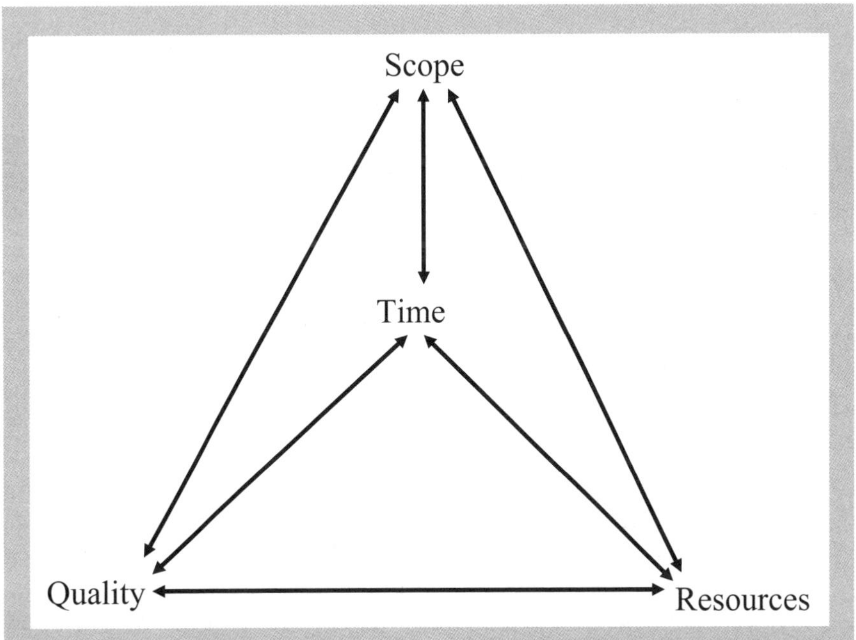

Figure 7.3 The interrelationship of the four main project drivers

Scope: What is to be produced, generally specified or defined in terms of tangible deliverables. Increasing project scope will require additional resources, a reduction in quality or the project timeline to be extended. The impact of continuously changing scope should not be underestimated and can result in continuously changing plans and requirements, leading to project failure. Proposed changes should be tightly managed and the implications for the project clearly explained to all the relevant stakeholders. Reducing scope in a troubled project can be used to deliver functionality sooner or improve project quality.

Time: The timeline as specified in the project plan. If the project is behind schedule, and the project manager wishes to deliver the remaining tasks in a shorter period of time, then the implications are to use more resources, reduce scope or to sacrifice quality. Sacrificing quality is the least desirable choice since it can have major repercussions on the future of the project.

Quality: The fitness for purpose of the system, and its ability to be extended and modified. Reducing quality will have major implications on future enhancements to the project and should never be sacrificed in core design areas.

The interaction of these drivers can be more complex than is implied in Figure 7.3. For example, repeatedly increasing the numbers of resources to try to ensure more rapid delivery of a project does not always have the desired impact and can result in even greater project slippage.[5] It does however provide a starting point for considering the implications of various project management decisions.

Co-ordinating and communicating project status

The importance of open communication cannot be overemphasized. It is important that expectations of project progress are managed and that current project status is communicated both internally and to project stakeholders. Just as with risk management, the aim is for no significant unexpected surprises. Status meetings must be held on a regular basis to review progress. Any developer should also be able to call a meeting at any time to discuss issues related to the project, and obtain assistance from fellow team members. Status reports should also include information concerning tasks completed during this reporting period, along with expectations for the next one.

Traffic light or red, amber, green (RAG) reporting is a high-level qualitative performance and risk indicator that is used in many projects. In a RAG report, the entire project, or well-defined units of it are each given a red, amber or green status. Green indicates that there are no problems with the piece of work and progress is being made as expected in the project plan, whereas amber acts as a warning to indicate that problems may be arising, which may result in the project not meeting its requirements (in terms of time, cost, quality and risk). A red status means that some key milestones either have been missed or will be missed unless corrective action is taken. The layout of a RAG report is similar to that of a risk report. The key results of the report are clearly laid out at the beginning, followed by a brief description that provides context to the report (Figure 7.4).

Issues will arise when multiple parallel development teams or individual developers work as part of a single project. These issues may be architecture, schedule, business or resource related. To ensure that the teams make effective progress with their work, as autonomously as possible, effective co-ordination will be required by either the project manager or a special team that provides leadership and co-ordination between the groups. This team's remit is to provide high-level management of the process, ensuring that the project team operates as efficiently and predictably as possible. It will also assist the project manager in deciding and implementing any remedial action that may need to be taken.

Risk mitigation

Throughout the project, existing risks should be continuously monitored and new risks identified and analysed. As mentioned in Chapter 1, for each risk (within the project plan) there are three alternatives:

1. *To accept the risk but do nothing for the moment.* The plan should however be stress tested to see what impact the associated events may have on the project.
2. *To remove the risk by taking a contingency approach.* Alternatives should be devised to deal with the eventuality of this risk being realized. This may be through undertaking (lower risk) backup tasks that could also address the requirements or developing alternative strategies to work around this situation should it occur. Which one is undertaken will depend on cost and the risk appetite of the project, together with the level of risk identified (quantified in terms of impact on the timescale, cost, deliverable functionality or quality of the project).

Project Status Report

For Period Ending 30/6/2003

Program Name: RiskEngine **Program Manager:** Martin Gorrod

Project Number: 12345

Scheduled Completion: 31/07/03

Forecasted Completion: 15/07/03

Summary

	Quality	Risk	Scope	Resources	Time
Red	☐	■	☐	☐	☐
Amber	☐	☐	■	☐	☐
Green	■	☐	☐	■	■

Summary

The RiskEngine Program is ahead of schedule and should, subject to no unforeseen issues, be completed two weeks earlier than scheduled in the project plan. The major risk impacting this project is that the Data Project will not be delivered on time. A contingency for addressing this will be to use the surplus effort to build a direct link from the RiskEngine System to the old Data System.

Quality

The initial expectations of the project are being met. This can be evidenced by:

- System response times exceed those specified by 50%
- 90% of acceptance tests are currently being passed

Risk

The primary risk impacting the RiskEngine System is the delay in the delivery of the new Data System. Although the RiskEngine System is likely to be delivered ahead of schedule, it cannot be implemented until the new Data system is available. The suggested action to mitigate this risk is to build a link to the old Data System that can be replaced when the new Data system is available. This will enable earlier implementation of the RiskEngine.

Achievements during this reporting period

The VaR engine has been fully implemented and passed integration tests.

Expected achievements during next reporting period

Completion of the reporting module to provide ad hoc reporting capabilities.

Figure 7.4 Example of an RAG report for project progress

3. *To remove or reduce the source of risk.* This may be by replacing inexperienced team members on critical sections of the project with others who are more experienced, modifying tasks to take a lower risk approach or developing prototypes to provide a feasibility study in order to further investigate any potential risks. Issue logs can also be used to highlight key sources of risk within the project that require rapid resolution. Resolution of these issues should be assigned to key project personnel and include the correct level of stakeholder involvement, if necessary, with resolution dates and a well-defined escalation policy. It may require forming small ad-hoc teams of experts (so called 'Tiger Teams')[6] to quickly study significant issues and perform specific analyses that were not included in the initial requirement gathering and analysis.

Many of the techniques discussed in Chapter 3 can be applied to assess the level of risk within the project plan. In particular, the techniques of KRIs, stress testing, scenario analysis and decision trees are all applicable. Some of the most common KRIs are:

- Tasks taking longer than expected resulting in delayed project completion and inefficient resource allocation
- Inability to complete the task as specified due to ambiguities in or incompleteness of requirements, which requires re-specification of the task and frequent changes to the resulting analysis.
- Loss of key resources
- Changes to or incorrect implementation of requirements
- Scope creep resulting in constantly extending project deadlines.

Anti-patterns can be also used to identify projects that are in crisis. These are common features or patterns observed either in architectural design, software development or the management of projects that commonly lead to significant constraints in any delivered solution or project failure.[7]

Deliver and review

The level of difficulty involved in obtaining acceptance of project deliverables is usually inversely proportional to the degree of stakeholder involvement and specification of any requirements, together with the level of expectation management during the project. Inadequate involvement of key stakeholders or poor specification and expectation management will only result in problematic acceptance. Once the project has been delivered and this stage of the project is complete, it is important to review and reflect on where the project succeeded and where it may have had shortcomings.

All team members should be included and asked to provide feedback on which parts of the process succeeded and which failed. This period of reflection should be non-judgemental, its aim being purely to provide feedback for improving the process, rather than to apportion blame. It should identify underlying causes so that transferable lessons concerning the entire project lifecycle can be learnt and applied to other projects. The primary objective of project management is to meet or exceed the expectations of the project sponsors. These expectations are typically expressed within the following categories:

- *Functionality:* The project delivers the required functionality.
- *Quality:* The project meets the stakeholders' expectations in terms of defect levels and extensibility/maintainability of system.
- *Cost:* The project delivers the desired functionality and quality at the anticipated cost (that is, within project budget).
- *Schedule:* The project delivers agreed system releases within the anticipated time frame. This high-level schedule should be agreed before development of the system.
- *Project Risk:* The level of risk associated with achieving the above is at or below the level expected or specified by the stakeholders of the project.

Evaluation of the process should compare the above with what actually occurred during the project, covering all the iterations of the project plan. Having determined any variances, the cause of these should be investigated and assessed. Typical questions that will arise from this process will include:

- Do variances and contingencies reflect tasks that were omitted?
- How do the estimating guidelines compare with the level of effort expended?

- Were the requirements adequately detailed, comprehensive and free of superfluous information?
- Could the development process be standardized, streamlined or otherwise made more effective?
- Are there ways to reduce future learning curves?
- Did the project identify and implement continuous improvement opportunities?
- How effective were the risk management process and any contingency measures?
- How well were expectations managed?

REQUEST FOR PROPOSAL (RfP) PROCESS

The decision to outsource

Whether an organization decides to develop a system in house or to outsource its provision will depend on a number of factors. This decision is likely to depend on:

- Importance of maintaining strategic control and whether the system to be developed represents a core competency for the organization.[8]
- Total cost of developing internally against the total cost of outsourcing, (including any legal costs and ongoing support and licensing costs) and how this relates to differences in the risks associated with each approach.
- The relative risks, both strategic and delivery, in outsourcing against developing internally. The change in operational risk arising from the transfer of internal development and support to an external vendor can be difficult to quantify but is an important aspect of any decision.

For many financial institutions, software is often not seen as a core competency or activity. As a result, driven by a desire to both reduce costs as well as access external specialized skills, many banks have moved towards outsourcing some of their technology operation,[9] purchased software products/toolkits or engaged external consultancies or software vendors to develop a system that meets their requirements. The recent focus on operational risk has also highlighted issues in managing risk inherent in the delivery and operation of complex technological systems and encouraged organizations to decide whether external third party providers can manage this more cost effectively and efficiently.

If the decision is made to outsource, the organization must ensure that the most appropriate supplier is selected. The aim of the RfP is to formalize the selection of the most appropriate supplier to deliver the required functionality in a competitive and open manner. The process formally notifies vendors that budget is available for this work and that a formal contract will be awarded at the end of the competitive proposal process. By clarifying these key (to the supplier) requirements, vendors should expend greater effort in the process than if it was just an initial inquiry or interest. The formalization of the process also ensures that all suppliers respond in writing rather than relying on informal discussion. These written responses can then be used as a basis for contractual negotiation.

The RfP supplier selection process is essentially an optimization problem where the supplier's ability to meet requirements in different dimensions is combined into a single score. The highest score can then be used to select the supplier that addresses the requirements in the most complete manner. This selection process may, however, be subverted by political issues and lobbying which will lead to a sub-optimal decision.

The RfP process will often require further clarification of actual requirements together with some hard negotiating on all aspects of the project. Any information provided by the organization issuing the RfP should therefore not weaken its negotiating position later in the process. Providing an RfP often dramatically extends the time required to procure systems and services. The benefits of a hopefully optimal and objective decision-making process arising from formalization into an RfP should however offset these costs. The process should begin in the same way as any other software project (Chapter 5), requiring an project proposal together with perhaps some initial requirements and feasibility analysis. At this point the processes will diverge. Whereas the analyst would then focus on converting these requirements into a system requirement, the RfP process becomes one of succinctly stating these requirements in a requirements outline.

Initial supplier selection

Before the RfP has been produced, it is important to gather information regarding the suppliers who are likely to be able to address the requirements and be willing to submit proposals. For a product-based solution, the RfP should be structured so that it utilizes open questions to discover the capabilities of the potential products and does not preclude possible suppliers by, for example, defining precise requirements that few or no products can address. If a more tailored approach is taken, through the use of toolkit providers and/or service-orientated firms that develop customized solutions, the requirements within the RfP can be more precise, defining exacting minimum requirements. The fundamental difference in approach between the purchase of a product versus a tailored solution means that this decision should be made before issuing the RfP. It will be difficult to compare vendors who utilize such a radically different approach using a single RfP and set of metrics. It is also unlikely that a strategy demanding a very specific customizable solution will be satisfied by the purchase of a product. The steps in this process are therefore to:

1. *Identify possible suppliers:* Various consultancies can perform this task, given general criteria and requirements.
2. *Obtain general information regarding the supplier:* This will involve understanding the supplier's capabilities, culture, business and technical strategy (and in particular how this strategy relates to that of the organization issuing the RfP). The aim should be to ensure that any vendor selected has a strategy and culture that is complementary to that of the organization.
3. *Typical cost of a supplied solution:* Most projects have some financial constraints so there is little point in selecting a vendor who is unlikely to deliver a project that costs less than the available budget.
4. *Perform initial due diligence work:* This may include informal discussions with clients of the supplier and viewing examples of their work at exhibitions or in initial sales meetings.

The steps above should provide enough information to determine which vendors are likely to be capable of addressing the RfP and should be included in the initial supplier list. This decision should also include factors such as:

- Geographical location and ability to provide timely support
- Experience in the problem domain
- Reputation and past experiences in dealing with the supplier
- Size of supplier
- Quality of work and any specific internal project or software processes that are supported
- Financial stability of vendor.

At the end of this process there should be a short list of three to four companies that should receive the RfP. Selecting too many vendors can make managing the interaction and selection process excessively time consuming and expensive. Selecting too few means that the process is likely to become uncompetitive and result in too limited a selection.

RfP outline

An RfP should provide the potential suppliers with enough information to create a proposal that will address all the concerns of the organization. It should contain:

Organizational overview
To provide the supplier with an organizational context and reason for issuing the RfP.

Assumptions and agreements
To highlight any constraints the proposal must meet and to ensure inappropriate proposals (such as those using technology not supported within the organization) are neither delivered nor considered. This section should also highlight any proposed penalty clauses or other legal restrictions.

Required proposal format
This should define the format and also ensure that proposals from different vendors can easily be compared. Defined tick lists and tables are often specified in order to simplify this.

Requirements
This should state the objectives of the RfP process, highlighting any project phasing requirements, prototyping or milestones that will need to be achieved, as well as the key functional requirements and any supporting training or documentation that will be necessary. These should be specified in sufficient detail to preclude misunderstandings and reduce the level of further clarification required. The statement of requirements should build on any functional prioritization, as well as adding any technical or process-related requirements. The basis of any cost calculations to be provided by the vendor should be clearly defined, specifying which costs should be included and excluded and how these costs should be broken down. Example areas of requirements and comments can be found in Tables 7.1 and 7.2.

Required proposal deliverables
Highlight the key sections that need to be included in the proposal. This may include information concerning the nature and costing for any engagement, company background as well as the specific development, quality assurance and testing approaches.

Additional documentation or system demonstrations required
This should provide supporting evidence and detailed information, if available, for any proposal deliverables.

Request for references
Vendor clients supplying references should have similar culture and requirements to those being specified in the RfP. This may however be problematic as many financial organizations will not wish to assist a potential market rival in their selection process. Any references should be from both recent and long-standing clients, in order to obtain different perspectives on the likely supplier/client relationship.

Who to submit the proposal to and contact point for RfP clarification
This person will act as a gatekeeper for the process, controlling the dissemination of information to the suppliers.

Summary of metrics used as basis for award of contract
The process for awarding the work should be as transparent as possible and clearly communicated to all potential suppliers. The key selection criteria as well as a metric for combining the degree to which the supplier can address the users' needs in each defined requirement should be spec-

Table 7.1 Example checklist of questions regarding a vendor's risk management solution

Functionality	Comments
Risk measures	Methodologies and measures implemented
Instrument coverage	Ability to handle structured products and other OTC derivatives and new instruments
Supported workflow	Do the screens and functionality support the trading style characteristics of the organization?
Integration	Ability to integrate into existing infrastructure
Performance	Processing volume and latency
Calculations	Quality and complexity of models implemented
Reporting	Capability and ability to customize
Regulatory	Ability to address regulatory needs
Reliability	Mean time between failures
Robustness	Availability of hot backups or standby systems
Scalability	How does the system scale with the addition of more hardware (horizontal and vertical scalability)?
Customization	What aspects of the functionality, screens and interfaces can be customized?
Quality of support	What are the service level agreements?
Cost	How is the product licensed; by number of users, locations, asset classes. What limitations are there on future maintenance costs and what are the likely integration and installation costs?
Upgradeability	Commitment of vendor to constantly improve software and match your business and technical strategy

ified, including other factors such as quality, cost, delivery and support and strategic risk (covering the financial soundness and past experience of the vendor). This metric will implicitly quantify acceptable trade-offs within the project, although the precise details of this are unlikely to be made known to the suppliers.

The increasing use of highly configurable or customized development solutions can dramatically complicate the selection process and can result in a perfect fit to requirements but with higher levels of delivery risk, strategic/enhancement risk and cost.

Table 7.2 Example checklist of questions regarding a market data vendor's solution

Data	Comments
Instrument coverage	Is it sufficient for current and future needs?
Quality	What are the source and quality of any market information?
Integration	Ability to obtain and use data in format provided
Support	What are the service level agreements?
Cost	How is the data licensed? Number of instruments, number of users accessing the data, number of geographical locations?
Commitment to continue and expand available data	Commitment of vendor to cover current and future instruments required

Timeline

This should highlight, as a minimum, the timeline for the RfP process, including the submission deadline and when any decision on supplier selection will be made. It should also outline other information such as when legal discussions will begin, the project start date and when any key milestones must be achieved. This will be important in assisting vendors with their resource allocation and determining whether they would be capable of entering into the process. Modifying the date a decision is to be made or varying the start and end dates of the project can seriously complicate this process for the supplier. It is therefore best to ensure that any time schedule is kept to. If this is not possible, all vendors should be promptly informed of any change, so that the implications can be factored in as quickly as possible.

The aim of the RfP process is to obtain a number of competitive and distinct approaches to addressing any requirements and meeting various constraints. The RfP should be structured so as not to act as a barrier to obtaining this information or encourage inappropriate proposals to be provided that will not meet unspecified requirements, and therefore be immediately rejected.

If the RfP contains confidential information, this should also be indicated in order to ensure that it does not become general knowledge within the marketplace. Generally, a non-disclosure agreement (NDA) is signed by all the parties involved in the process to ensure this does not occur.

Communication between organization and vendor

Any communication between the organization and the vendor should be controlled in order to ensure that no supplier obtains an unfair advantage in terms of understanding of the proposal decision process. This may be achieved by formalizing this interaction and ensuring any disclosed information is distributed to all potential suppliers. Typically this process is more informal, but must be managed to ensure that the decision process is not subverted. How much information the organization chooses to divulge, especially in the early stages of the RfP process, is up to those involved. As mentioned earlier, it should provide sufficient detail to allow the supplier to provide the required information, but not so much that any advantage the organization has in later negotiations is lost.

Once the RfP deadline has been met, an experienced and diverse team of experts should validate the proposals, providing different perspectives and views on the responses. This will require technical, business and support knowledge in order to fully access the implications of any proposal. The evaluation process should not penalize a vendor simply because they have provided a more detailed response to a requirement while another has left its statement more ambiguous or omitted important detail. Any such points should be clarified with the supplier to ensure that an objective fair comparison can be performed.

Managing the supplier relationship

Many organizations end the RfP process by providing feedback to all unsuccessful suppliers on why they were not selected. This has the advantage of ensuring that the process is seen as a fair and unbiased one, as well as maintaining good relationships with each supplier involved in the process. This may be important in the future when further RfPs are produced or if contractual negotiations with the initially selected supplier fail and another has to be used.

The contractual stage is when expectations between the vendor and organization are defined and clarified, with fine-tuning of aspects of the supplier's proposal. This will explicitly define each party's rights and liabilities throughout the engagement, legally clarifying issues such as support levels, pricing and payment schedules (based on various deliverables and licensing terms), warranties, dispute resolution, termination, confidentiality, intellectual property ownership, and so on. The contract may include penalty clauses or bonuses for attaining target levels, in order to motivate the supplier throughout the engagement. As a result, a number of metrics will need to be defined in a 'balanced' manner (Chapter 1) in order to effectively manage the delivery of the solution. The pre-contractual negotiation is essential in setting the basis for what may be a long-term relationship.

Any engagement will result in a number of risks and these should be identified and mitigated if necessary. Managing these risks will require ongoing monitoring and management of the relationship, as with any other project. Fundamentally, any client/supplier relationship will need to go beyond clarifying how functionality and support are packaged and delivered; it will require a much closer rapport. It is therefore important to ensure that the manner in which the organization and supplier will work together both now and in the future is agreed as early in the process as possible. This should address how new requirements may be accommodated or how tailored functionality can be added to the solution, either by the vendor or by another third party. One of the key risks of any external relationship is how differences in the strategic direction of the two companies will be managed and any implications for the organization of vendor tie in.

Working with a vendor is an ongoing relationship, which will hopefully last a significant period of time and needs to be managed as such. As a result, it is important to ensure that the internal staff for the project work as a team with staff from the supplier. Project risk can be significantly increased through the addition of internal and external dependencies. Monitoring project progress can be complicated and impeded by communication issues across company boundaries and it should be anticipated that both the client and the vendor will at some point either be late or cause problems with the delivery or installation of the system. Ensuring there is an appropriate mechanism to resolve any such issues will be critical in preventing damage to the relationship with the vendor. Any such damage will only make project success even more unlikely.

Fixed and variable priced contracts

The proposal from a vendor may be fixed priced, variable priced or a combination of the two (for example based on a fixed price for a core product with integration costs based on the amount of effort expended). Fixed price contracts involve project risk transfer in that a defined cost is charged for the work irrespective of the actual cost incurred. As a result, vendors are likely to include a pricing premium to compensate them for taking on this risk. Because of the difficulty in quantifying software project risk, this premium can be significant if the requirements are not viewed as being well defined. Payments for these types of projects will follow a payment schedule defined in the contract, which should be associated with project milestones or deliverables.

Variable priced contracts are typically based on time and material costs incurred by the supplier. They require the client to pay for actual chargeable costs incurred by the supplier on a regular ongoing basis until completion or termination of the project. This exposes the client to the cost implications and uncertainty associated with the project. As a result, these types of projects need to be closely monitored, with realistic estimates of likely costs obtained before the start of any work. A project plan must be used to monitor progress and highlight variances on an ongoing basis. The separation of user and delivery team across two different companies can act as a significant barrier to monitoring project status, which can result in some unpleasant and costly surprises to the client.

Notes

1 R. Brealey and S. Myers, *Principles of Corporate Finance* (McGraw-Hill, 2002)
2 J. C. Hull, *Options, Futures and other Derivatives* (Prentice Hall, 1997)
3 D. Egolf, *Forming Storming Norming Performing: Successful Communications in Groups and Teams* (Writer's Club Press, 2001)
4 R. Templar, *Fast Thinking Appraisal: Work at the Speed of Life* (Prentice Hall, 2000)
5 F. Brooks, *The Mythical Man-month: Essays on Software Engineering* (Addison-Wesley, 1995)
6 S. McConnell, *Software Project Survival Guide* (Microsoft Press, 1998)
7 W. Brown, R. Malveau et al., *Antipatterns: Refactoring Software, Architectures, and Projects in Crisis* (John Wiley 1998)
8 R. Grant, *Contemporary Strategy Analysis* (Blackwell Business, 1995)
9 Finextra, 'Barclays outsources desktop technology to EDS' Finextra.com (4 June 2003)

CHAPTER 8

Quality management and testing

Just as sequences of events can lead to losses from sources of risk within the organization, losses due to defects in software occur because of a sequence of interactions with the system that uncovers those defects. The aim of the testing process is to increase the expected mean time between failures as well as reducing the potential loss that arises when a failure occurs (the *return* aspect of the risk/return equation). Reducing the magnitude of any loss may necessitate adding functionality that ensures potential sources of risk are discovered and resolved as soon as possible. This can be achieved by performing system reconciliations or monitoring certain KRIs within the system.

This leads to two approaches to removing defects from within software. The first is to focus on the events and generate event sequences to validate that the software behaves as expected (that is, there is no uncertainty in outcome). If the outcome is not as expected, the software is *debugged* to discover the source of that failure. The second approach is to focus on the sources of risk and remove them from the software, without considering the sequence of events that could result in failure.

The first strategy is the traditional approach to testing; the tester develops scenarios and stress tests that ensure the software operates correctly when dealing with a range of frequent event sequences, as well as unlikely sequences of events. The low probability event sequences will often focus on the handling of error scenarios arising from unexpected user interaction, or unlikely sequences of system interactions or surrounding infrastructure failure. The second approach moves us into techniques and processes for developing robust and error-free code[1] as well as formal software specification and verification.[2]

THE SOFTWARE TESTING PROCESS

Testing is often seen as the final step in the delivery process. Its aim is to ensure that the delivered software meets the specification for the system and is 'fit for purpose'. Treating testing as a separate and final stage in the software development lifecycle can, however, result in a number of undesirable surprises at the end of a project when delivery and deployment of the system are expected, not delays arising from having to correct the software. By separating testing from the development and requirements process, developers often do not feel accountable or responsible for this aspect of the project. Instead, testing should be seen as an integral part of the software development process with an important role to play throughout the project lifecycle. Frequent and ongoing testing will ensure that:

- Functionality and specified requirements are implemented correctly.
- An objective assessment of progress is produced that can be linked to milestones within the project plan; completed and missing functionality is clearly identified by the successful or unsuccessful execution of the tests.
- Regressions in the development process are identified. This occurs when ongoing development causes previously implemented functionality to fail.
- Inconsistencies between specification and implementation are detected.
- Unspecified behaviour is highlighted early in the project.

The aim of the testing process is to discover software defects before software delivery and deployment. These defects may arise from *bugs* (which are the incorrect implementation of correctly understood requirements), from correctly implementing misunderstood requirements or from missing functionality that has not been included in the development plan. Detecting the results of correctly implementing the wrong functionality can be difficult if the software is not independently verified and tested, based on the actual requirements rather than an interpretation of them.

Making the testing process integral to the development process also shifts the resourcing of this task to earlier in the project, and enables the requirements for testing to be closely integrated with (and to extend) the requirements and specification process. This reduces the likelihood that tests will be derived from misinterpretations of the requirements. It also enables acceptance tests to be defined upfront before implementation so that they do not distract or distort the development process.

Completeness of testing

The goal of the testing process is to ensure that all code paths are verified as supporting the required functionality. Essentially the problem is one of defining a minimum spanning set of test scenarios that include all possible sources of failure or error. To achieve this aim is impossible for all but the simplest of systems or sections of code. Instead we revert to a risk-based approach to testing. Just as with any risk management strategy, managing risk within the software process should focus on the prevention of high probability failures and the areas of the system (that is, sources of risk) where failure can result in large or catastrophic losses. These can be determined and visualized using techniques such as risk assessments or by producing a probability/ impact matrix.

The development process shows us that when software is written the same code paths are often used to handle similar operations. There is therefore no benefit from repeatedly testing a piece of code with similar inputs. How we define what is similar will require some level of understanding of the implementation in order to appreciate when different execution paths are likely to be utilized. This will tend to be at the extreme range, boundary levels or with unexpected inputs. For example, when testing the payout of a financial option,[3] the tester should use price inputs that are below, at and above the strike price as well as extremely high or low input values. Unexpected inputs may include entering negative prices into the system.

Testing concentration

Since the aim of testing is to try to discover defects in the software, the more ways there are for a piece of software to fail, the more tests there should be. The level of testing for a section or unit of code should therefore be comparable with the number of execution paths in that code. As a result, thin client applications will require less testing than fat client applications. Similarly, software that maintains an internal state that changes its behaviour will require greater testing than one that does not, due to the larger number of possible execution paths.

Performance testing should be used where the area of functionality is likely to be a performance bottleneck. Potential performance bottlenecks should have been identified as part of the architectural design but can also be highlighted through the use of performance monitoring tools.

Measuring software risk

The risk management techniques of Chapter 3, which are used to assess operational risk, can also be used to measure risk in the software development process. From a testing perspective, these risks will arise because of the inability of any software development process, like any human activity, to not fail in some manner at some point in time. Risk therefore arises from the inability of a software process to deliver bug-free code that exactly meets the system specification. These failings will then lead to an unexpected loss arising from the unexpected behaviour of the system. Key risk indicators are often used to highlight potential risk or failure within the software development or testing process and may be based on:

- Bug reporting rate as an indication of software quality.
- Bug reporting rate during regression testing as an indication of quality of bug fixes without impacting other functionality.
- Ratio of fixed bugs to new user-reported bugs in a release as an indication of quality of regression testing.
- Resubmission rate of bugs as an indication of problems in the specification or unit testing of changes associated with a bug.
- Testing coverage in terms of percentage of code executed when performing various tests. This can be relatively easily determined using various automated test coverage tools.

- In object-orientated design, the number of lines of code to classes, number of methods per class and distribution of code across classes as an indication of code quality.
- Code defects per line of code for a given user to indicate poor coding quality.

As with any risk monitoring process, a dramatic growth in the level of a KRI acts as a warning indicator that risk is increasing and that the project may be failing due to an inherent problem in the software process.

Levels of testing

Rather than simply testing the entire system and ensuring it behaves correctly for a wide range of event sequences, testing is often performed at various levels of the system. Testing low-level units of software enables the process of code validation to be divided up into more manageable pieces and ensures that testing is embedded within the development process. Whereas the sequence of events that a system may need to deal with is very large, each building block within the system will typically only have to deal with a small subset of these events. Testing can therefore be simplified by testing the interaction of these blocks separately and validating that each is correctly implementing the required functionality. This also enables each block to be stress tested in a manner that may be difficult when it is embedded within a complete system; testing the strength of a bolt within a machine can be more easily achieved by stressing the individual bolt rather than the entire machine.

Embedding testing within the development process also permits testing to begin the moment a unit of code has been successfully completed, providing an objective validation that the piece of work has been completed (rather than leaving testing until all system level functionality is available). As software evolves over time to address changing requirements, it is important to ensure that simple changes to a system do not suddenly result in numerous errors resulting from failures in other implemented functionality (which may arise indirectly from the change). This highlights the importance of ensuring that the individual building blocks within the system and any assumptions of their behaviour are well understood and tested.

Testing may be either *black box* or *white box* in nature. With black box testing, only the public interfaces and externally visible behaviour are used to test the software, treating the unit to be tested as a 'black box' where specific implementation details cannot be seen. The only assumption made is that the piece of functionality being tested should meet the defined specification for the unit. As a result, it is also known as specification testing. White box or glass box testing uses the developer's knowledge of how the functionality is implemented to derive the test cases and may also access private interfaces and data to ensure the correct behaviour. Because its aim is to test the structure of the code and ensure it meets the unit specification, it is also known as structural testing. As with black box testing, the aim of white box testing is also to validate that the specification is correctly met.

Because white box testing makes assumptions about the code structure, these tests can be expensive to maintain. Any change to the software that changes the code structure (even if the observed behaviour remains the same) can break the test. This can result in misleading test case failures. These tests can, however, provide more complete test coverage because they can utilize an understanding of the specific implementation to ensure all code paths are tested. Due to their sensitivity to code changes, they are usually utilized towards the end of the project, when the code base is more stable. White box testing is especially useful when testing software that maintains state. Often this state is not visible externally but can easily be verified by white box testing to ensure its behaviour meets the state transition behaviour derived during the analysis stage of the project. Testing occurs at the following levels:

Unit testing

Testing of an individual self-contained package of software to ensure that it meets its specification. These tests are usually written by individual developers (for efficiency and cost reasons) because they will understand the precise specification being met by the unit of code. All but the most trivial code changes should have unit tests associated with them, in order to verify the change has been correctly implemented. The unit tests should cover the changed functionality as well as verifying that other expected behaviour is unaffected.

Integration testing

Verification that the individual units of software interact and work together in the expected manner. These tests should include fairly long (perhaps even end-to-end) processing paths but the focus is on testing intervening software units and their interaction (for example exception handling, persistence of data, transactions and so on.) They will consider various partitions of the system functionality into logical sections of (overlapping) functionality. Even if all the underlying units of functionality have not been developed, *stub* functionality can be implemented that provides enough of an appearance of functionality to support any higher level process flow testing. This approach is often used to validate high-level connectivity and performance requirements but results in additional development effort to write the required stubs. The resolution of integration issues often requires the involvement of a wide range of project members and so can be difficult and time consuming to solve. As a result, any such issues should be resolved as rapidly as possible.

System specification testing

This refers to testing of the entire system as seen by an end user, to ensure it meets the user requirements. If a use case approach is employed in the requirements phase, the use case can easily be used as the basis for black box system specification testing, verifying the behaviour and interaction of all the units required to implement the use case. System specification testing is an essential project-tracking tool in that it provides a natural quantitative milestone indicating progress towards project completion. It becomes an executable (and so measurable) equivalent of the specified requirements. If the requirements change, tests will fail until explicitly fixed to reflect the altered system behaviour. Interfaces into other systems outside the scope of this project will need to be simulated through the use of simulation software and data. As a result, it will not verify the integration of the software into the production environment, only that it will integrate based on the assumptions and current understanding of those systems (encapsulated in any simulation software).

User acceptance testing (UAT) and deployment or installation testing

UAT is intimately related to the scope of a project. The delivered functionality is defined by the scope of the acceptance tests or some subset thereof, executed on the target user platform and environment, integrating into other external systems within the organization. UAT is usually performed by a group which directly represents the end users and is unconnected with the project team. It is the final check that the system meets the specified requirements, running in the actual production environment (or one virtually identical to it). UAT is the final stage in testing. It relies on:

1. Verification that the system has been correctly implemented, based on passing all the relevant tests.
2. Validation that the requirements document, which the system and UAT is based upon, correctly specifies what the stakeholders actually want.

> This is achieved by verifying that UAT reflects the actual usage of the system and will rely on the quality and completeness of the requirements gathering process. By defining and verifying the UAT requirements early in the project, many potential issues with the user requirements can be resolved.

At the end of this testing, the decision is made whether the system is or is not accepted. If it is not, the system is returned to the software development team for rectification (or in extreme cases, project termination). Only if the requirements gathering process and the development process have both been correctly executed will the system pass UAT.

Types of testing

In order to address the many requirements of testing, different approaches are used to test for specific types of software failure. The relative importance of each of these types of tests will depend on the user requirements, but all should be present to some degree:

Operational tests
This is the most common type of test and verifies behaviour under expected operating conditions. This may also include the behaviour that occurs when processing onerous or incorrect data that is likely to be frequently received.

Regression tests
Regression tests are vital in the later stages of software development. They verify that changes to the system have not resulted in the failure of previously working functionality. This is extremely important when frequent bug fixes are occurring to the system. Levendel[4] has noted that developers generally introduce one new bug for every three that they fix. Developers should therefore consider writing additional regression tests when fixing bugs in order to verify that additional defects are not being introduced. Regression tests are often based on the reuse of other types of tests. Because they should be frequently or continuously performed, in order to highlight regressions in the system, they should be automated wherever possible.

Performance tests
Performance tests verify that the system is capable of achieving the required level of processing specified in the requirements, under different types of load or event sequences. They can be problematic to perform if the

testing environment is not identical or very similar to the production environment. If this is not the case, adjustments must be made to the performance test results so that they are comparable with what will be expected in the actual production environment. It is important that this task is not left until UAT.

Load tests

Load testing verifies the behaviour under different levels of processing load. Typically this concentrates on full load (where the data volumes and number of users accessing the system are at the expected peak or continuous load levels specified in the requirements), stress testing (where the maximum specified levels are attained) and overload testing (where these levels are exceeded to investigate how the system behaves). Although overload scenarios should not necessarily provide the expected behaviour that occurs under normal operating conditions, it is important to ensure that they do not result in any undesirable side effects which cause the system to fail in a catastrophic manner. In other words, failure must be 'graceful'. Load testing should also cover running different user operations at the same time to ensure there are no undesirable timing or other side effects from performing certain tasks concurrently. As for performance testing, a test environment which is identical or similar to that of the final production environment will be required.

Failure tests

As well as testing the correct behaviour of a system under expected inputs, the system should also be stressed to investigate its behaviour under unexpected input conditions, whether this arises via the user interface, in interactions with external systems or through the internal failure of parts of the system. Failure tests often demonstrate deficiencies in the requirements document by highlighting unspecified behaviour under certain conditions. The aims of these tests are to systematically use the system in a manner it was never designed to address. These tests should cover any timing issues or race conditions in using the system, together with failure of infrastructure such as networks, databases and servers. They should also ensure that the system restarts or failover support operates as expected in the event of a serious system failure.

Usability test

Usability tests highlight poorly specified behaviour and assumptions in the user interfaces, and any failure to adhere to style guides. These tests are usually performed manually, verifying that screen layouts, error messages and other pieces of information are displayed in a consistent and usable manner. Because developers tend to focus on functionality rather than usability, many systems can be difficult and cumbersome to use, requiring the complex or unintuitive use of mouse and keyboard to access certain parts of the screen. Many of these issues are obvious the moment the user interface is used under the same time and workload pressures that the end users will face. However, these issues are often not highlighted when developers perform simple usage testing, using trivial or low data-input volumes.

All the tests above should link back to the original requirements and any inconsistencies or unspecified behaviour should be highlighted so that the requirements can be updated and revalidated with the stakeholders. As a result, the functionality and behaviour of the system to be tested should be decided in collaboration with the test manager, senior business analysts, lead software engineers and system architects. Each will be able to provide a different perspective and understanding of the likely failure points of the system.

Once a test has been passed, it should continue to be so in subsequent testing. One of the first work assignments for the test team after running the tests should be to investigate any that are failing. The cause of any failure must be determined and resolved. Because of the side effects caused by the failure of one section of code on another, ignoring failed tests for too long can seriously impact the development process, as it will be difficult to determine the true cause of any failure. This is especially important if the failure is in core functionality that other development will rely on. Because of this a key set of tests, called *smoke tests* are often defined and must be passed before changes are propagated throughout the development team or more detailed testing is performed.

The testing process

Testing, like all other sections of the software development lifecycle, must be carefully planned and not performed in an ad hoc manner. Whenever test cases are run, it is important that this occurs in a predictable and reproducible manner. It is then possible to reproduce test failures and compare the percentage of tests passed in a consistent manner. The implications of this are that any test environment must:

- Return itself to a known state before executing any test scenarios
- Execute any test using defined inputs
- Ensure test results are repeatable by reducing any system unpredictability arising from sequencing or timing issues. This can be achieved by utilizing the same system configuration and load characteristics on each test run.

Both the level and the completeness of testing to be implemented should be decided, communicated to the entire project team and estimates provided for inclusion in the project plan. The interrelationship between different tests should also be determined so that time is not spent on addressing failed integration tests when the underlying unit tests are also failing. Adequate documentation must also be maintained explaining how the tests should be run, the aim of the test and linkages into appropriate requirements and analysis documentation. The general testing approach is to separate the inputs to the system into:

- Initial system state and configuration that defines the system load and data at the start of any testing
- Test data and stimuli that are received and processed by the system
- Simulator configuration defining how any external interface simulators will behave when interacting with the system.

By separating out these different types of data and stimuli, it is possible to reuse test data, test programs and initial system states and configurations. They can then be employed in different combinations, in order to generate a larger number of test scenarios. For example, by changing the system configuration it is possible to extend operational tests to be load tests. Similarly, by using different test data, the processing of different portfolio and instrument types can be investigated under similar conditions.

The testing process (Figure 8.1) will take the input data and generate some type of output. This may be graphical output or data sent to external systems. This output is then compared against a baseline or expected output.

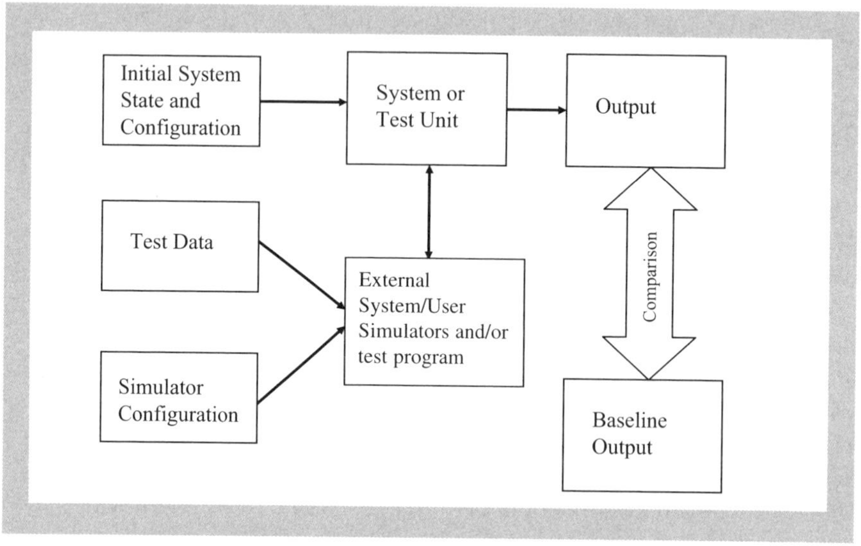

Figure 8.1 The testing process

If the output from the test is the same as the baseline output then the test is passed. Differences between the output and the baseline will indicate a failed test, the cause of which must be determined. This may be due to:

- Incorrect baseline output
- Change in test data, test program, simulators or configurations
- Change in system specification
- Incorrect or unimplemented system behaviour
- Incorrect test environment configuration or set-up

If the cause is due to a change in system behaviour or specification, resulting in the system no longer meeting the user requirements, or due to an error in the test program, the error should be assigned to an appropriate member of the development team. The testing team can resolve other causes of test failure by either modifying the test data or regenerating the output baseline so that it matches the expected output.

Although as much automation as possible is desirable, this must be weighed against the cost of setting up such environments and any maintenance required. For example, some GUI testing tools can be highly sensitive to changes in the GUI layout. Since this is an area that often changes with user feedback, it is also an area of automated testing that can result in exceptionally heavy maintenance early on in the development process. As a result, initial testing is often performed manually while there are frequent changes, before being automated when the GUI is more stable.

Test reporting

As with any risk management process, the testing process should maintain a record of the results of testing, together with a description of those results, so that progress and setbacks can be clearly monitored over time. This information can be used to derive KRIs and highlight individual sources of risk within a project. For example, the performance of individual developers can be monitored by tracking the frequency of defects within their code or the time taken to resolve failed regression tests.

Having performed the test, it is important that the results are communicated to all those involved in the software project. This not only increases transparency of the process, aiding project management, but also provides information for testing meetings where common experiences between all the team (testers, developers, business analysts, project managers) can be shared.

A priority or test score should be assigned to the passing of each test. For some tests, such as performance or stress tests, different scores may be attained when the system is able to process higher volumes or handle ever more complex failure cases. The evolution of these scores and the tests passed then provides an independent record of project progress that can be monitored and linked into managing the project plan. To support this monitoring process, additional test notes can be added to the final test report that give more subjective or summary information. This provides context to the progress of the testing at any particular moment in time.

TOTAL QUALITY MANAGEMENT

The aim of testing within the software development process is to examine various behaviours of a system and compare these to the baseline requirements. It is, however, difficult to ensure high quality software purely by testing and debugging it. Instead quality must be embedded throughout the software development lifecycle and built into the software process. As noted in Chapter 4, the later a bug is discovered, the more expensive it is to fix. By reducing the number of bugs in the software and ensuring implemented functionality is correct first time, costs can be dramatically reduced.

Total quality management (TQM) tries to provide management and control structures that focus on ensuring quality and constant ongoing process improvement throughout the project. Quality is defined as being those qualities that will lead to stakeholder satisfaction. TQM must involve all project members with an aim to instil a culture of developing high quality code that adheres to any coding standards and is delivered to schedule and budget. Reviews and testing then become merely a validating process, certifying that the software does indeed meet the user requirements. Many techniques for software process improvement have been developed to provide developers with the discipline and tools to manage their performance and software quality.[5]

Software refactoring

Refactoring[6] is a disciplined approach to improving the quality of software or architectural design in terms of maintainability and structure without introducing new behaviours, after the initial implementation has been written. Software should be neither over nor under engineered; it should implement what is necessary to meet current functional and quality requirements in a maintainable manner. Over-engineered solutions, often produced in the hope of providing additional future flexibility and sophistication, can lead to complex software which takes longer to develop and is also more difficult to understand and maintain. Similarly, under-engineered solutions require significant changes or rewriting to handle even the simplest changes, which may ripple through the design. Instead, a balanced approach is needed where the software is no more complex than it need be but is structured so that it can be refactored to support additional functionality as required, in an evolutionary manner.

Refactoring often involves the clarification and simplification of the refactored code, removing any duplication or poor design. This may involve the refactoring of software into accepted *design patterns*. Design patterns can improve the comprehensibility of code by basing the design on well-documented and understood approaches. Developers should, however, beware of using patterns when they are not appropriate; a condition known as being 'pattern happy'. It is also absolutely essential that the ability to refactor is not used as an excuse for poor quality design or code.

Reviews

Various types of review process can be used to improve software quality. These reviews may also be extended to include documentation and testing procedures in order to ensure the appropriateness and correctness of any requirements and testing being performed. Reviews should be performed frequently during the development process, typically coinciding with delivery milestones that mark the completion of a section of code or piece of functionality. The review process, just like other aspects of software development, is iterative, dynamic and constantly improving through refactoring and refinement. During the first iteration, a large number of issues are likely to be uncovered. The appropriate project team members will then need to resolve these issues before further reviews occur. In following reviews there should be fewer and fewer issues, until all those involved in the review process approve the resolution of all the highlighted issues. Although ensuring convergence and agreement of the resolution of any issues can be difficult to manage, the process has the advantage that the whole review team will be the owner of the end product. The question of who causes a defect to occur should then never arise, as it will be the responsibility of the entire team to ensure a defect-free system is produced. The 'author is no longer here, so nobody understands this code' situation will also be eliminated, reducing any maintenance risk in the project.

Code and design reviews

Code and design reviews are formal meetings where approaches and models are discussed with all interested parties for comments and approval. Frequent review and assessment of the proposed design and architecture is key for any project. Only by reviewing assumptions, design decisions and progress can project risks be highlighted and then mitigated. By involving all key personnel in decision making at the earliest possible point, the quality of decisions should be greatly improved. This review can act as a break point for the team to refocus on what has been produced and enable the project to change direction if it is off course. It also provides individual developers with a high level 'helicopter view' of the project, putting their effort into perspective, and permitting them to raise any issues that they may not previously have been aware of. Even if no changes are made, it can help act as a milestone for the team to acknowledge their achievements so far and also provides an open and visible marker for the project manager. These reviews can also prevent group denial of outstanding but unaddressed issues before they become a major problem later in the project.

Code inspection

Slightly less resource intensive and more informal, the code inspection process requires the review of any changes to or new pieces of functionality by an independent developer who is familiar with the overall solution and any development standards. This should also cover associated documentation and unit or regression tests. As with other qualitative approaches to risk measurement and reduction, code inspections provide a holistic but not necessarily complete approach. Code inspections can also be used to cross-train team members in different parts of the code, creating a sense of collective ownership. This has the advantage of helping to create an open culture and reduce any specific dependencies on individuals within the project team, increasing resource fungibility, which reduces project risk. The inspection process should ensure appropriate architectural standards and patterns are adhered to and that the reporting of errors, raising of exceptions, and persistence of data are all handled in an identical manner, using common design patterns where appropriate.

The aim of code inspections is to highlight defects in the software and design process or deviations from various standards, thus improving code quality and maintainability. The inspection process should highlight any incorrect assumptions in the use of other pieces of code which could result in system failure or incorrect operation. Developer egos or opinions should not be allowed to dominate this process, and any coding standards should be common sense and accepted by the entire project team, rather than being blindly enforced dogmatically. The failure to adhere to design or coding standards will result in the system becoming more inconsistent and difficult to understand and maintain, all of which will increase project risk.

Code walkthroughs

Similar to code inspection, this is when a developer responsible for a section of code leads one or more members of the development team through various scenarios and stress tests for that code. These other developers should ask questions, make comments concerning the implementation, highlight possible errors or missed cases and non-adherence to standards. The very process of articulating code behaviour and explaining coding decisions can often enable the developer to realize failings or omissions in the code. This process should also highlight any *antipatterns*. Software antipatterns[7] are patterns found within code that impose certain constraints, limitations on maintainability or failings into the code structure. They can have a major impact on code quality and should be removed by refactoring.

VALIDATING, VERIFYING AND BACKTESTING APPROACHES AND MODELS

Any approaches used either to develop software or as the basis for modelling risk within the organization will be subject to a number of uncertainties and potential failings:

- Is the approach or model appropriate given the context of the organization and the risks it takes?
- Is the approach or model correctly implemented?
- Does the outcome of actual events support the hypothesis on which we base our decisions?

This introduces three tasks that need to be performed:

1. Validating that an approach is appropriate given the types of risk or organizational context.
2. Verifying that it is being correctly implemented and used.
3. Scientifically testing any assumptions by statistically comparing expected and actual outcomes and ensuring that they do not significantly disagree.

These three tasks can be seen most effectively in the verification and validation of risk models used to price and risk manage financial instruments, but similar techniques also apply to selecting an appropriate software development process in order to assess, manage and mitigate development risk.[8]

Model risk

Models are simplifications of reality, with inherent assumptions and deficiencies. As a result, these assumptions must be investigated to ensure that they are likely to be valid, model inputs must be verified to ensure that they are correct and model outputs should be tested against actual events and losses to ensure that expected and actual outcomes do indeed agree (Figure 8.2). By both validating and verifying processes and models it is possible to ensure that any deficiencies do not result in significant failures in the risk management process. All models, because of their inherent assumptions, will have limitations and conditions when the model will fail and not match real world behaviour. Managing model risk is concerned with understanding when and why they might fail, and ensuring models are improved if they are not able to

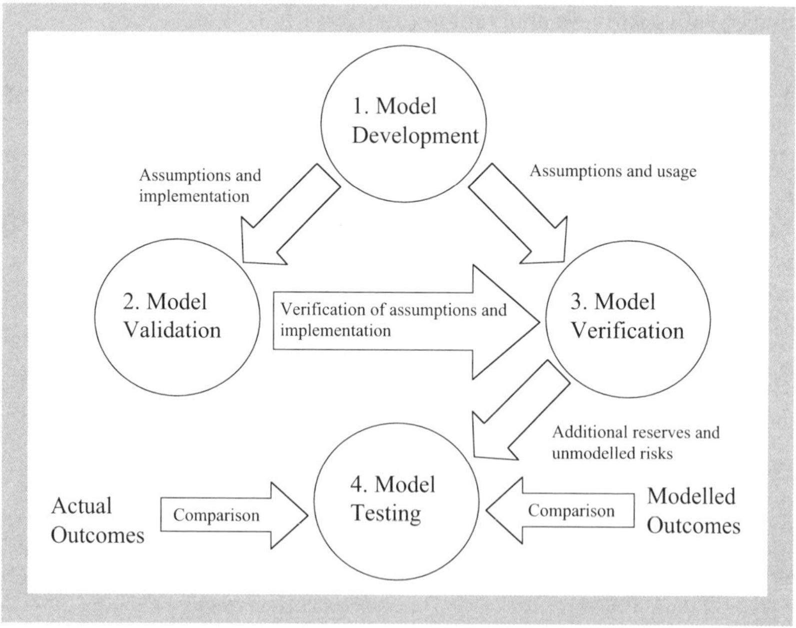

Figure 8.2 Interaction of model development, validation, verification and testing groups

adequately reflect actual risk. Within most financial organizations there are four interacting tasks performed around the risk modelling process that support this aim:

1. Models are developed by various model development groups within the organization. For pricing and risk managing market and credit risk in individual traded instruments, these groups are likely to be associated with the trading operation that will utilize their models. Because operational risk permeates the entire organization, these models, as with the models used to aggregate market and credit risk across the organization, tend to be centralized in risk management groups. This group is responsible for deciding what assumptions will be made by the model, given their understanding of the risks being modelled. These assumptions will then be highlighted to the traders, risk managers and risk validation group.
2. The models are validated to ensure that they are correctly implemented, with any assumptions or deficiencies analysed and documented, based on any potential differences between actual expected and modelled event behaviour. Only by understanding these models and modifying them where necessary can the risk manager and trader have any confidence in the resulting risk information and identify the occurrence of events that may result in the models failing. Model validation usually occurs in risk validation groups or is undertaken by external auditors, who are independent of the model development groups.
3. Once the deficiencies of any models have been understood, the use of these models together with the correctness of any model inputs must be verified. Model verification ensures that these models are not used inappropriately and the sources of any input parameters are correct; any model will be designed for use in certain situations that exhibit the behaviour assumed in the model. This task is often performed by a control function within the organization. Any risk arising from unmodelled risks, model mis-specification, unsuitability or uncertainty in the input parameters will have had reserves made against it in order to provide an additional buffer to the calculated regulatory and economic capital. These reserves retain some of the trading P&L so that any reported trading profit is more conservative than it would have been, having been reduced to account for potential unmodelled future loses or risks.
4. Models should also be tested and compared (or *backtested*) against actual events to ensure that predicted and actual losses do indeed

agree. Any discrepancy between expected outcomes and actual outcomes must be statistically acceptable for any probabilistic models and within acceptable accuracy limits for exposure-based approaches. If this is not the case, it is likely that any risk mitigation strategies implied by these models may not in fact have reduced the risk profile as expected. Model event sensitivities together with the actual occurrence of various events are often compared against any P&L in order to provide some level of *P&L explain*, where the occurrence of various events is associated with individual returns that comprise the total P&L. This can highlight situations where P&L cannot be adequately explained, which may highlight a deficiency in the model or an area of risk which is not being monitored or included in this explanation process. The nature of scientific and model testing in particular is that models can only be rejected, not validated as always being a true representation of reality. This is clearly problematic when trying to verify models that deal with large impact, low probability events, which is a concern for operational risk modelling. Even where a model has been shown to be deficient, the cause of that deficiency may be due either to inaccurate or incorrect subjective model input parameters or a flaw in the assumptions of the model.

A new business process is usually implemented to ensure that new types of instrument can be risk managed, settled and accounted for before any transactions are executed. This may require the provision of ad hoc functionality that feeds into the usual risk management, settlement and accounting systems within the organization. The volume of these new types of transactions will however be limited until the associated operational risk can be reduced through the implementation of more robust processing mechanisms. Often the initial processes will rely heavily on spreadsheets and manual processes to make up for the deficiencies of existing systems. As a result, they will have high levels of operational risk associated with them.

Backtesting

Whenever risk is measured it is important to compare actual against predicted outcomes in order to ensure that the two do indeed agree. The most common form of this type of testing is the backtesting of P&L against VaR, which is often a regulatory requirement.

P&L is an inherently backward looking measure. It indicates what profit or loss has been made by a business unit, and will comprise realized (which arises from an actual cash flow, possibly by selling a position in a financial instrument) and unrealized P&L (which arises from changes in the current market value of financial instruments). Unrealized profit may equally be lost in the future; what is important are the forward looking measures such as expected return and any associated risk. The aim of backtesting P&L is to validate the risk predicted by a model against any actual losses and to ensure that they are not statistically significantly different. For VaR, this is achieved by measuring P&L and ensuring that any VaR limit is not exceeded more frequently than the calculated confidence level would imply.

When validating VaR, the reported *'dirty'* P&L is modified to omit any sources of profit or loss that are not included in the VaR model. This resulting *'clean'* P&L does not include any P&L arising from intra-day trading, new trades or changes in reserves that may be taken over the time period used in the VaR calculation. This figure should only include P&L arising from market moves, carry/funding costs and market-related adjustments. Many organizations also backtest against dirty P&L or compare dirty and clean P&L to ensure that there are no unexpected or unexplained differences between the two. Significant divergence can indicate aspects of risk that are not being captured or monitored by the risk process. Dirty P&L is often much easier to measure because it represents 'bottom line' P&L that will be recorded in the GL. It is also the underlying driver of actual losses for the organization that will impact its financial viability.

Although the VaR calculation is typically a one sided test in that it focuses only on potential losses, it can also be used to determine the likelihood of profits being much higher than expected. This figure can then also be validated against P&L to further validate the model. The cause of any exceptions should be thoroughly investigated to understand whether they are due to statistical effects or deficiencies in the data or modelling process.

Processes such as backtesting also have complex reporting and analysis requirements so that the precise source and cause of any discrepancy can be determined. When backtesting VaR, the backtesting may need to be applied at the subportfolio level, in order to discover what types of instrument or trading strategy have caused this discrepancy.

Backtesting approaches can also be used to compare the realization of risks (those problems which did occur) within a project against its various risk measures (those problems that could occur), in order to verify their accuracy. Where these project measures are shown to be deficient or inappropriate, they should be replaced by measures that are more likely to provide early warning signals. Similarly the effectiveness of any testing procedures and expected defect levels can be compared against actual end user reported defect levels.

REPLACING EXISTING FUNCTIONALITY

One of the most difficult requirements to address is the ability to account for any discrepancy in the output from the existing system and that produced by the new system. It is not unusual for unfounded confidence to be placed in the existing system, even if it is understood to be deficient. The project team will then need to show that any discrepancy is due to a failure of the existing functionality and not due to a defect in the new system. As a result, there is usually a period when both systems are run in parallel and the outputs from each are compared. Unfortunately, differences will arise not only because of previously undetected defects in either system, but also from:

- Differences in input data, which will include any data concerning sources of risk together with risk events that cause any losses
- Differences in the methodology used to measure risk
- Differences in the representation of that risk.

Being able to precisely reconcile two systems can be extremely difficult, if not impossible to achieve, and can end up just confirming that the specification of each system is indeed different. Some level of comparability (Figure 8.3) may, however, be achieved by:

- Inputs into the new system being filtered or modified to match those of the existing system
- Output from each system being transformed into a comparable form.

It is important to be able to ensure that there are no unexplained material discrepancies and that any explanation does not arise from a failing in the new system, otherwise the stakeholders are unlikely to have enough confidence to wish to deploy the new system. The level to which this reconciliation process is performed will depend on the

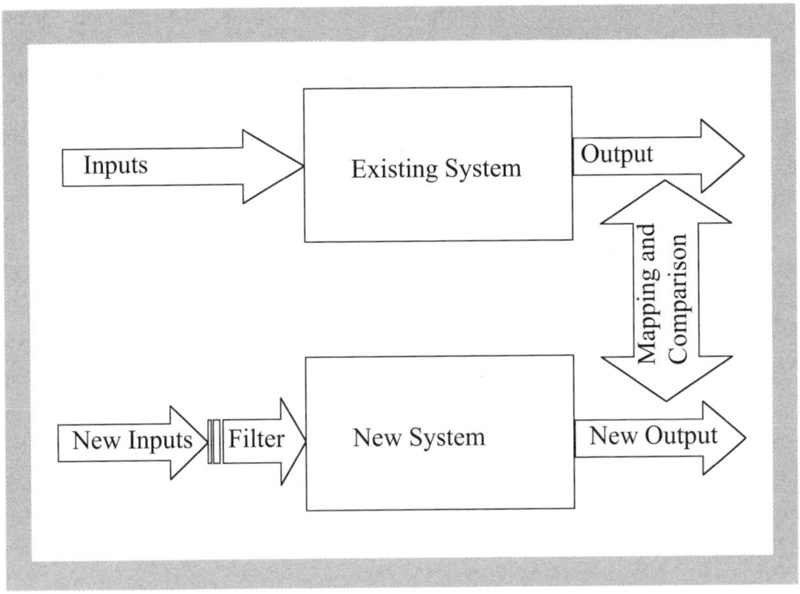

Figure 8.3 The system reconciliation process

amount of other testing executed and the level of material discrepancy that occurs. This process is often one of diminishing returns and the risk/return trade-off must be carefully managed. Transparent prototypes, developed using less robust or performant tools such as spreadsheets or mathematical workbench tools, can help to verify new functionality by creating a baseline to compare against the output from the new system. Provided these prototypes can be independently verified, it should be possible to convince any stakeholders of the correct operation of the new system in specific cases where it significantly differs from the existing system.

Notes

1 S. Maguire, *Writing Solid Code* (Microsoft Press, 1993)
2 R. Backhouse, *Program Construction and Verification* (Prentice Hall, 1986)
3 J. C. Hull, *Options, Futures and other Derivatives* (Prentice Hall, 1997)
4 Y. Levendel, 'Reliability analysis of large software systems: defect data modelling', *IEEE Transactions on Software Engineering,* **16** (2) Feb 1990 141–52

5 S. Zahran, *Software Process Improvement – Practical Guidelines for Business Success* (Addison-Wesley, 1998)
6 M. Fowler, *Refactoring – Improving the Design of Existing Code* (Addison-Wesley, 2000)
7 W. Brown, R. Malveau et al., *Antipatterns: Refactoring Software, Architectures, and Projects in Crisis* (John Wiley and Sons, 1998)
8 W. Florac and A. Carleton, *Measuring the Software Process: Statistical Process Control for Software Process Improvement* (Addison-Wesley, 1999)

CHAPTER 9

Deployment, configuration and change management

The term *configuration management* refers to how the software process deals with recording and managing change. This includes the issues of source code control, versioning, building and deploying the system, as well as defect and change tracking. Controls should be built in to the change management process in order to ensure that all required activities and tasks are performed before the release of any system. For example, a problem report should exist and have been approved prior to the modification of any software or documentation; review activities should have been completed before allowing changes to be visible to other developers.

The configuration management process highlights the iterative nature of software development. Rarely is a system ever developed and deployed with no further changes being required. Managing this process from both a risk and a resourcing perspective is essential for the ongoing success of the project.

DEFECTS AND CHANGE REQUESTS

The aim of any configuration management process is to control software development activities from both a productivity and a risk perspective as well as to ensure that any resources are correctly deployed within the project. This can be especially important when managing defects and change requests (Figure 9.1) as the new tasks arising from this are unlikely to have been explicitly included in the initial project plan.

It is important to distinguish between code defects (functionality that has been incorrectly implemented), system configuration issues (incorrect functionality due to internal or external data or system set up) and change requests (functionality that has been implemented according to the requirements specification, which has now changed). The drivers for these types of problems are distinct in that:

- Defects arise from the software implementation process
- System configuration or data issues arise from the incorrect deployment of the system or incorrect data or data maintenance processes

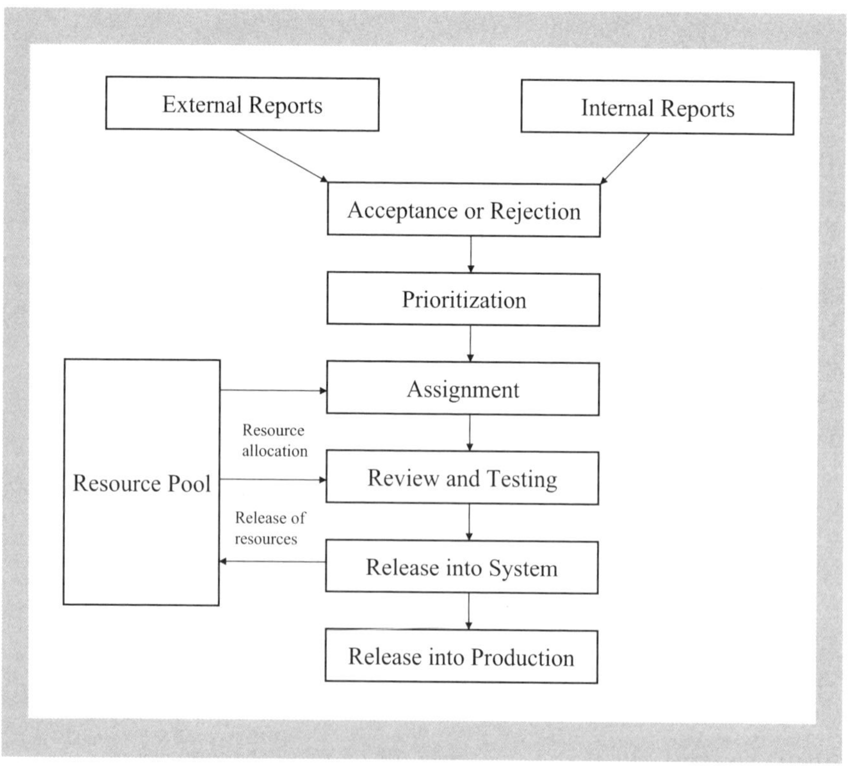

Figure 9.1 The defect and change request management process

- Change requests arise from failure of the communication and validation of requirements between the business analyst and the stakeholders, or a misapprehension or misunderstanding of the true requirements by the stakeholder.

Managing the risks associated with each of the above can be very different. Defects can often have as much impact as a small change request and should not necessarily be treated too lightly. An explicit process for prioritizing the removal of any known defects should be defined. This will ensure that the resolution of any defects takes an appropriate place in the project plan, without unnecessarily impacting any critical delivery milestone dates. Batching a number of related defects together into a single task can be used to increase the efficiency of this process; when making a change within a section of code, it is usually most efficient to perform other similar changes that impact the same area of code at the same time. When defects are serious or where their resolution may have significant side effects, it may be necessary to treat them more like change requests in order to ensure any impact on the project is well understood.

Change requests tend to have a much wider impact on the overall design of a system; correcting a code defect typically only impacts the section of the code where the defect can be found. Changes in functionality can, however, require modification to the design and interaction of a number of disparate parts of the system. Change requests also impact the project plan because they increase or change project scope. The number of change requests that are included within a release of a system can have serious consequences for project delivery, a point discussed in Chapter 7.

For these reasons, change requests need to be managed explicitly. All change requests should be given due consideration when proposed, but they must be reviewed and approved in order to determine their impact in terms of cost, project schedule, quality and risk. This impact needs to be understood by all the parties (stakeholders and project team) concerned. The aim of any change control process must be to protect the project from unnecessary changes and ensure that any changes that are proposed have been well thought out and specified. Because work on change requests competes with other work, it must be explicitly managed and made visible within the project plan. In this way the stakeholders are less likely to be surprised if or when delivery dates start to slip due to the impact of these changes.

If the change occurs early enough in the project and is clearly related to an ongoing or not yet started task, reworking the tasks within the project may enable the request to be included within existing project work, perhaps with less slippage than originally estimated. However, not all change controls will fit into existing work in this way and so new tasks will need to be created and assigned resources. Again, similar change requests should be grouped together and performed as a single task.

SOFTWARE PROBLEM REPORTS (SPRs)

Software defects or requests to change functionality should be reported to the project team through a well-defined process. This usually involves the production of a software problem report (or SPR), which defines the nature of the problem and provides complete traceability and status monitoring for the problem. SPRs can be generated either internally within the project or by end users. As a result they may relate to either externally visible system issues, or internal software and design-related issues. An SPR should capture enough information to fully define the nature of any problem and will need to contain details such as:

Person raising the SPR
This should also highlight whether the SPR is being raised internally within the project or by an external user.

SPR identifier
A unique identifier, usually automatically assigned, that is used to track the SPR and assist in traceability.

External reference identifier
If the user or support groups also assign this SPR a unique identifier it too should be recorded to assist reconciliation within the SPR process.

Category and area relating to SPR
This should provide enough information to determine the team that will be responsible for resolving the SPR. It should also categorize the nature of the SPR, which may be a software defect, change request, error in documentation, support issue, configuration issue, failure in the testing process and so on. Many users will assume that any behaviour that does not agree with their understanding of what the system should do is a defect in the system. As a result, some defects are likely to be modified to change requests after further clarification and discussion.

Summary and description
High-level description of the nature of the problem, with a more detailed description of the defect or change request. This should detail why the reported problem is an issue.

Severity (critical, serious, non-critical)
Categorization of the severity of the problem. This may be changed after investigation of the cause of the SPR and on further discussion with the users or project team.

Status
The status of the SPR. This may be one of:
Mistaken: the SPR was incorrectly reported
Duplicate: of an existing SPR (in which case this SPR should be linked to the existing SPR, in order to ensure traceability)
Active: an active SPR whose state may then be one of:

- New – initially reported
- Verified – verified and confirmed as being an SPR
- Allocated – detailing the resources responsible for its resolution
- Under investigation – detailing cause of the SPR, estimated effort required to resolve and any proposed solution. This step may also determine the true cause to be an external data or configuration issue that requires no change to the system. Once the problem has been investigated the priority of the SPR may be modified depending on the cost and benefit of addressing it
- Fixed – the developer has resolved the SPR
- Tested/reviewed – an independent test and review of the change has been performed

Integrated into stable release: fix has been integrated into the development system.

Version of system SPR relates to and any specific environment details
This will assist in replicating the SPR by being able to relate it to a specific version of the system. Any environment-specific information can also help verify that it is not due to the deployment environment.

How to repeat
Before an SPR can be resolved, the underlying cause of the problem must be determined. The cause of any problem and the point at which it is apparent can be in totally different parts of a complex system. Knowing

how to repeat the process that resulted in the SPR will ensure that any cause can be more easily determined. If the steps taken to repeat the behaviour reported in the SPR are incomplete or incorrect, it can be exceptionally difficult and time consuming to determine the exact sequence required to reproduce it.

Version of files the fix is included in
This will indicate at what point the change is made in the source code control system. It will assist in ensuring it is included or omitted from a future production release of the system.

A key control in this process is to ensure that different people perform the roles responsible for modifying the status of an SPR. This introduces independent verification of resolution or progress in resolving the SPR.

SOURCE CODE CONTROL

Source code or version control[1] is the process of managing and versioning changes to project artefacts. Even for a single developer the benefits are clear. It provides both a history of changes (usually with a description of why any change was made) and the ability to view and recover information as of some previous point in time. Source code control is an important process in attaining the higher CMM levels, providing traceability and a clear audit trail of any changes – what was changed, by whom, why and when. When multiple people work on the same project artefacts for overlapping or multiple releases of a system to different deployment environments, the issues of co-ordination and controlling changes become considerably more complex.

Concurrent development, where multiple developers work on the same code base, is a fact of life. One of the major problems arising from this is that the work performed by one developer is likely to depend upon or interact with that produced by other developers. In order to verify the correct operation of the integrated system, this dependency or interaction is a key requirement at certain stages of the development process. However, prior to the completion and testing of each unit of work, this can lead to interference between different development streams, making the process of concurrent development unworkable.

The source code control system permits members of the project team to obtain (or *check out*) copies of project artefacts such as software or documentation, which they can then work on privately. Their changes will not be visible to others until they commit or *check in* those changes to the source code control system. This check-in process ensures that the version which is being updated is the same as the version on which the modifications have been made. If this is not the case, and more recent changes have been checked in since this artefact was checked out, then these overlapping changes must be merged together into a new version of the artefact where none of the overlapping changes are overwritten or lost (Figure 9.2).

The merge process produces a new version of an artefact, which tries to include both the changes in the version being committed together with any changes that have been checked in since this version was obtained from the source code control system. These overlapping changes may conflict or be difficult to resolve. This can result in a complex and time-consuming process that can introduce additional risk into the project through the possibility that some changes are lost during this merge process. Reoccurring defects or omitted functionality will then result.

The problem of conflicting overlapping changes within the source code control system can be prevented by developers obtaining *locks* on artefacts

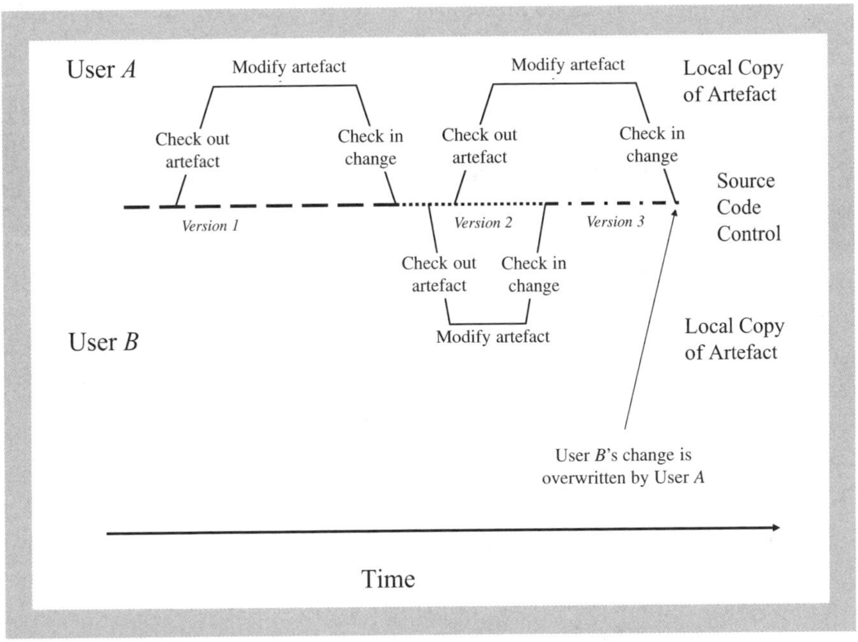

Figure 9.2 Non-conflicting and conflicting changes of artefacts under source code control

that they wish to modify. These locks prevent other developers from changing that artefact until the lock has been released, which occurs once any changes have been committed into the source code control system.

The process of locking or merging changes into the source code control system results in an essentially linear sequence of changes being performed and checked in, one after another. This is an acceptable approach where each individual change is self-contained and, once made, should be included in the version available to the entire project team. It does not, however, support the concept either of different groups of developers sharing and working on essentially different versions of the system (which will be merged together at a later date) or of artefacts being checked in when they are in an incomplete state and so should not be seen by other members of the project. Permitting developers to privately check in artefacts in an incomplete state provides them with all of the benefits of source code control (being able to return to a previous version, look at changes and so on) but without having to make these changes visible and possibly interfere with other development.

The ability to utilize the source code control system so that developers can check in changes that not all other developers need to see is supported by having a *branching* model. This permits the code base to be isolated at a given point of time so that concurrent development by different groups or individuals then causes the code paths to diverge from each other until any changes are ready to be integrated and merged back together. The initial branch from which development diverges is called the mainline branch and is the branch into which all changes will need eventually to be combined. *Tags* are often used within source code control systems to link together individual versions of items within the source code control system that combine into a single working release of the system. An example of the branching process can be seen in Figure 9.3. The branch names are depicted by boxes, with tagged versions of each branch represented by circles, and the addition of features as diamonds. The merging of a branch into another or back into the mainline can be seen as dashed lines.

The branching process has the benefit of ensuring consistency and reliability, with developers able to modify and share changes with certain other developers using the same branch, but to not impact those who are using different branches. This enables significant changes to certain parts of a system to be made without impacting other development. Once those changes have all been completed and tested, the branch can then be merged back. The aim of this approach is to reduce the chances of large-scale changes breaking the mainline, which is typically used as the basis

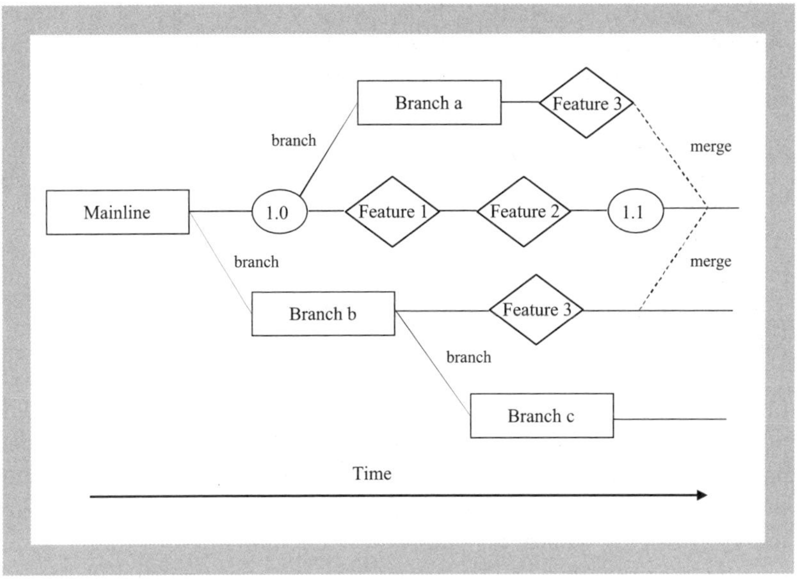

Figure 9.3 Example of a branching diagram

of ongoing development. It can increase developer productivity but results in the additional overhead of increased co-ordination within the project and the merging of numerous isolated changes into a single integrated view of the system at some point in the future. There are two extremes to branching policy:

Early branching
Each developer creates a branch from the mainline and works on that from the very start of the project. These changes are then merged back into the mainline at appropriate points in the development.

Deferred or lazy branching
Each developer works on the mainline unless or until working on a major task that conflicts with or could disrupt the work of other developers. This type of branching can be used to remove the need for *code freezes* where developers cannot commit their changes until a stable, tested version of the system can be generated and tagged. Instead of creating a code freeze, a separate release branch is created while development continues on other branches. Once the release is stable it is merged back into the mainline.

As well as having a branching policy within the project, there should also be a merging policy. This will indicate how frequently branches should be merged and who should be responsible for performing this and resolving any issues from the merge process. The frequency of merging will dictate how early on in the development process problems and risks arising from integrating different development efforts are highlighted. Being able to detect these issues early in the development process will however be at the expense of having to perform a frequent or continual merge effort. Ideally, changes should not be combined into the mainline branch until any resulting merged code has been successfully run and tested.

It should be clear that the branching process can increase both project risk and productivity. The project workflow should be decomposed into separate lines of development that can then be recombined back into the mainline branch so as to maximize productivity but with the least amount of additional effort and risk from performing any merge process. There are many policies for determining when branching or merging should occur. The precise approach will depend on the nature of any concurrent development and the risk appetite of the project.

The project's risk appetite for branching is, however, likely to change throughout its life; early on in the development it may be less risk averse than when the system is in production. The project manager may be willing to trade-off greater productivity against a higher level of risk at the start of a project, which will not be acceptable when maintaining a system already being used in a production environment. This implies that the branching policy of a project may change over time.

When selecting a source code control system, the following may be required:

- Distributed repository in multiple locations.
- Accessibility in a performant manner from all development locations.
- Integration with the chosen development environment, processes and tools.
- Concurrent users and support for adequate branching.
- Links to the software problem reporting and project management system to ensure traceability.
- Efficient visualization of different versions of information under source code control.

- Ability to perform validation checks before information is checked in to certain branches. This can be used to ensure that unit or smoke tests are passed before any changes may be committed and helps to ensure the stability of the software within the source code control system and prevent incorrect functionality impacting other developers.
- Transaction support for complex wide-ranging changes. For example, all the changes are checked in together or none are; this ensures that a consistent set of changes are always checked in, rather than permitting the check-in of some to succeed and others to fail, possibly due to previously unnoticed merge conflicts.
- Event triggers so that committed changes can notify other users or start build processes.
- Ability to determine which artefacts are being modified (or are checked out).
- Viewing of a history of changes for artefacts within the source control system.
- Visually comparing differences between different versions of artefacts.
- Versioning of artefacts and ability to revert to a previous version (even if it has been deleted) as of some given date.
- The ability to synchronize to the latest or a previous version of an artefact.

MAINTAINING TRACEABILITY

The configuration management process must help to ensure traceability is maintained. Defects and change requests must be associated with given versions of the system and the impact of any change must ripple and be recorded throughout the development process. This should update all aspects of the project and ensure the information is synchronized and versioned. In particular, change requests will modify the requirements, which will modify the analysis and design and hence the implementation (Figure 9.4). These changes to the requirements will also need modifications to be made to any tests associated with these changed requirements. Failure at any point in this chain of dependencies will result in an implementation that will fail during the software testing phase, either because the unmodified tests do not now match the output from the modified implementation or because the implementation does not reflect the latest requirements that are included in UAT.

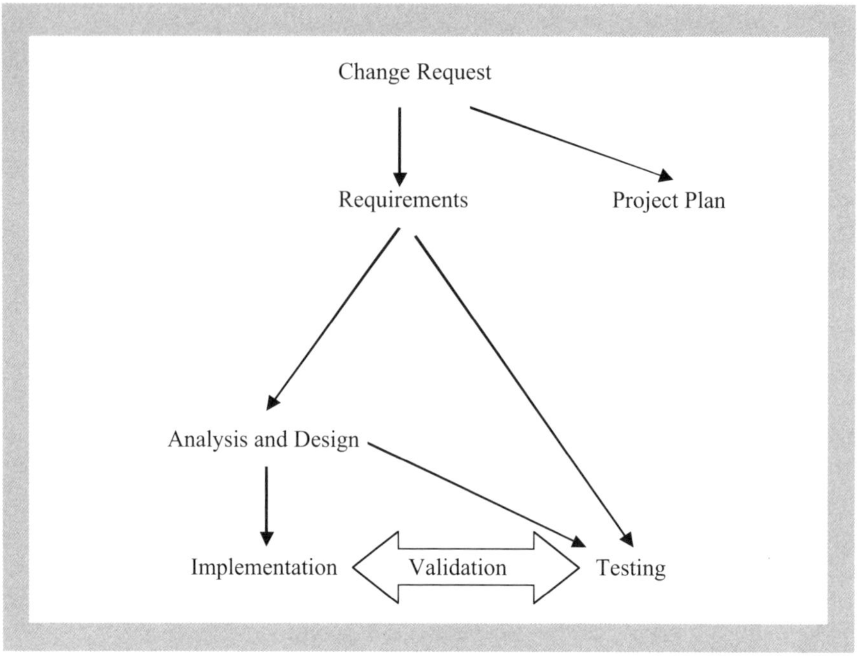

Figure 9.4 The impact of change requests on traceability

VERSIONING SYSTEM RELEASES

The aim of versioning releases is to indicate the compatibility between different versions of a system, or components, and modules within a system. It also provides a tag to identify versions of artefacts within the source code control system used in a given release, against which change requests and defects can be reported. There are many approaches to versioning software but the generally accepted approach is to break down a release into:

Major release
This indicates significant change or improvement in a system or software component that is usually associated with a change in an interface or externally observed behaviour. This will mean that major releases are not *backward compatible,* that is they cannot be replaced by earlier major releases.

Minor release
This is a feature enhancement of a non-trivial nature that does not change any existing interfaces or behaviour of the system. As a result, compo-

nents or systems can be upgraded to a version within the same major release with a higher minor release number without any noticeable change in existing functionality.

Incremental or point release
This does not add any new features or functionality, and is purely used to address and correct defects within the system or component. It will not modify any interfaces or specified behaviour.

Typically this results in a version number of the form X.Y.Z, where X indicates the major release number, Y the minor release number within that major release and Z is the point release number. The version may also be clarified by further alphanumeric characters highlighting certain types of intermediate release during the development process such as:

Development or build release
Used for development use, this represents a stable version of the system on which further development should occur. It provides a stable version of core functionality where key aspects may be overridden by functionality being implemented and developed locally to each developer or development team.

Snapshot release
A development release which is tagged within the source code control system.

Release candidate
A snapshot release which is built and installed into the quality assurance (QA) environment for full testing and quality assurance. This may lead to a release into the production environment.

Alpha release
A snapshot release for development testing that has not yet been fully tested.

Beta release
These are previews of releases that can be used to showcase new, not fully tested functionality, or to provide an early fix to software defects. They are also release candidates for testing in the QA environment, having passed initial testing in the build environment. While beta releases should not be used as an excuse to deliver poor quality, they are

delivered 'as is' with no guarantees concerning quality until they have been fully certified by the quality assurance and testing process.

Hot fixes or patches
Quick fixes to existing released code to address a major defect discovered in the production environment. The changes incorporated into a hot fix will usually be performed on a branch in the source code control system that is associated with the current production release. These fixes, or a more complete solution that will address this defect, will need to be incorporated into the current mainline branch before the next release into the production environment.

Major version releases are the most difficult to manage because they are associated with changes to interfaces or the behaviour of the system. Changes that impact the way in which the system integrates and interacts with other external systems will require the co-ordination of the release with associated changes in those other external systems. This close-coupling dramatically escalates deployment risk by increasing the number of systems within the organization that will need to be upgraded at the same time. Upgrading systems is inherently risky, as any modification to a system may introduce unforeseen problems or defects.

DEVELOPMENT, BUILD AND TESTING ENVIRONMENTS

The build process is concerned with the conversion of software into an executable system. Tools exist which will automate the build process and determine the various dependencies of sections of code on each other, so that this process is performed in the correct order.[2,3]

Development, building releases, testing and UAT should ideally all be performed in different logical (but not necessarily different physical) environments. This logical separation will prevent changes in one environment impacting one of the other environments in an unexpected manner. Each of these environments has different characteristics that are aimed at increasing productivity within that environment, but which could undermine the tasks being performed in the other environments if they are not separated:

Development environment
Characterized by the development of code checked out from the source code control system, with individually customized developer environments, sharing some common, stable functionality provided by the devel-

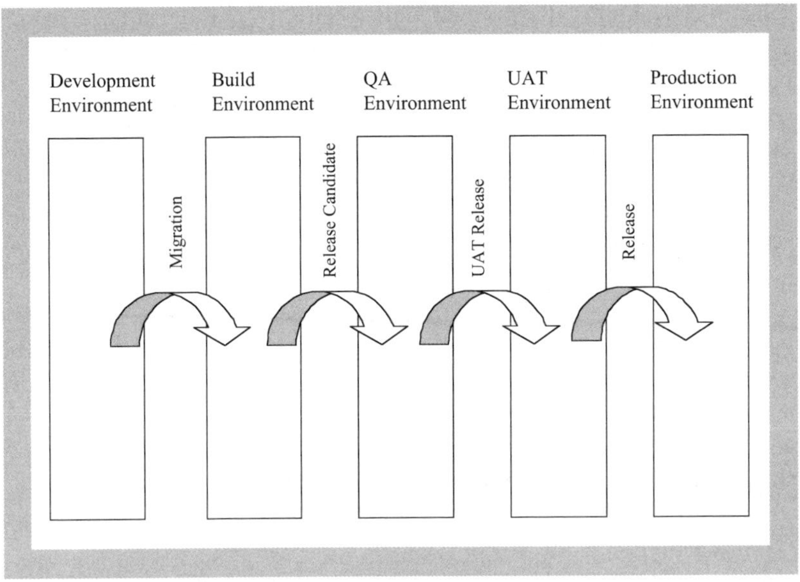

Figure 9.5 The different software environments used within a project

opment release that is generated in the build environment. Local unit and other tests will be executed in this environment to ensure that new functionality does not destabilize the build release of the system.

Build environment

A consistent single view of what is currently classified in the source code control system as being a stable version of the system under development. Each individual developer's copy of the system will eventually be checked in to the source code control system and combined to produce a group development copy that must be validated as being stable and correct. This copy then becomes the project's new development release that is used as the basis for ongoing development changes. This process is known as *migration.* Any code that is not within the development release branch (which may be the same as the mainline) of the source code control system or is local to a developer will not be accessible in this environment.

The build of the system in this environment therefore ensures that unexpected functionality does not inadvertently enter into the stable build of the system. The results of this build should be automatically tested to ensure that there are no regressions or failing functionality.

This process should also publish to the project team the results, errors or warnings from the process. It may also apply a build tag to the files included within the source control system, once the build is accepted as stable, in order to produce a snapshot release, as well as generate any automated documentation. The build process may even show what changes have been committed since the last build, together with the name of the developers responsible for the change. This can be important in identifying potential culprits of *build breakages* when the system fails to build or tests fail. By tagging the files used within each snapshot release traceability can be improved, permitting defects and unexpected behaviours to be associated with given versions of the code within the source code control system. It also permits changes that result in non-stable builds being quickly identified and removed if necessary, as well as the ability to build the system as of some previous snapshot release in the event of a serious breakage in the build process.

QA environment

An environment devoid of any development, build or system tools that are not available within the production environment. Release candidates of the system are installed into this environment and fully tested. Its aim is also to verify that any installation scripts or instructions are correct and that there are no unexpected dependencies on features of the development or build environments, such as unexpected or outdated versions of external libraries or components. The environment should be identical or very similar to that of the production environment and is therefore also the obvious place for performance and load-based testing.

UAT environment

The UAT environment is similar to the QA environment. Once a release has been verified in the QA environment by the project team, it will then be tested by the end users or some team responsible to them. This acts as a final independent check to ensure that the release meets any specified requirements and will be accepted by the end users. The UAT process is often formalized through a sign-off process where completion of the specified user acceptance tests derived from the requirements marks the formal completion of the delivery of a project. Traceability of requirements and a well-documented sign-off process confirming the requirements, as well as managing expectations throughout the life of the project, can be key to ensuring that this process can actually be performed.

Production environment(s)
The deployment environment(s) where the system is finally used by the end users. This should be an environment that is physically different from any of the others to ensure that the system and its performance are not adversely impacted by any development activity.

In order to ensure consistency between the results of this process in each of the development and build environments, a single build process should be implemented which customizes itself to the specifics of each environment. Utilizing a number of different independent build processes in the individual developer and then build environments will only increase the amount of maintenance required for this process, as any change will need to be made repeatedly for each individual environment. This will increase the likelihood of inconsistencies entering into each process resulting in different outcomes and behaviours in each environment.

SOFTWARE DEPLOYMENT

The final stage of a project is the deployment of the system to the end users. It is a critical point in the project, as it does not matter how good the system is, if it cannot be utilized then the project is guaranteed to fail. As a result, deployment should be included as an explicit task within the project plan and planning and risk assessment performed from the start of the project. Deployment introduces two new groups into the process, in addition to the end users:

Support staff
Front line support for the system, addressing any known issues (and how they can be worked around), general usage of the system and configuration issues.

System administration staff
Support of the underlying infrastructure and third party software such as operating systems, middleware, databases and so on as well as administrative tasks such as performing backups and installations.

In order for each of these groups to be able to perform their tasks, they must be adequately trained and informed of their role in the operation of the system. If these support and system administration operations are centralized or standardized within the organization then they will also introduce constraints on the project, dictating how the system must be packaged for installation, what third party software may be utilized and whether it can be supported, and what form any training and documentation should take.

Initial deployment

The initial deployment of a system is usually associated with some larger business process re-engineering effort that will result in new processes and workflows being implemented within the organization. This will require staff training and perhaps even new skills. The impact of this entire process and any possible associated risks must be carefully assessed and monitored if the project is ultimately to be deemed a success.

The first deployment of a system will also be associated with additional integration and data migration tasks concerning how the system is to be made available or *rolled out* to users. This deployment may be performed either incrementally or in a single step or *big bang*. The risk profiles and costs of these two approaches differ dramatically.

Systems can be categorized according to their user base and the functionality they provide to that user base. These two dimensions provide the major options for incremental system deployment:

- Deliver system to a subset of users or location by location
- Deliver only a subset of the total functionality
- A combination of both of the above.

The degree to which functionality can be delivered incrementally will depend on which functionality is viewed as being critical to the business process and whether the system design permits any functionality to be delivered in an incremental manner. This will also depend on whether subsets of functionality may be easily integrated into the current infrastructure and used to support or extend existing system functionality.

Incremental delivery enables new system behaviour to be closely monitored for a few users or localized pieces of functionality. This will limit the impact of any unexpected system failure and so reduce deployment risk. If the roll out is to a subset of users, there is also the option to transfer processing back to the old system in the event of a system failure, provided any relevant information can easily be transferred between the old and new systems. This is not an option if the old system (or blocks of functionality) are completely decommissioned. Incremental delivery does, however, result in additional costs from maintaining and supporting both the new and old systems. It can also greatly complicate data flows and any data migration strategy into the new system (if this is required), which again increases deployment risk.

Rolling back functionality

At some point the deployment process will fail or a release will be installed that is unstable or does not support some critical functionality. Resolution of this problem is then either to provide a manual fix or patch to the new system that enables it to be installed and operate correctly within the production environment, or to roll back the new installation, leaving the system and functionality in its previous state. The roll back process is one that must be carefully managed; any installation process must ensure that the version of the system being replaced can still be made available in the event of an emergency. The upgrade process does not, however, just impact the internal functionality of a system. It may also be associated with changes in the internal state and persistence of information as well as changes in interfaces or the representation of external data (Figure 9.6).

The new version of the system may require some of the persisted data to be modified, augmented or reorganized. Problems will arise in the roll-back process if the changes to this data or the interfaces to external systems are not compatible with those of the previous release. If this is the case, these changes must be reversed, relying on any data transformation to be reversible or on the ability to replace it with a copy of the persisted data before the installation of the new version. Time is often critical in such decisions, and the implications of each approach need to be carefully considered. The safest manner to support this process is to back up or save all aspects of the old system, which will be replaced or modified so that they can be reinstalled if necessary. If the new system has modified information then rolling back to the start-of-day configuration will require any persisted changes to be reapplied to the system. This may need to be performed manually, which will not be a feasible option if it results in a huge amount of effort, or for any resulting logged data updates to be automatically replayed on the old system. Designing such features into a system can significantly reduce deployment risk.

Deployment risk, associated with co-ordinating and rolling back major releases that impact several other systems within the organization, can also be reduced by ensuring that the system to be deployed is capable of

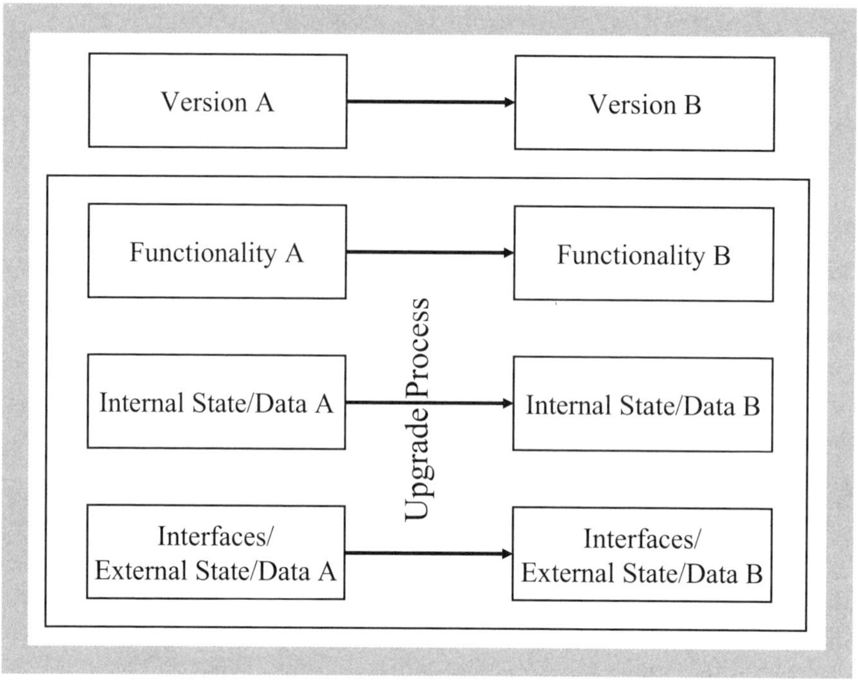

Figure 9.6 Changes arising from the upgrade process

supporting the interfaces and behaviour of the previous major release as well as that of the new release. Configuration information may then be used to enable the system to support whichever interfaces and behaviours are required. This loosens the coupling between systems, permitting the roll back of an external system to occur without also requiring all associated systems be rolled back.

Global deployment

System installation is a complex task, especially when multiple locations and pieces of hardware are involved. Manual deployment processes for installing and updating a system are only an option when there are a limited number of sites to which any system must be deployed. Such processes are usually prone to error, expensive to perform and unacceptably slow. Although patch releases to address critical system failures may need to be performed manually, the intention should always be to automate this process. This is especially important for systems in financial organizations, due to the frequent and rapid requirement for updates to functionality. Because financial software is often deployed globally, this installation process must be able to deal with timed releases in the future, when trading or risk processing is not occurring. The global nature of financial markets across different time zones means that there is rarely a single point in time when a system can be rolled out simultaneously to all locations without impacting the business operation in one of them. Because of this a phased roll out around the globe is often required. The installation process must therefore be robust and able to resolve local installation issues and problems, as well as being able to deal with periods when different locations may be using different versions of a system.

Release notes

Release notes are used to inform those external to the project of the changes that have been made since the last version of the system. These changes will arise from differences in the deployment of the system or corrections to defects and change requests resulting from the completion of a number of externally or internally defined SPRs. The release note should be a simple document laid out in a standard format that includes the following information:

- System summary and other identification information, including release version number
- Installation notes, including system requirements
- New features and enhancements (linked to externally defined SPRs)
- Bug fixes (linked to SPRs)
- Known problems and 'work arounds'
- Notes and contact information, including details on user training or documentation updated.

These release notes may be sub-divided depending on the group they are aimed at, providing different details of information to the support staff, system administrators or users. Release notes should also be distributed in advance of any installation in case they highlight potential problems for these groups which will need to be resolved before the release can occur.

TOOLS AND PROCESS AUTOMATION

Tools and process automation can and should be used throughout a software project. This not only helps to enforce standard approaches and procedures within a project but can also reduce the time and risk associated with performing certain repetitive tasks, as well as enhancing resource productivity. The benefits of any tools must, however, be weighed against any additional overhead in utilizing them. A simple checklist to be considered is:

- Administration requirements
- Likely productivity improvement
- Cost of acquisition and maintenance
- Learning curve requirements
- Previous experience or recommendations from other project teams
- Support for the tool, both internally and externally
- Ability to customize operations as needed
- Limitations of how the tool may be used, accessed and integrated with other tools
- Likely increase or potential for errors and therefore additional project risk in using the tool
- Ease of use and performance considerations.

The danger in not automating repetitive tasks, especially if they are likely to become more resource intensive during the project (such as with testing), is that they will be performed less and less rigorously as the task burden increases. This is especially likely to occur when pressure to deliver is greatest at the end of a project and when there is the least amount of time to address such issues. In the QA and testing process, this can lead to poor quality testing which dramatically reduces software quality and increases the risk of project failure.

The level of automation can range from the generation of code fragments from analysis and design diagrams through to the authoring of test cases from specifications of user interaction with a system. The reverse process of generating documentation directly from code fragments can help increase traceability and ensure that both documentation and code are always kept synchronized. Although such automated processes can derive information about what a design or section of code does, it is often difficult to understand the reasons why or define the problem being solved without further developer input. This will fundamentally limit the degree to which the entire software lifecycle can be automated and the degree of reverse engineering that can be performed within a project. Tools such as debuggers, memory management analysis and performance monitoring tools are key to any software project and ideally should be standardized across all projects within an organization. This will also facilitate the reassignment of resources between projects.

Notes

1 D. Bolinger and T. Bronson, *Applying RCS and SCCS: From Source Control to Project Control* (O'Reilly & Associates, 1995)
2 J. Tilly and E. Burke, *Ant: the Definitive Guide* (O'Reilly & Associates, 2002)
3 A. Oram and S. Talbott, *Managing Projects with Make* (O'Reilly & Associates, 1992)

PART III

Trends in Risk Management Process and Technology

CHAPTER 10

The future of risk management technology

Current market conditions at the turn of the new millennium make it difficult to predict the future for risk management and its associated systems. Uncertain and volatile environments are, however, likely to increase the importance of risk management as the organization's primary defence against losses arising from this uncertainty. The merging of many large financial institutions in the 1990s has resulted in a more competitive financial marketplace, just as the world has been exposed to economic and political stresses and uncertainties. The lower trading volumes seen in some markets have highlighted the importance of controlling fixed costs, whereas the relative buoyancy of the fixed income market[1] has highlighted the need to maintain a diverse market risk exposure in order to ensure overall profitability.

The future is likely to see a continuance of this focus on risk management, costs and operational efficiency. The desire to reduce costs may lead to greater outsourcing and the transfer of certain operational risks to third parties. Offshore sites have highlighted the comparative advantage[2] of using highly trained staff in lower cost regions such as India, China and Russia. Some of the trust and operational risk issues are still to be worked out and there may well be some realization that the actual risks in such an approach are higher than anticipated.

The drive for efficiency and lower costs has been a major factor behind electronic trading and the creation of electronic rather than physical marketplaces or methods of interaction. This has resulted in increased automation of many trading processes and led to very different business models from those used in the past. Some of these new electronic marketplaces such as electronic communication networks (ECNs) and alternative trading systems (ATS) first appeared in the mid-1990s in the US as an additional, lower cost and extended trading hours marketplace for equities trading. They have extended to many different types of instrument (covering fixed income bonds, credit default swaps, FX) and have broken down the dealer monopoly, permitting clients to trade directly with each other without the use of an intermediary. They have also increased competition by having a number of competing brokers displaying prices in a single electronic market. As well as adding considerable transparency to the markets, these electronic markets have helped reduce transaction costs and have increased trading volumes.

The move to electronic marketplaces and the provision of (or ability to provide on demand) firm tradable prices, rather than *indicative* prices on market data provider screens or in telephone quotes, has added additional complexity to the trading operation. Although they have removed some of the volume constraints and risks associated with excessive manual intervention in the trading process, they have also introduced new operational risks. Rather than losses arising from manual errors, they now arise from defects and failures of the technology used to automatically generate prices or commit to trades, as well as the possibility of electronic failure in the communication links or electronic marketplace itself.

There have been a number of embarrassing events arising from either system related failures or errors arising from the interaction between users and their supporting technology.[3] The focus on developing safe systems and processes where a single failure in the workflow cannot result in a significant loss is only likely to become more important in the future. Many of the inefficiencies and manual interventions that provided the opportunity and time to detect potential errors have been automated away. The speed of current markets has removed the opportunity to retract incorrect trading instructions, making it even more important that everything is performed correctly, first time.

The growth in the number of electronic marketplaces has also presented three additional major challenges on the trading desk:

1. Trading on multiple electronic market places at once.
2. Trading high volumes at high speeds.

3. Integrating market data, risk management information and trading functionality into a single view. This must be able to manage the potentially rapidly changing positions, risk exposures and trading conditions.

These changing demands and the likely ongoing amendments to the Basel 2 Accord will keep risk management firmly in the spotlight for the foreseeable future. Some of the implications of Basel 2 are still not fully understood by the markets. What this implies is that systems developed to address current perceived risk management needs are likely to rapidly evolve as the implications of the framework become clearer and evolve over time. This will increase the requirement for any risk management infrastructure to be extensible and to address changing market requirements.

There has also been a step change in the way people view risk and an increasing interaction of risks in different markets. Historically, financial institutions and regulators have thought in terms of different categories of risk that were independently managed. Depending on the type of trading, this defined which type of risk tended to dominate and would be the focus for risk management. Current market conditions, the cross asset class nature of many complex structures and the current mix of risk within an organization are, however, resulting in a reassessment of this. Corporate bond trading is now intricately connected with the trading of credit derivatives, government bonds and swaps. What we are seeing is a convergence in the trading of what were historically seen as separate business areas.

RISK MANAGEMENT IN THE FUTURE

The different categories of risk interact in a complex manner, impacting the total risk exposure of the organization (Figure 10.1). For example, market conditions tend to drive trading volumes, which in turn impact operational risk. Similarly, economic conditions impact interest rates, which in turn can affect the cashflows and solvency of companies and hence their credit quality.

It therefore seems likely that the risk management system of the future will need to address this increasing complexity in how risk is perceived and be able more efficiently to aggregate, model and combine risk information from across the organization. It will then be possible to manage business areas based on the total risk taken, rather than on

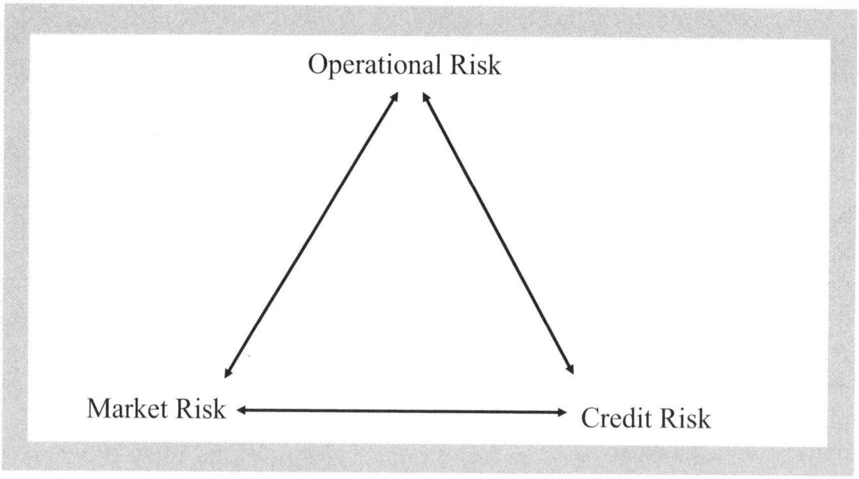

Figure 10.1 The interaction of different types of risk

a subset which is seen as being the dominant risk. When trading a given financial instrument, there will always be a combination of market, credit and operational risk:

- *Market risk:* changes in the value of the instrument arising from changes in market variables
- *Credit risk:* changes in the value of the transaction arising from the likelihood of counterparty default or changes in the underlying credit quality of the company the instrument is based upon
- *Operational risk:* potential losses arising from operational failures in the trading, management and settlement of the instrument.

Often a separate group or department will manage the risk associated with each of these categories. Market risk and some types of pricing-related credit risk are typically managed by a market or corporate risk function; other types of credit risk and credit exposure by the credit department; and finally, operational risk by newly formed operational risk groups. Given their interrelation, it seems highly unlikely that organizations will be able to maintain this division of responsibilities for different types of risk. Assessing risk exposure by examining a single type of risk, asset class system or geographical location will always be misleading and leaves the organization vulnerable to an unexpected combination of correlated market, operational and credit risks. Similarly, regulators now require significantly more complex analyses and reporting that cannot be undertaken without sufficiently sophisticated, highly integrated risk management technology.

The advantages of having a complete, consistent and current view of risks within the organization should be clear. Once a framework exists for obtaining this information and analysing it, there are a number of additional key competitive advantages that can be obtained:

- The risk information can be used to improve the manner in which the organization is run and improve how risk capital is allocated. This moves the risk management framework from one which is a purely defensive measure, ensuring all potential losses are understood and monitored, to one which adds economic value to the organization.
- Reusing the functionality embedded in the risk management framework to add value to the organization. If an open framework is utilized that enables functionality to be easily reused and deployed in other areas, then this capability can be leveraged in new directions.

In an increasingly competitive marketplace, financial organizations are trying either to compete against each other on cost or to provide additional added value services to their clients. Risk management is not only important to financial organizations, it is also important to their clients. If an organization has invested a large amount of money and effort in developing comprehensive risk management functionality, then making some of this functionality available to its clients could provide an important additional service. It could enable clients to monitor, in real time, the status of any of their financial transactions and the amount of risk they are exposed to. To be able to achieve this, the system must have been developed in a scalable, flexible and modular fashion that enables certain information and functionality to be made available over different delivery channels such as the Internet, with minimal additional cost.

The previous generation of 'closed' black box risk management solutions could never achieve this. However, the move towards scalable frameworks with standardized and reusable functionality means that the additional cost compared with the potential customer benefits may make this a reality in the future.

RISK TRANSFORMATION AND COST BENEFIT ANALYSIS

Risk mitigation, system and process change is all about risk transformation and cost benefit analysis. Rather than risks being completely removed, the actual outcome is usually that the risk to be mitigated *is* reduced but that *some* of it is transformed into a different, and hopefully easier to manage type of risk. Whether any transformed risk is actually easier to manage will depend on the organization. This risk transformation process again highlights the interaction between market, credit and operational risk. For example, if traders offset some market risk in a portfolio by entering into a customized financial transaction directly with a client, they will reduce market risk but increase credit risk arising from potential counterparty exposure. They may also increase operational risk if the systems and processes are ill equipped to handle this new transaction.

This highlights the importance of considering the total risk associated with a transaction and how any potential return may change and associated total risk may vary through risk mitigation. Analysing the cost and benefit of possible risk mitigation strategies should therefore consider any new risks that will be introduced, as well as the cost of mitigating this risk (Figure 10.2).

Previously, technology has been seen as a key source of competitive advantage for financial organizations and an important way of removing operational risks associated with excessively manual processes. However, many organizations are reassessing the affects of this risk transformation

Figure 10.2 The cost–benefit equation

and how project risk and technology risk may now be significant sources of risk that they are ill equipped to manage.

This reassessment has partly been driven by a realization that many projects have resulted in costly failure and the defect levels and flexibility of many systems have resulted in those systems needing to be replaced a short period of time later. Far from achieving competitive advantage or reducing operational risk, many organizations have instead ended up with significant losses from project or system deficiencies and minimal benefit. Managing this aspect of risk within the organization is likely to be of even more importance in the future. It will require improvements in the way projects are managed and the use of more appropriate technologies and development processes that reduce project risk and provide more cost-effective and higher quality solutions. These solutions will need to evolve with the organization and ensure that it can maintain its competitive position by rapidly responding to any changing requirements.

STRATEGIC VERSUS TACTICAL

Strategy is concerned with the bigger picture of where we are today, where we wish to be in the future (in order to be profitable and to survive) and the gap between these two views of the world. Any chosen strategy should address the bridging of this gap. Tactical approaches on the other hand focus more on current requirements to address immediate needs and ensure short-term survival.

Approaches to developing risk management solutions are often categorized as being either tactical or strategic in their scope. Typically what is meant is whether the focus is short or long term. When the focus is overtly short term, the tendency is for longer term objectives to take a secondary focus, resulting in strategic drift away from where the organization wishes to be in the future (Figure 10.3). This can often lead to a case of 'mortgaging the future for quick gratification today'. This need not always be the case and links back to the concepts of taking a balanced approach.

Any project should not only consider short-term needs in isolation, but also ensure that any solution can evolve to address longer term strategic requirements. As a result, strategic business goals should drive the strategic IT goals within the organization, ensuring that current technology can evolve to support the business objectives (Figure 10.4). It is important to view Figure 10.4 correctly; technology should support business goals and be driven by them, not necessarily the other way around.

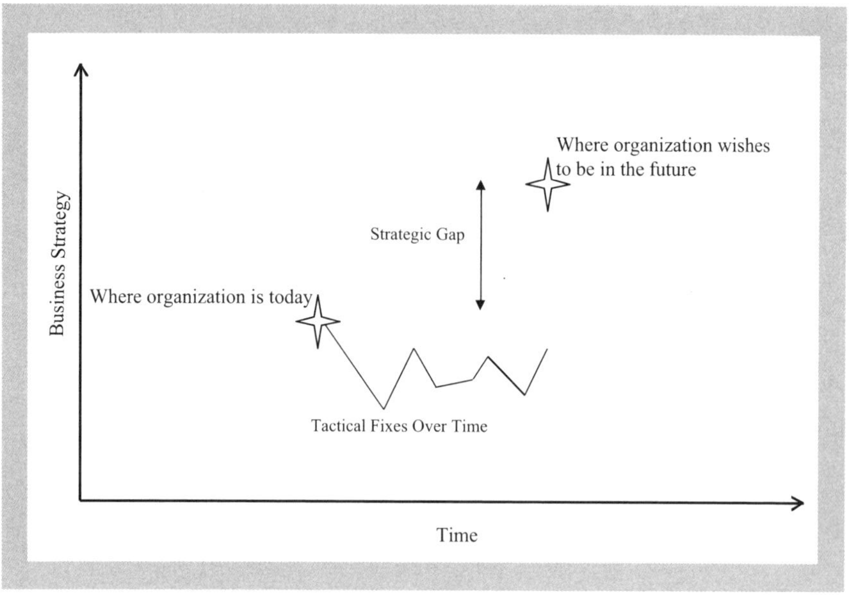

Figure 10.3 Strategic project drift

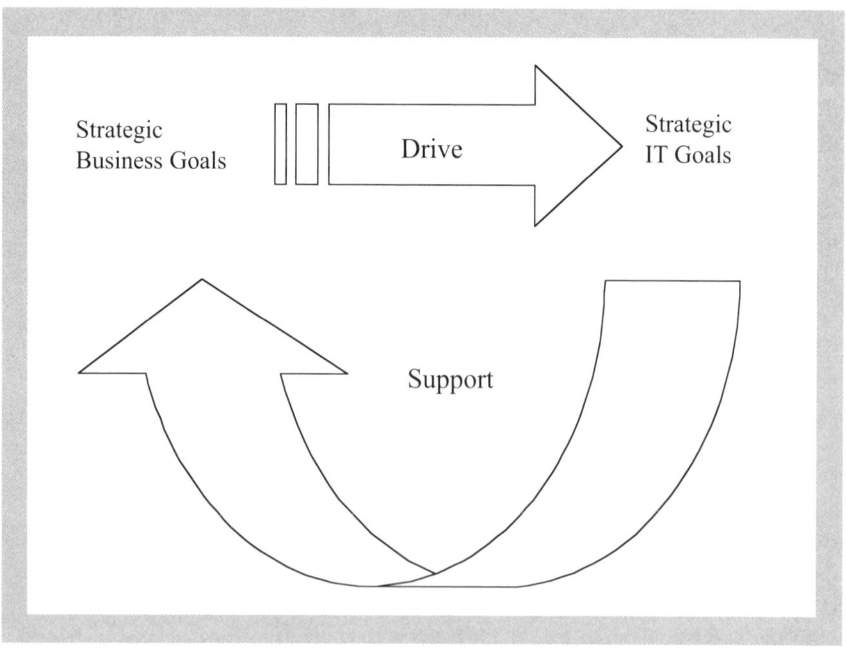

Figure 10.4 The strategic road map

The IT strategy should define a clear upgrade path that extends existing technical capabilities within the organization both in terms of the delivery of new technology as well as supporting the current technology. The IT strategy should not require the complete re-engineering of existing systems, which would be a prohibitively expensive, time-consuming and high risk strategy. Instead it should permit existing systems and technology to be leveraged and reutilized in an incremental evolutionary manner towards the desired strategic technical architecture. Previous approaches of viewing software as a disposable commodity have resulted in expensive and high risk approaches to system development. Given the current cost and time constraints in implementing new solutions, this is unlikely to be acceptable in the future.

STRUCTURAL PROJECT RISK

The track record of many projects within financial organizations is generally not good; many fail to deliver what is expected from them. Although total project failure is not that common, many projects end up failing in a strict sense in that they are over budget, deliver less functionality than initially specified, take longer than expected, or are difficult or costly to maintain and cannot evolve with the organization.

This is not a problem that is purely confined to financial organizations. If most technology projects are assessed against their original project requirements, an amazing number can be judged to have failed. Phillips found that, depending on how strict a definition of project failure is used, over 80 per cent of software projects can be judged to have failed in some manner.[4] There are, however, common reasons for project failure, such as:

- Inadequate management of requirements and scope creep
- Ambiguous and imprecise communication among team members, exacerbated by the different backgrounds and levels of understanding within the team
- Undetected inconsistencies in requirements, design, and implementation
- Insufficient testing
- Inadequate or qualitative (rather than quantitative) assessment of project status

- Failure to identify and manage risk
- Uncontrolled change propagation and lack of any change management process
- Excessively manual processes and procedures.

This situation is problematic for many organizations; they understand the need to improve their risk management systems but are disheartened by the observed failure rate of many IT projects. Rather than managers aligning themselves to projects that have a high likelihood of failure and will adversely impact their careers, there is a tendency to make do with existing functionality, enhancing it with low risk but ineffectual modifications.

The cognitive biases mentioned in Chapter 1 also lead to organizations oscillating between developing systems internally and outsourcing this development. Whether the last project failure was associated with an in-house or outsourced project, often drives the decision for the next project.

Although many organizations will compare the cost of the two approaches, few do this in a structured manner and address the issues of risk transformation and strategic risk. Outsourcing may remove the risk of internal project failure but this has been transformed into the risk of external project failure and strategic risk, arising from a divergence between the vendor's and the organization's view of the future.

Whichever approach is taken, it is important that the organization has the capability to manage the delivery of a risk management solution, be it internally or externally developed. There are many KRIs which can indicate that there is a high level of inherent risk associated with projects within the organization and that the project management process should be reviewed for possible failings. Some of the most obvious KRIs are:

- Frequent project failure
- Long lead times between enhancements
- Irregular frequency of releases
- Many incompatible systems
- Multiple failed RfP processes.

Projects in crisis tend to abandon defined processes and the key monitoring and planning tasks in an effort to focus all resources on delivering the project. This is often just at the point when assessing and mitigating risk is vital to ensuring the successful delivery of the project.

Any project manager in an environment that is exhibiting signs of high levels of structural project risk should stop and assess the underlying causes before proceeding. It is likely that, working within the same organizational constraints and using similar resources, future projects will also fail unless remedial action is taken. This is an important lesson of risk management; if a risk assessment highlights a significant level of risk then it is likely that, unless mitigating actions are taken, events will occur that make that risk a reality.

Because each organization is unique, it is difficult to take a universal approach and apply a generic RfP or software development approach that is guaranteed to work. Instead, the unique process that works for a particular organization must be 'discovered' and developed over time. Once an approach has been proved successful within the organization, it is important to leverage this experience and apply it to other, similar problems.

The view of unique projects that address unique business requirements combined with common frameworks that address common process issues found within the organization can help leverage generic project experiences. This should lead to standardization in aspects of project management, development processes, testing and infrastructure that are

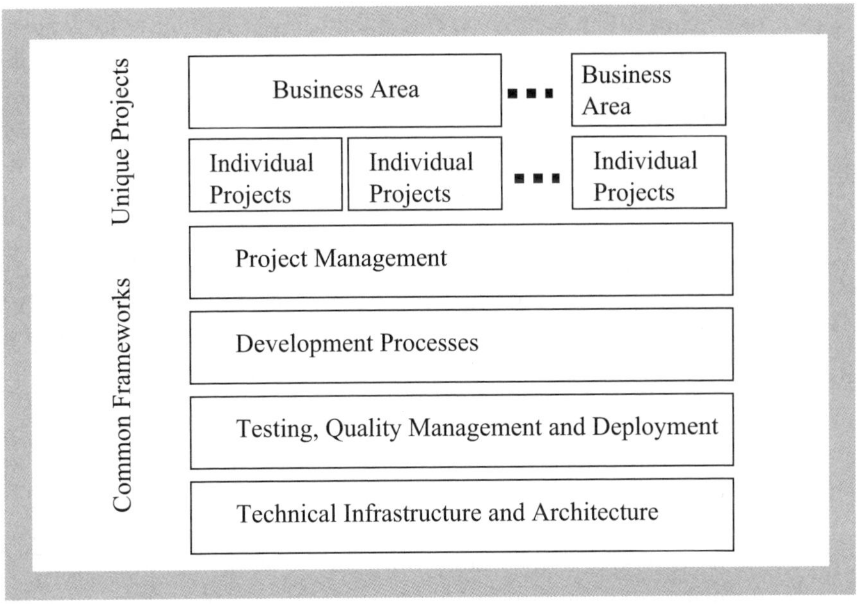

Figure 10.5 The move towards common frameworks

indeed common across the organization. By standardizing these aspects of the projects, common resource pools can be utilized across certain aspects of different projects, reducing resourcing issues.

What is important is to apply standardized processes and resources where there are generic problems, but ensure that each project contains specific resources, skills and processes to address the unique requirements of each business area problem (Figure 10.5). Projects can just as easily fail through the use of too generic an approach and resources that cannot address or understand the specific issues within the business area.

FLEXIBILITY AND MANAGING THE UNKNOWN RISK

Probably the most dangerous risk to an organization is the risk that it knows nothing about. van der Heijden characterizes events into three different types.[5]

1. *Unknowables:* Events that cannot even be comprehended
2. *Structural uncertainties:* Events which can be comprehended but which do not happen frequently enough to be assigned a probability (for example stock market crashes)
3. *Risks:* Events that happen with frequent enough regularity for a probability to be assigned (for example daily price movements) and the probability of a loss of a given size occurring to be calculated.

The impact of these different types of events can be managed by calculating the probability of losses arising from any known risks, scenario testing for structural uncertainties and having a flexible environment and tools to spot new (as yet undefined or unnoticed) unknowable risks. As a result, it is especially important for the risk manager to be looking for the weak signals that indicate new sources of risk.[6] These will be hidden among all the background noise of other (known) risks within the organization.

New sources of risk may arise from new types of residual or basis risk arising from implementing different business models and changes in external market behaviour leading to imperfect hedging or management of existing risks. The key requirement will then be to ensure that internal processes and systems can be quickly enhanced to capture information concerning these new risks so that they can be adequately managed.

A flexible and extensible risk management system will therefore be essential to enable existing information and functionality to be extended to monitor new risks arising *externally* from changes in the market or regulatory environment, and *internally* from changes in the organization's business model.

MAINTAINING COMPETITIVE ADVANTAGE

The nature of the software delivery process is that it can take a significant amount of time to develop and install a new system. While this can be acceptable in a relatively static environment, the dynamic nature of financial markets means that this is not an option. In order to capture potentially lucrative trading opportunities, financial organizations need to be able to modify their processes and systems. As a result, 'build once and never change' is not an option.

Spreadsheets have often been seen as the solution to providing the ultimate flexible environment for performing ad hoc calculations and manipulating and managing information. Ad hoc analysis and complex formulae can easily be implemented in a familiar and powerful environment. In their proper place, spreadsheets are the ultimate adjunct to the risk management process. However, they can result in an environment that:

- Is difficult to scale
- Offers poor performance; spreadsheet macros and cell calculations perform poorly compared with other types of implementation
- Lacks the robustness and failover capability of other approaches
- Has poor levels of security; typically an all or nothing approach
- Is a difficult one in which to implement controls, audit trails, versioning or monitor changes
- Is difficult to integrate with, resulting in excessively manual processes. Even where integration occurs, simple changes in spreadsheet format can result in the process failing. This can dramatically increase operational risk
- Only allows single user access/updating, which can lead to problems in effectively sharing information within the spreadsheet.

The major deficiency is probably the significant effort required to control and monitor the data and calculations performed within the spreadsheet. Their flexibility means that significant effort is required to ensure that the spreadsheet contains no errors or omissions and is not modified so that errors are introduced into it. This function often provided through laborious and expensive *spreadsheet audits.*

Some of these issues can be addressed by performing some of the more complex or computationally intensive processing in external components. Often these external components have been installed locally leading to a problem on Microsoft platforms known as 'DLL hell',[7] whereby issues arise in using different versions of these components required by the different applications. Installing a new component or dll required by one application then tends to break another, leading to a support and maintenance nightmare.

DEVELOPMENT APPROACHES

The limitations of traditional development approaches have been brought to the forefront by an increasingly demanding and dynamic marketplace. Financial organizations need to obtain improved returns on their investment in technology and reduce the risk of project failure, but be able to rapidly produce customized and flexible solutions. This is quite a challenging set of requirements.

In order to obtain a better return on any investment in technology the software development process must either:

1. Improve resource productivity through the use of more efficient tools, programming languages and development environments
2. Reduce the amount of software to be developed through reuse of existing software or next generation programming languages that reduce the amount of software to be written.

The need to utilize customized solutions has always meant that a reasonable percentage of a system must be written or modified to meet the precise requirements of the organization. Although more efficient tools and development environments have helped to improve development productivity, recent focus has been on trying to reduce the amount of software that needs be written. There have historically been two extremes of approach to this; to utilize application frameworks or software libraries (Figure 10.6).

Application frameworks provide both design and code reuse in a common framework that enables the application developer to insert

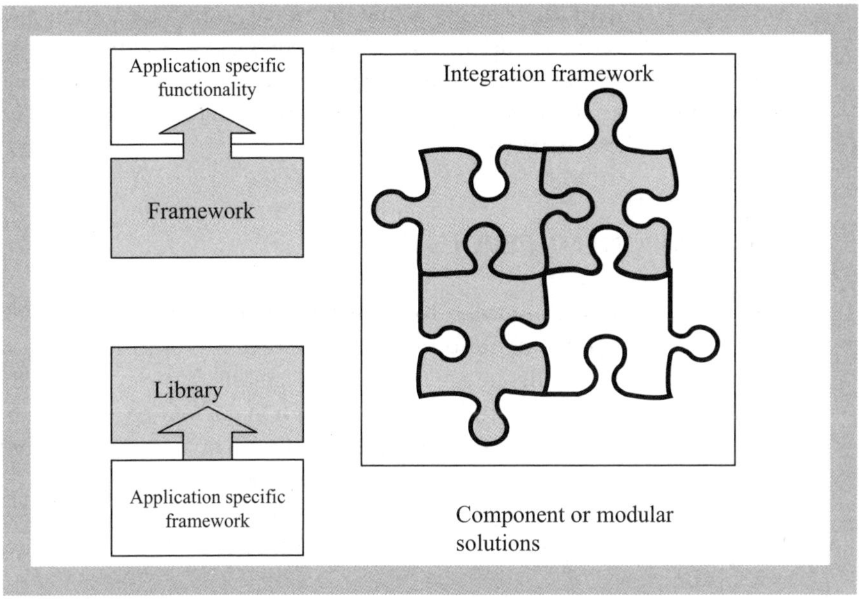

Figure 10.6 Approaches to developing risk management solutions

application-specific functionality at certain defined points in the framework. This approach has been used by many product vendors, who provide a system that enables client-specific functionality, such as financial calculations and risk measures, to be inserted into the framework. Libraries provide the other extreme of building blocks of common functionality that can be utilized in a complete solution. When building a risk management solution, the application developer must develop the framework into which these library building blocks are fitted.

Both these approaches have been problematic. The application framework has provided high levels of reuse but insufficient customization and flexibility; only certain functionality can be customized at certain points in the workflow. Libraries have provided some levels of reuse but a significant amount of the application must still be written.

Recently, a third approach has been utilized by many vendors and financial organizations, based on the reuse and development of components or modules within a well-defined technical integration framework. These components are connected together using the framework, which provides the common technical functionality required to build large enterprise applications and enables large units of functionality to be reused.

Project risk can be dramatically reduced through the reuse of proved, pre-tested functionality. The Meta Group found that reused code only had 25 per cent of the defects found in newly developed code and enabled solutions to be deployed 40 per cent faster.[8] Having a reuse strategy can provide a significant advantage to financial organizations that need robust solutions that address the rapid product evolution seen within the financial markets.

THE COMPONENT REVOLUTION

Component-based approaches to solution development have proved particularly effective in building risk management solutions. Their inherent flexibility results in extendable applications that can be quickly developed. Time is increasingly being seen as a major source of competitive advantage, so being able to enhance and deliver risk management solutions in a timely manner is becoming even more important.

Component technology also offers a more risk-averse and cost-effective approach. Gone are the large-scale expensive projects of the past. New systems must:

- Make greater use of prewritten code (that is improved reuse)
- Leverage existing systems, reducing the amount of functionality to be rewritten
- Have better integration and less manual intervention, improving operational efficiency and reducing operational risk.

Components that provide the core functionality of a system will enable developers to focus the majority of their efforts on building applications which address the specific functional and workflow requirements of the organization rather than generic system and business functionality. Tailored functionality that gives an organization its competitive advantage can be integrated with these common components to quickly deliver customized solutions where a significant proportion of the final solution is prewritten. Components that are written once but used everywhere within the organization can also resolve inconsistency issues in calculations and approaches to risk management.

Traditional approaches to software development have led to the close coupling of functionality, which is embedded into a single compiled unit within an application. This has made it difficult to upgrade functionality or to reuse and standardize approaches across the organization. The use of CBD permits customized systems to be developed that facilitate some of these key requirements for any risk management solution; reusability, flexibility and replaceability.

The concept of component-based development and component technology has been with us for some time. CORBA, DCOM, COM+ have all supported this approach and have been around since the mid-1990s. One may be forgiven for asking why, if the component-based approach has existed for so long, there is not yet a flourishing market for prewritten components? This was an issue raised by Grady Booch in an article in 2001.[9] He believed that one of the reasons for it was the absence of an accepted technical infrastructure for component-based development. It was not until the release of Java2 and the J2EE platform in 1999 that there has been any truly enterprise-scale platform standards for CBD. At this point Java moved from being 'just' a programming language to being a true component model for building enterprise-scale component applications. This was soon followed by Microsoft's announcement of .NET in 2000 (being the final evolution of DCOM, MTS/COM+ into Microsoft's Distributed Internet Applications Architecture (DNA) and then onto .NET). The arrival of these improved frameworks for developing component technology may mark the beginning of the next major technical design revolution; the commercial arrival of component technology. Although many within the technology industry see the technical case as clear, the movement to any new technology is often seen as high risk. It is therefore often avoided unless there is some compelling event that increases the importance of the component approach.

Booch also highlighted another reason why we have not yet seen a flourishing commercial component market. The competitive advantage that can be gained from an organization componentizing its assets should mean that it would be better off using those components to dominate the market rather than trying to sell them. This would tend to imply that although we may see an increase in the private, internal market of components within an organization, this might not evolve into a growing public market.

The Component Based Development and Integration Forum (www.cbdiforum.com) has noted a similar failure for a flourishing component market to evolve. In its 8 May 2003 newsletter, it highlighted the organizational structure issues that prevent enterprise-wide IT initiatives. These structure issues will also act as a barrier to high levels of component reuse within an organization. To address these issues, the problems associated with relying on key services under the control of other groups will need to be resolved. This trust and service guarantee problem can be resolved, just as risk managers have had to resolve issues in obtaining guarantees on the provision of data from around the organization for use in the risk management process. Whether they are willing to continue this struggle in ensuring the provision of certain key functionality and calculations is still uncertain.

According to Clemens Szyperski,[10] an additional issue has been that critical mass has not yet been reached in the component market. Once it is reached, Szyperski sees a 'vortex' forming that will draw in traditional solutions. If a component-based solution can utilize a 'best of breed' approach, with the most appropriate components used from different vendors, they will be able to leverage off a shared development effort that will rapidly perfect each individual component. Those organizations who maintain a proprietary component approach will fail to leverage the benefits from this shared development and increasingly be sidelined.

It may be that the reuse argument for using component technology will fail in the same way as it did for justifying object-orientated approaches; only time will tell. Despite this, both component- and object-orientated development approaches have provided improvements in the efficiency and maintainability of software. It therefore seems likely that they will both play a key role in developing risk management systems in the future, even if they are not a panacea.

THE INTEGRATION AND INTERFACE GAP

The component revolution in some ways has complicated the integration challenges within an organization. The current two dominant approaches of J2EE and .NET will need to co-exist with previous component technology standards as well as a range of existing systems and legacy applications. This will further complicate the mix of technologies found throughout the marketplace and within any specific organization, with no single technology dominating. As a result, integration and interoperability will become ever more important.

.NET is likely to dominate in the user environment because of its ability to easily integrate with the existing Microsoft environment, especially applications such as Microsoft Word and Excel. The flexibility that the Microsoft Office environment provides for users to easily generate customized reports and analyses, seamlessly copying information from one application to another should not be underestimated.

Because of this, if J2EE is used to provide middle-tier functionality, it will need to easily integrate with .NET-based solutions. J2EE and .NET are therefore likely to have to co-exist in many organizations.

The existence of two component environments does result in some advantages; each is likely to want to try to dominate over the other resulting in a competitive cycle of enhancements and improvements.

The integration issue is also important in determining whether Szyperski's arguments for the evolution of a public component technology market will really evolve. This will require the ability to utilize components from multiple vendors, and for these to seamlessly work together. The new component frameworks are providing a number of standard mechanisms for certain tasks, such as locating components and security, that will enable different components to integrate more widely within an organization's IT infrastructure. This also relieves the components of the need to implement such features in a proprietary manner, which can be a significant barrier to integration. In the absence of common technology, data representations, interfaces and rules for interaction, there is, however, an integration chasm that must be crossed. Constraints concerning the ability to modify existing legacy applications mean that trying to achieve a common approach may never be possible. Instead, the concept of an integration layer that ensures that components developed by different vendors or development groups within an organization can interact may prove critical to the success of component technology. Just as with EAI software, this will need to transform between different data representations and manage different models for component interaction. The overhead of achieving this integration must not, however, result in unacceptable performance implications.

CONCLUSION

Developing a risk management system is not simply a question of writing software. It requires a complex interaction of many different people and skill sets within the organization. It also requires a deep understanding of the problem, the ability to determine what needs to be achieved and the ability to develop and execute a plan of action. The aim of this book has been to provide an overview of the tasks that need to be performed and some of the key aspects of risk management and software development that will need to be understood. There are no 'silver bullets' for solving the many problems that you are likely to face, but hopefully by understanding what some of the key issues are likely to be you will be forewarned.

Below is a list of ten key points to consider both when running a risk management group as well as a project developing a risk management solution. Risk is everywhere within an organization. What is important is that those risks are identified, monitored and measured and their implications understood and mitigated if necessary.

1. Ensure there is a strong risk oversight group covering all the types of risk within the organization. This oversight group will act as a sponsor for the development of any risk management solution.
2. Ensure adequate awareness and training and the creation of a risk aware culture.
3. Develop written policies and agreements of what needs to be achieved or performed.
4. Assign clear roles and responsibilities.
5. Conduct a risk assessment and benchmark any approach.
6. Establish early warning systems to highlight increases in risk or expected loss.
7. Establish adequate reserves and contingency plans.
8. Establish your risk appetite and risk limits.
9. Always take a balanced approach.
10. Continually identify, monitor, evaluate and mitigate risk.

Notes

1 M. Richards, 'Merrill Lynch 2Q Earnings Rise 61 Percent', *Yahoo!News* (15 July 2003)
2 R. Grant, *Contemporary Strategy Analysis* (Blackwell Business, 1995)
3 Finextra, 'Traders head for the pits as Globex falls over' (Finextra.com, 2 May 2003)
4 D. Phillips, *The Software Project Manager's Handbook – Principles that Work at Work* (IEEE Computer Society Press, 1998)
5 K. van der Heijden, *Scenarios: The Art of Strategic Conversation* (John Wiley, 1996)
6 D. Mercer, *Marketing Strategy: The Challenge of the External Environment* (Sage, 1998)
7 M. Loney, 'Microsoft promises end to "DLL hell"', *ZDNet magazine* (6 March 2003)
8 D. DiNunno, *Reuse Productivity – IT Performance Engineering and Measurement Strategies* (Meta Group, April 2000)
9 G. Booch, 'The illusion of simplicity', *Software Development Magazine* (February 2001)
10 C. Szyperski, *Component Software – Beyond Object-orientated Programming* (Addison-Wesley, 1999)

Appendix

RISK MANAGEMENT SYSTEM PROVIDERS AND CONSULTANTS

The risk management vendor marketplace contains a large number of possible suppliers of risk management products, toolkits or consultancy services. They cover risk throughout the hierarchy, from hedging on the trading desk to complex portfolio analysis and VaR calculations. This Appendix contains a list of some of those vendors categorized as product, toolkit or consultancy providers. Those suppliers categorized as consultants offer some level of consulting service rather than just professional services in implementing their product. Each supplier's area of expertise at the high-level risk management groupings of operational, credit or market risks are then given. If you are looking for a supplier for a specific requirement, a more detailed analysis of the precise coverage of the sources of risk included (specifically instrument coverage for market and credit risk) will be required. This information, however, tends to be constantly updated as products and services are expanded to cover current market requirements.

Company	Type	Website	Operational risk	Credit risk	Market risk		
					Equity	IR	Comm
3V Finance	Product	http://www.3vfinance.com			X	X	X
Accenture	Consultancy	http://www.accenture.com	X	X	X	X	X
Acrys Consult GmbH	Consultancy	http://www.acrys-consult.com	X	X	X	X	X
Acrys Consult GmbH	Product	http://www.acrys-consult.com	X				
Advanced Portfolio Technologies	Product	http://www.apt.com			X	X	
AFA Systems	Product	http://www.afa-systems.com			X	X	X
Algorithmics	Product	http://www.algorithmics.com	X	X	X	X	X
Andrew Kalotay Associates	Consultancy	http://www.kalotay.com				X	
Andrew Kalotay Associates	Product	http://www.kalotay.com				X	
Anvil Software	Consultancy	http://www.anvil.com			X	X	X
Anvil Software	Product	http://www.anvil.com			X	X	X
Application Networks	Product	http://www.application-networks.com		X	X	X	
Ascendant Technologies Inc.	Product	http://www.ascendant-tech.com		X	X		X
Ascendant Technologies Inc.	Consultancy	http://www.ascendant-tech.com		X	X	X	X
Axiom Software Laboratories	Product	http://www.axiomsl.com	X	X	X	X	X
Barra, Inc.	Product	http://www.barra.com			X	X	
Bloomberg	Product	http://www.bloomberg.com			X	X	X

Brady Ltd	Product	http://www.bradyplc.co.uk			X	X	X
C/S Solutions Inc.	Product	http://www.cs-solutions.com	X				
Calibrex International Corporation	Consultancy	http://www.calibrex.com				X	
Calibrex International Corporation	Product	http://www.calibrex.com				X	
Calypso Technology	Product	http://www.calypso-tech.com		X	X	X	X
Cap Gemini Ernst & Young	Consultancy	http://www.cgey.com	X	X	X	X	X
Card Decisions Inc.	Product	http://www.carddecisions.com	X				
CMS BondEdge	Product	http://www.cmsbondedge.com				X	
Cognotec	Product	http://www.cognotec.com				X	X
COMIT Gruppe	Product	http://www.comit.ie	X	X	X	X	
Credence Analytics (I) Pvt. Ltd	Product	http://www.credenceanalytics.com		X	X	X	X
dbs Financial Systems Ltd	Product	http://www.dbsfinsys.co.uk	X				
Decision Software Inc.	Product	http://www.dsoftware.com				X	
Digital Risk Solutions Ltd	Consultancy	http://www.digitalrisksolutions.co.uk	X				
Digital Risk Solutions Ltd	Product	http://www.digitalrisksolutions.co.uk	X				
Fernbach Software S.A.	Product	http://www.fernbach.com	X	X		X	
Financial Objects	Toolkit	http://www.finobj.com		X	X	X	X
FinancialCAD	Toolkit	http://www.fincad.com			X	X	X

(Continued)

Company	Type	Website	Operational risk	Credit risk	Market risk		
					Equity	IR	Comm
Fitch Risk	Product	http://www.fitchrisk.com	X	X			
Fitch Risk	Consultancy	http://www.fitchrisk.com	X	X	X	X	X
FNX Ltd	Product	http://www.fnx.com			X	X	X
GFI	Product	http://www.fenics.com					X
IBM Global Services	Consultancy	http://www.ibm.com	X	X	X	X	X
Imagine Software	Product	http://www.derivatives.com			X	X	
Integral Development Corporation	Product	http://www.integral.com			X	X	X
Intermark Solutions	Product	http://www.intermarkit.com			X	X	X
Investment Support Systems Inc.	Product	http://www.inssinc.com				X	X
IQ Financial Systems	Product	http://www.iqfinancial.com		X	X	X	X
Iris Financial	Toolkit	http://www.irisfinancial.com			X	X	
IRIS Integrated Risk Management ag	Product	http://www.iris.ch	X	X	X	X	X
Kawaller & Company, LLC	Consultancy	http://www.kawaller.com			X	X	
KWI	Product	http://www.kwi.com					X

Lepus	Consultancy	http://www.lepus.co.uk	X	X	X	X	X
Lombard Risk Management Ltd	Product	http://www.lombardrisk.com		X	X	X	X
Long View International Ltd	Product	http://www.lvi.com			X	X	
MathCAD	Toolkit	http://www.mathsoft.com					
Matlab	Toolkit	http://www.mathworks.com					
Mathmatica	Toolkit	http://www.wolfram.com					
MB Risk Management	Toolkit	http://www.mbrm.com		X	X	X	
Measurisk	Product	http://www.measurisk.com			X	X	X
Methodware	Product	http://www.methodware.com	X				
Montgomery Investment Technology Inc.	Toolkit	http://www.fintools.com			X	X	
Montgomery Investment Technology Inc.	Consultancy	http://www.fintools.com			X	X	X
Murex	Product	http://www.murex.com		X	X	X	X
NumeriX Corporation	Toolkit	http://www.numerix.com		X		X	X
Oasis Management	Product	http://www.oasismanagement.com				X	X
Oasis Management	Consultancy	http://www.oasismanagement.com			X	X	X
Open Link Financial Inc.	Product	http://www.olf.com		X	X	X	X
OpRisk Limited	Consultancy	http://www.opriskconsulting.com	X				
Optionomics Corp.	Product	http://www.optionomics.com			X		

(Continued)

Company	Type	Website	Operational risk	Credit risk	Market risk		
					Equity	IR	Comm
OptionVue Systems International, Inc.	Product	http://www.optionvue.com			X	X	X
ORC Software	Product	http://www.orcsoftware.com			X	X	X
PFS TraderTools LLC	Product	http://www.tradertools.com					X
Portiva Corporation	Product	http://www.portiva.com	X				
Portiva Corporation	Consultancy	http://www.portiva.com	X				
Principia Partners	Product	http://www.ppllc.com		X	X	X	
Providus Software Solutions	Product	http://www.providus.com	X				
Raft International	Product	http://www.raftinternational.com	X	X			
Random Walk	Consultancy	http://www.randomwalk.com			X	X	
RCS Riskmanagement Concepts Systems AG	Product	http://www.risksys.com	X	X			
Red2Green Canada Inc.	Product	http://www.red2green.ca		X			
Red2Green Canada Inc.	Consultancy	http://www.red2green.ca		X			
Reuters	Product	http://www.reuters.com			X	X	X
Risk Reward	Consultancy	http://www.riskrewardlimited.com	X	X	X	X	X
RiskAdvisory Software Inc.	Product	http://www.riskadvisory.com					X

RiskAdvisory Software Inc.	Consultancy	http://www.riskadvisory.com					X
RiskCare Ltd	Consultancy	http://www.riskcare.com		X	X	X	X
RiskMetrics Group	Product	http://www.riskmetrics.com		X	X	X	X
royalblue financial plc	Product	http://www.royalblue.com			X		
RxSoft GmbH	Product	http://www.rxsoft.de				X	X
SAS Institute	Product	http://www.sas.com	X	X	X	X	X
SavvySoft	Product	http://www.savvysoft.com		X	X	X	X
Screen Consultants	Consultancy	http://www.screenconsultants.com	X	X	X	X	X
Sophis	Product	http://www.sophis.fr		X	X	X	X
Standard & Poor's Risk Solutions	Product	http://www.standardandpoors.com		X			
Suite LLC	Product	http://www.suitellc.com				X	
Suite LLC	Consultancy	http://www.suitellc.com	X	X	X	X	X
Summit Systems	Product	http://www.summithq.com		X		X	X
Sungard	Product	http://www.sungard.com		X	X	X	X
Front Capital (Sungard)	Product	http://www.front.com		X	X	X	
Tamesis Ltd	Product/ Toolkit	http://www.tamesis.com		X	X	X	X
TechHakers Inc.	Toolkit	http://www.thi.com				X	

Continued)

Company	Type	Website	Operational risk	Credit risk	Market risk		
					Equity	IR	Comm
Tetrix Solutions	Consultancy	http://www.tetrix.co.uk	X	X	X	X	X
The Kamakura Corporation	Consultancy	http://kamakuraco.com		X	X	X	X
The Kamakura Corporation	Product	http://kamakuraco.com		X	X	X	X
Theoretics Inc.	Product	http://www.theoretics.com				X	
Trema Group	Toolkit	http://www.trema.com		X	X	X	X
Triple Point Technology, Inc.	Product	http://www.tpt.com					X
Ubitrade	Product	http://www.ubitrade.com		X	X	X	
Wall Street Systems	Product	http://www.wallstreetsystems.com		X		X	X
Xenomorph	Product/ toolkit	http://www.xenomorph.co.uk			X	X	

Index

D

E

S

T

U